W9-AAM-845

WITHDRAWN

Rough Justice

Also by Peter Elkind

The Smartest Guys in the Room:
The Amazing Rise and Scandalous Fall of Enron
(coauthor with Bethany McLean)

The Death Shift

ROUGH JUSTICE

THE RISE AND FALL OF
ELIOT SPITZER

Peter Elkind

PORTFOLIO

PORTFOLIO
Published by the Penguin Group
Penguin Group (USA) Inc., 375 Hudson Street, New York, New York 10014, U.S.A. • Penguin Group (Canada), 90 Eglinton Avenue East, Suite 700, Toronto, Ontario, Canada M4P 2Y3 (a division of Pearson Penguin Canada Inc.) • Penguin Books Ltd, 80 Strand, London WC2R 0RL, England • Penguin Ireland, 25 St. Stephen's Green, Dublin 2, Ireland (a division of Penguin Books Ltd) • Penguin Books Australia Ltd, 250 Camberwell Road, Camberwell, Victoria 3124, Australia (a division of Pearson Australia Group Pty Ltd) • Penguin Books India Pvt Ltd, 11 Community Centre, Panchsheel Park, New Delhi—110 017, India • Penguin Group (NZ), 67 Apollo Drive, Rosedale, North Shore 0632, New Zealand (a division of Pearson New Zealand Ltd) • Penguin Books (South Africa) (Pty) Ltd, 24 Sturdee Avenue, Rosebank, Johannesburg 2196, South Africa

Penguin Books Ltd, Registered Offices:
80 Strand, London WC2R 0RL, England

First published in 2010 by Portfolio,
a member of Penguin Group (USA) Inc.

1   3   5   7   9   10   8   6   4   2

A portion of this book first appeared in *Fortune*.

LIBRARY OF CONGRESS CATALOGING IN PUBLICATION DATA

Elkind, Peter.
Rough justice : the rise and fall of Eliot Spitzer / Peter Elkind.
p.   cm.
Includes index.
ISBN 978-1-59184-307-8
1. Spitzer, Eliot. 2. Governor—New York (State)—Biography. 3. Attorneys general—New York (State)—Biography. 4. Spitzer, Eliot—Marriage. 5. New York (State)—Politics and government—1951–   6. Political corruption—New York (State).   I. Title.
F125.3.S73E45 2010
974.7'043092—dc22   2010001975
[B]

Printed in the United States of America
Set in Sabon LT Std
Designed by Daniel Lagin

For Stephen, Landon, George,
Adele, and Sam

Author's Note

I T HAS BEEN NEARLY TWO YEARS SINCE ELIOT SPITZER WAS abruptly transformed—as though by a ray gun fired by space aliens—into "Client 9." While not exactly the expanse of history, enough time has passed for some perspective.

Spitzer is evidence of how modern times have compressed the natural rhythm of everything—even scandal. He leapt onto the national stage overnight—and vanished in a moment. In the period it has taken me to write this book, he has performed what passes for him as penance, and has already begun a comeback. As with many things about this hyperkinetic man, it may prove too much, too soon. But Spitzer isn't the sort to accept a contented life—or even an extended stay—sitting on the sidelines. (Or, for that matter, to salve his soul and reputation performing charity work with Honduran refugees.) For reasons of ego, temperament, ability, and conviction, he remains hell-bent on making his mark in the public arena, no matter how bloodied and beaten that leaves him.

Spitzer's fall wasn't the first sex-based implosion of one of our icons—and was quickly followed by others. But it was surely among the most improbable, as measured by the chasm between public image and private reality. A man born and bred to act on cold facts and reason proved all too hot-blooded and human—revealing first his temper, then his temptations. He damaged himself with the first and committed hara-kiri with the second.

I began working on *Rough Justice* twenty-two months ago, not long after Spitzer resigned as governor of New York. I had written extensively about his Wall Street crusades as attorney general in the pages of *Fortune* magazine, my journalistic home, and profiled him there as well. This book benefits from that work. But the story took me many places I had never been—from the gothic corridors of the New York capitol to the fantasyland of high-priced hookers.

I became interested in telling this story right after the scandal broke, after learning of the news on my BlackBerry during a spring-break ski trip with my family. Alex Gibney, the Academy Award-winning documentary filmmaker, had the same thought. We had worked together as he produced his film on Enron, based on the book I coauthored with Bethany McLean, *The Smartest Guys in the Room.* We quickly agreed to collaborate again, only this time preparing our separate projects concurrently, sharing ideas and information along the way. This has proven a remarkably productive partnership.

This book relies, in good part, on an intimately detailed, contemporaneous written record. Through Freedom of Information requests, investigative files, and the openness of others, I gained access to a treasure trove of documents: private diaries, handwritten notes, unsent letters, and—so fitting for a story about Spitzer—thousands of e-mails. They helped piece together a remarkable tale. But ultimately, the book benefits most from the often-painful candor of the many people I interviewed who lived through these events. That starts with Spitzer himself.

This is not an "authorized" book. Its conclusions and revelations about him—some admiring, some harsh, some startling—are entirely my own. Yet Spitzer, whom I first met in college, began speaking with me early, when he was saying nothing in public, and continued doing so regularly through the completion of this project. Our conversations covered every aspect of his life and work, often in great detail. Spitzer is not a naturally introspective man, and many of my questions were uncomfortable. Ultimately, he was remarkably forthcoming, even reflective, tackling almost every question I asked. He asked nothing more than that I treat him fairly. I am grateful for this trust and cooperation.

Silda Wall Spitzer politely declined my repeated requests for an on-the-record interview. The quotations attributed to her come from my 2005 interview with her for *Fortune,* those who have spoken directly with her, and published interviews elsewhere. In 2005, I also interviewed Spitzer's parents, Bernard and Anne, and his siblings, Emily and Daniel.

The world of prostitution, for obvious reasons, was tough to crack. In the end, Alex Gibney and I came to a detailed understanding of life inside Emperors Club VIP—and its dealings with Eliot Spitzer. I interviewed its founder, Mark Brener, three times in jail before his sentencing, and benefited greatly from conversations with his criminal defense lawyers. Alex conducted a remarkable interview with Brener's young partner, Cecil Suwal, after purchasing an option to acquire fiction film rights to her planned memoir; this is the only circumstance in which anyone was paid in connection with an interview for this book. I also spoke to Suwal several times in January 2010. Emperors Club VIP booker Temeka Lewis has said nothing to the press, but her attorney shared his insights. I also obtained scores of secret text messages from inside the Emperors Club during 2007. Although Ashley Dupré declined repeated interview requests, we spoke with two others who are far more knowledgeable about both Emperors Club VIP and Spitzer's involvement. Neither woman has been previously identified or interviewed. To protect their privacy, we have changed their names; other than the usage names used by escorts, they are the only pseudonyms in this book. "Tammy Thomas" worked as a phone booker at Emperors Club VIP for about seven months; she spoke with me at length. "Angelina" was an Emperors Club VIP escort; Alex conducted a wide-ranging tape-recorded interview with her, as well as several follow-up sessions. Both were candid about their experience; both had extensive dealings with the mysterious "George Fox."

Eliot Spitzer's fatal misdeeds were private acts of marital infidelity— the very sort that some of our greatest presidents had gotten away with from the dawn of the republic. Those days are clearly over. In the modern media age, it's impossible to put the genie back in the bottle. Character matters—and so do laws. But it's worth giving a moment of thought: should we care so much about personal flaws when our government—and our financial system—is so hobbled by the sort of incompetence, greed, and corruption that hurt everyone? These pages, I hope, offer a window into how things work—and how they don't: on Wall Street, in our houses of government, in the hearts and souls of our political leaders.

—PETER ELKIND, FEBRUARY 2010

Man is conceived in sin and born in corruption and he passeth from the stink of the didie to the stench of the shroud. There is always something.

—WILLIE STARK, *ALL THE KING'S MEN*

Contents

Rough Justice

Introduction

I T WAS COLD AND BARELY DAYLIGHT WHEN LLOYD CONSTAN-
tine arrived at 985 Fifth Avenue in Manhattan, a stone's throw from
the Metropolitan Museum of Art. The media horde that would soon
gather outside had not yet begun to arrive. Constantine, a regular visitor,
stepped quickly into the lobby. The doorman, crisply dressed in his black
uniform, waved him through into the elevator.

The urgent summons from his old friend had come the night before,
in a shocking phone call. "I have to resign," the fifty-fourth governor of
New York had told him. "As early as tomorrow, it will be reported in *The
New York Times* that I've been involved with prostitutes."

"It's late," responded Constantine, a wealthy antitrust lawyer, after
briefly hearing out his friend. "I will be at your apartment at 7 A.M. And
I certainly won't abandon you. It can't be as bad as you think."

But, of course, it was.

Constantine had known the governor for a quarter century. He'd
watched every step of his magical political rise: his breathtakingly narrow
election as New York's attorney general; his audacious, media-grabbing
crusades against corporate corruption and greed; his ascent to the national stage as the moralizing "Sheriff of Wall Street," America's most
feared enforcer; and his inevitable election as governor of the nation's
most important state in a record landslide—bigger even than those of
Teddy Roosevelt, Al Smith, and FDR. All this had spurred giddy talk
about his prospects for becoming the first Jewish president.

Constantine's friend had arrived in Albany vowing to clean up New

York's notoriously corrupt and dysfunctional state government. He'd deliver a balanced budget on time, provide healthcare to the uninsured, bankroll needy school districts, breathe life into the moribund upstate economy—and do it all in the sunshine, out from behind closed doors, without favors or backroom deals. He'd spoken to friends of wanting to leave a historic legacy, to offer a national model for activist government in the post-Reagan age. "The light of a new day shines down on the Empire State once again," he'd thundered, standing coatless—*just like JFK!*—in a drizzly chill during his inaugural address on New Year's Day. His election promised "a new beginning," an administration "as ethical and wise as all of New York."

But nothing had gone as planned. During fourteen months in office, he'd stumbled from one crisis into another, often disasters of his own making. To Constantine, he'd seemed inexplicably . . . *different*—distracted and unfocused, given to impulsive judgments and fits of rage. Lesser adversaries—the pygmies of Albany—were bedeviling him.

Now, Constantine concluded, he suddenly understood. His friend had been harboring a terrible secret: he had a toxic drip seeping into his brain. From the first day of his tenure, New York's governor had known that he was doomed—a political dead man walking. The only question was when the end would come.

Constantine stepped off the elevator onto the eighth floor; 985 Fifth was an "elite rental"—a three-bedroom like apartment 8B, with lovely views of Central Park, went for more than $17,000 a month. Inside, Constantine was immediately greeted by the familiar profile of his old friend, plastered on so many magazine covers over the years—the lean frame, the big ears, the jutting jaw. Only now the predatory countenance was gone. He was the hunted, not the hunter. The governor's wife of twenty years, Silda, stood near her husband, but there was a palpable chill between them. Both were in tears, looking shattered.

"Welcome to a Greek tragedy," said Eliot Spitzer.

———

It was during 2008, the year Eliot Spitzer fell, that America began to learn the consequences of its madness. The venerable investment-banking houses of Bear Stearns and Lehman Brothers collapsed, buried beneath the weight of unregulated investments in high-risk mortgages. A fund manager named Bernie Madoff confessed to operating a $50 billion Ponzi scheme. AIG, the global insurance powerhouse, became a ward of the state. Merrill Lynch was auctioned off for a pittance. Citigroup struggled to survive. The nation spiraled into recession.

It was a hard time to be Eliot Spitzer. New York's former governor stewed as he watched all this from the sidelines. He'd warned Washington about subprime debt. He'd prosecuted AIG for cooking its books. He'd taken scorching heat for a showcase lawsuit over grotesque executive pay. Most of all, he'd preached the perils of greed and hubris, and deregulation run amok. Despite all his early tribulations as governor, he would have been heralded as a Cassandra, and a major player in the national debate about how to fix the mess—perhaps even President Barack Obama's choice for U.S. attorney general.

Instead, Spitzer was cooped in a converted conference room at his father's Manhattan real estate office, nominally presiding over a family business empire that ran itself, reduced to wielding his political influence through a column for an online magazine. "I get up in the morning, make breakfast for the girls, put them on the bus, come to the office, read the papers, and I say to myself ten thousand times: '*I should be doing something else.*'" He spoke wistfully to me of the days when "issues were important, not my sex life."

I began meeting with Spitzer in early June, less than three months after he'd resigned, while the possibility of criminal indictment still hung over him and he remained publicly silent. We spoke regularly over the next year and a half, mostly face-to-face. Spitzer is not, by nature, a reflective man. "I don't believe in psychiatrists; I don't do introspection," he'd blurt during our early discussions, whenever a question sought self-analysis. But now he was left to contemplate his extraordinary fall, and the memories were searing. The creeping inevitability of exposure and political ruin. The excruciating Sunday-afternoon confessions to his wife and three teenaged daughters. Silda, devastated and teary, standing beside him before the entire world as he tersely acknowledged behavior that violated "any sense of right and wrong." The crushed expressions of his young staff, who had attached their lives to his promise. And, of course, the open celebration of his enemies. The cheers on the wooden floor of the New York Stock Exchange. The angry billionaire who stared into a TV camera and proclaimed, "We all have our own private hells. I hope his private hell is hotter than anybody else's." *How had this insanity come to pass?*

Overnight, Spitzer had become a tabloid joke—THE LUV GUV, ELIOT MESS, CLIENT NO. 9, the papers called him. No humiliation was out of bounds—no detail about his "horny habits," no comment about his marriage. *"Silda, are you leaving him?"* a columnist for one of the city's tabloids had bayed, as the Spitzers rushed off from a final press briefing without taking questions. In print, that same scribe had berated New York's first lady for not racing into divorce court, branding her "a doormat," an "ass-coverer," and an "enabler" for her husband, who deserved to "burn."

In the days that followed, Constantine had been so concerned about Spitzer's mental state that he arranged for close friends to take turns checking in on him, placing the former governor under an informal suicide watch. "I've known people who killed themselves," says Constantine, "and I felt the concern was warranted." Months later, Spitzer privately scoffed at the thought that he might take his own life. But he quietly acknowledged his pain. "However bad you think it might have been," he said, "it's been exponentially worse."

———

In an age that treasures celebrity, there is a certain voyeuristic fascination in watching a famous man blow himself up. Eliot Spitzer's self-immolation provided the quintessential morality play—indeed, the very sort that he'd served up during his years in public office. Spitzer was a white knight: an Ivy League–smart, Fifth Avenue–rich political reformer with a perfect family—a man who had wielded moral indignation like a broadsword. Why, Spitzer had even *prosecuted* escort services as attorney general— and promoted a law during his time as governor that stiffened criminal penalties for johns. Now he stood revealed as a hypocrite, a flawed crusader who harbored a secret life consorting with expensive prostitutes.

Spitzer's rise was almost as improbable as his crash, and the tale of how he got there does much to explain how it ended. His political career had been nurtured in a privileged and emotionally repressed upbringing; launched with noble, almost naïve, intentions; and fueled by a potent mix of creativity, fierce intelligence, and bristling ambition. By midlife, Spitzer had become a superstar, reshaping entire industries and collecting billions in penalties and fines. He had gone after some of the most powerful people in America—and become one of them himself. Always, he'd flown close to the sun, daring the consequences, until they finally arrived.

No politician who has soared so high has fallen so fast. No unraveling has dashed more high-minded hopes. No demise has inspired more celebration among well-connected enemies. Spitzer publicly acknowledged that he had been undone by his own weakness and "stupidity"—that he ultimately had no one else to blame. But he privately suspected that the investigation and exposure of his misdeeds had murkier origins—that he was the victim of a political "hit." And on that front, there are indeed hints of intrigue.

Spitzer's private and public paths had taken him into strange, treacherous terrain: lonely, intoxicating worlds of sex, power, and politics. He'd toppled an arrogant insurance mogul bent on revenge; done business with a sweaty Russian-born pimp who evangelized about spirituality and macrobiotic diets; become target practice for a dirty-trickster consultant, who cast himself as the Joker tormenting Spitzer's Batman; and become intimate with a pampered Jersey girl who chose turning tricks over a life without Louis Vuitton. The intersection of their lives had powerful consequences for all involved.

At the core of the story, of course, is a marriage. Within moments of Spitzer's public confession, the image of the stricken Silda literally standing by her man had lit up the blogosphere with debate about conjugal behavior in the twenty-first century. Eliot's political demise was, in fact, not even Silda's first marital nightmare—a painful (if far less public) shock had come twenty-five years earlier. Yet in the months after Spitzer's fall, Silda had not only remained committed to her husband but had actually come to regard him as a felled crusader—a casualty of the powerful forces he had courageously taken on.

As the unfolding financial meltdown left him feeling strangely vindicated, Spitzer (especially in private) became increasingly unbound. He scoffed at those who complained about his prosecutorial "bullying" as New York's attorney general. The loudest such complaints came from "little entities like Citibank, Merrill Lynch, and AIG," he told me. "I will *never* apologize for how I've dealt with them. Look how they've destroyed our financial system! If anything, I was too *soft*!" Had he overstepped his bounds, in public turf battles with the Justice Department and the SEC? "When did they ever do anything without our kicking the shit out of them first?" Spitzer replied. "They were intellectually moribund. They didn't know how to follow their nose to find out what was going on in corporate America." New York's state legislature, he declared, was full of people who were "fundamentally corrupt." As for *The New York Times,* his bible since childhood: "I use it to wrap fish."

On the subject of his involvement with prostitutes, Spitzer was considerably less plainspoken during these early conversations—insight on that would come later. Though Spitzer was loath to admit it—psychological problems were for the weak—he had been in counseling with Silda for months, seeking to save his marriage and understand his actions. How *could* he have done what he'd done, despite the certainty of discovery, despite the enormous stakes, despite the absolute knowledge that his enemies would be merciless if he stumbled? Spitzer had his speculations, but preferred retreating to the shibboleth that every man has his flaws. "Rational people do irrational things," he liked to say. The Spitzers took comfort in, of all people, the words of Oscar Wilde:

"Every saint has a past, and every sinner has a future."

PART ONE
THE RISING

Never talk when you can nod. And never nod when you can
wink. And never write an e-mail because it's death. You're
giving prosecutors all the evidence we need.

—ELIOT SPITZER, FEBRUARY 2006

Chapter 1: Ironbutt

BACK IN THE DAYS WHEN ELIOT SPITZER WAS KNOWN AS "THE Sheriff of Wall Street," journalists usually told the story of his early life as a building block for hagiography. Given the later events that transformed him into "the Luv Guv," there is a natural temptation to revisit the past, this time in search of pathology. Reality, of course, is both subtle and complex; there are few "Rosebud" moments. But looking back, there are unexplored clues to understanding what was to come, both good and bad.

Two anecdotes feature prominently in virtually every account of the childhood of Eliot Laurence Spitzer, born on June 10, 1959. We'll call the first "The Spitzers Play Monopoly." The second: "Dinner with the Spitzers." It is no accident that both star Eliot's father, Bernard, a towering figure in the lives of his three children.

In the first episode, young Eliot, perhaps six or seven, is across the Monopoly board from his dad, who by the mid-1960s is an actual real estate tycoon. Improbably, on this day, the youngster has gained the upper hand, controlling a vital piece of Monopoly property—perhaps St. James or Boardwalk. Bernard orders Eliot to sell, presumably for a pittance; young Eliot dutifully complies, and is soon reduced to both bankruptcy and tears. This, Bernie later told writers, taught his son a vital lesson: never defer to authority. "I play to kill," he explained drily, in the Spitzer way, offering the truth wrapped in a veneer of humor.

Dinner with the Spitzers was an equally harrowing affair. The family patriarch was contemptuous of what he calls "idle chitchat." *How was your day at school? How are you feeling?* Bernie didn't want to hear it. Indeed, Eliot says he has literally never heard his father talk about the weather. Instead, the Spitzer parents transformed their large Tudor home in Riverdale, a wealthy wooded enclave in the Bronx, into a running class in critical thinking, most conspicuously during family dinner, convened on Tuesday, Thursday, and Sunday nights. (Other days, Bernie and Anne would eat alone, leaving their offspring to the live-in housekeeper.) Around the table, each of the three brainy Spitzer children—Eliot's older sister, Emily, became a lawyer; his older brother, Daniel, a neurosurgeon—would take a turn leading the nightly debate on a single topic. Subjects ranged from the war in Vietnam to how a steam engine works to the economic implications of double-digit inflation. Carl Mayer, Eliot's close college friend and an attorney himself, likens it to eating with the panelists from *The McLaughlin Group.* "It was not the typical American household. You'd sit down, and the father would lob some grenade, and Eliot would start screaming." Recalls Daniel Spitzer: "We had a huge fight one time about the definition of 'desert'—whether it could include the Antarctic. My father was often a devil's advocate. He knows that if everybody sits there and agrees with him, nobody learns anything."

In print, these Darwinian scenes were invariably (and correctly) deployed to explain the origins of the youngest child's hypercompetitiveness and his extraordinary seriousness of purpose. As Eliot put it, "They raised us to be thoughtful and get into the issues, with an intensity." But these episodes also describe a certain emotional deficit—a household with little patience for introspection and self-doubt, personal weakness and pain. The Spitzer children recall their upbringing as "strict," "super-rational," and "highly regimented"—sometimes, as Eliot once put it, "at the expense of the warm and fuzzy stuff." Indeed, in the acknowledgments page of his college senior thesis, Spitzer offered thanks to his family—not for their love and support but "for being always understanding when events challenged the validity of my analysis."

There was no coddling in the Spitzer household. In a 2005 interview, Anne Spitzer joked to me that her third child was "ignored," before adding: "I can safely say that Eliot certainly wasn't hovered over. . . . My philosophy was, if there was a problem, they'd let us know." The Spitzers were devoted parents who loved their kids and taught them to care about giving something back to the world. But their expectations were often insurmountable, simple praise was rare, and the cutting banter was constant.

It surely must have been daunting to have a father who always played the intellectual tough guy, and parents bent on taking their children down a notch. Carl Mayer once recalled finishing a tennis game with his friend and being greeted by Anne as he walked off the court. Said Mom: "I hope you kicked Eliot's ass!" In this family, vulnerability—and even sickness— was a sign of weakness, an impediment to further attainment. It is no accident that Eliot Spitzer, suffering from a bad cold one day as an adult, quickly boasted, "I haven't taken a sick day in twenty-four years." Lloyd Constantine, Spitzer's friend for most of his adulthood, sums it up this way: "What Bernie did was create an atmosphere of total egalitarianism: 'If you're nine and you can take me down, just go ahead! Take your best shot, kid!' If you want to indict him for something, it's that he created this warrior."

Whatever emotional impact all this may have had on their youngest son, it is clear that Bernie and Anne offered an extraordinary model for achievement. After Spitzer became Wall Street's most feared regulator, his critics reflexively accused him of failing to understand how business really operates. In truth, his family offers one of those genuinely magical American success stories—the sort of capitalist bootstrapping that Ayn Rand would have admired.

Bernie Spitzer and Anne Goldhaber were both raised by struggling Austrian Jewish immigrant families on New York City's Lower East Side. Bernie, whose father, Morris, owned a print shop, grew up in a thirty-dollar-a-month cold-water flat. Anne's dad was a rabbi. They met during summer break at the Weinreb Hotel, a resort in the Catskills Borscht Belt, where he played saxophone in the band and she worked as a babysitter. Anne was fourteen; Bernie, at eighteen, had already graduated from public high school and earned a degree in civil engineering from City College. They married three years later, after he returned from the Navy, in 1945.

By the early 1950s, after finishing a master's at Columbia, Bernie Spitzer had launched a career that would make him one of New York's most successful builders. He specialized in high-end Manhattan properties with views of Central Park. He also built the city's largest apartment building, the fifty-five-story, 865-unit Corinthian, transforming the site of an abandoned airline terminal near the Queens–Midtown Tunnel into a gargantuan luxury condo tower.

A tall man with bushy eyebrows, Spitzer was an exacting old-school gentleman. Everyone who worked at Spitzer Engineering, as his business was modestly named, addressed him as "Mr. Spitzer." Even now, says Jeffrey Moerdler, the Spitzers' real estate lawyer, "I wouldn't dare go to Bernie's office without a suit on. I have never seen him without a suit and tie." In the New York real estate community, according to a 1991 *New York Times* story, Spitzer was known as "an insightful taskmaster"; the Corinthian's architect called him "the most organized and demanding developer I ever worked for." Spitzer shrewdly set aside the lower floors in his premium buildings for premium commercial tenants: doctors' offices. According to Moerdler, he became the largest individual owner of Manhattan medical-office space. Flashier New York developers rode the market's wild cycles in and out of bankruptcy court. But Spitzer built and held his projects, did much of the design work in-house, and avoided high-leverage deals. He retains a stake in about a dozen premium buildings—a portfolio, says Moerdler, that renders the Spitzer family "recession-proof."

All this success, of course, made the Spitzers very rich, with a fortune that peaked at more than $500 million. As Eliot was growing up, the Spitzers enjoyed a large house, memberships in private clubs, and ruling-class-type recreation: ski trips to Vail, tennis, and squash. Yet they loathed ostentation. Eliot wore hand-me-downs and didn't get his first suit until after college; Daniel rode his sister's old bike. Anne, who held two master's degrees herself (English and psychology), always worked—first at her sons' high school, then at Marymount Manhattan College, where she taught until the age of seventy-seven. Even after he had become rich, Bernie cut his own hair, and drove himself to the office in a battered Plymouth station wagon, prompting business peers to remark, "There goes the million-dollar man with the thousand-dollar car." Says Daniel: "We were not spoiled. We were given opportunities. We were not given a lot of material goods."

Being raised by "the ultimate rationalist," as Eliot puts it, also meant setting aside religious practice. In a 2005 interview for a *Fortune* profile of his son, Bernie Spitzer told me that he rebelled against his Orthodox Jewish upbringing after going to temple as a child and being "surrounded by people who were praying and who didn't understand what they were saying in Hebrew. . . . I went through all the ritual, and concluded I was not a ritualist." As the Spitzer parents saw it, you could be an intellectual or a person of faith—but not both. Though their children were raised as Jews, Eliot never had a bar mitzvah, the Jewish coming-of-age ceremony, and the family didn't even belong to a synagogue. The Spitzers celebrated Jewish holidays at home, where the parents would lead discussions about the meaning of the occasion. "It was a philosophical household," says Bernie. "It was the ethical-moral precept of Judaism I wanted them to respect, not the ritual."

———

Looking back, many of those around Eliot Spitzer view his entire life as an unbroken preparation for elective office. Bernie was sometimes even described as "a Jewish Joseph Kennedy." Eliot Spitzer calls that nonsense—growing up, he certainly dreamed he might someday be appointed to a substantial government post (perhaps even secretary of state), but he never imagined himself dashing across New York, chasing votes and kissing babies. Yet weighing Spitzer's past, it is hard to escape the sense of a young man being groomed—and grooming himself—for elected office.

He attended—and excelled at—elite private schools: New York's Horace Mann, Princeton, and Harvard Law. He was absorbed in public issues from an early age: by ten he'd begun a lifelong morning ritual of poring over *The New York Times*; at fourteen, he subscribed to *Foreign Affairs*; as a college freshman, he sometimes went home on weekends to fulfill his duties as treasurer of the Ben Franklin Democratic Club in the Bronx. Spitzer was incredibly disciplined: marveling at his ability to sit motionless in a library study carrel for hours, friends at Princeton nicknamed him "Ironbutt." And he was ferociously competitive. Though pudgy in high school, he co-captained Horace Mann's tennis and soccer teams. (His parents attended only a single match.) In soccer, he recalls playing the role of "enforcer," charged with taking out opponents. "You play hard, you play rough, and hopefully you don't get caught," he memorably joked to Stephen Colbert in 2005. "He was smart and ambitious from a very early age," says Jason Brown, a Horace Mann friend who accompanied Spitzer to Princeton and Harvard Law. "If 'W' is one model of coming to politics, by waking up when you were forty—oh, my God, Eliot is the antithesis of that. He did not suffer from a dissolute youth."

Just blocks from the Spitzers' home, Horace Mann was an all-male bastion of liberal Jewish intellectual ambition. (The first girls arrived in Eliot's senior year.) Its distinguished alumni include LBJ biographer Robert Caro, civil rights leader Allard Lowenstein, economist Robert Heilbroner, and *New York Times* Pulitzer Prize winner Anthony Lewis. Guided by its Latin motto, *Magna est veritas et prævalet*—"Great is the truth, and it prevails"—Horace Mann preached the transcendent power of knowledge and logic. Spitzer would fervently embrace this gospel.

Nearly everyone there was bright and privileged, and used the measures of the East Coast elite to keep score. Who was *really* smart—and in what way? Everyone was acutely conscious of SAT scores. (Eliot's, a near-perfect 1590, invariably found their way into print decades later.) Among top students in this competitive cauldron, for whom going to college at the University of Pennsylvania was viewed as failure, the ultimate goal was getting into Harvard. (Emily Spitzer was already there.) Young Eliot had successfully chased virtually every brass ring, every conspicuous measure of achievement. But here, he fell short, to his bitter disappointment. College English professor Bob Faggen, who attended Horace Mann at the time, recalls seeing Spitzer in the school's main building after the college letters arrived, slamming a locker door and kicking a backpack. A respected history teacher even wrote a letter of protest to Harvard, appealing the rejection, but to no avail. Eliot would have to settle for following his brother Daniel to Princeton.

———

At Princeton University, a place where many students took themselves too seriously, Spitzer stood out for his earnestness and sense of purpose. "He was a twenty-two-year-old guy who was already acting like a forty-two-year-old guy," says Stuart Mieher, one of his college roommates. Spitzer awoke at 6 A.M. to drink black coffee and pore over the *Times* in his dorm room. He rarely cut a class. Most of all, he immersed himself in student government, which many on campus viewed as a joke (only about a third of students bothered to vote), an ego playground for aspiring "politicos."

Spitzer's only previous foray into elective politics had ended badly. He'd lost a solemn bid for seventh-grade class president at Horace Mann to his friend Jason Brown, who had ridden into office on the slogan "Don't Be a Dope When Things Are Down; There's Still Hope If You Vote for

Brown!" As a high school senior, Spitzer had subsequently displayed the requisite measure of cynicism, including this quotation on his yearbook page: "The worst thing about political jokes is that some of them get elected." (He also quoted Hamlet, the troubled prince who meets a tragic end.) But at Princeton, he started running for office virtually from the moment he arrived. After plastering the campus with earnest leaflets (VOTE PERFORMANCE!), he won election as chairman of the student government while just a sophomore. Wary of falling short, he hadn't even told his parents he was running.

Spitzer had eagerly plunged into the small, swirling pond of student politics: seeking endorsements, giving speeches, forging compromises, dealing with the press—the campus press, that is. This was his first performance as an elected executive, and its sobriety was not stylistically different from what came decades later. Upon election, he told *The Daily Princetonian* that his first goal was to "initiate necessary changes to make the committees more effective and more rapidly functioning bodies." While his friends participated in demonstrations against university investments in apartheid South Africa—and even an occasional sit-in—Eliot promoted resolutions and negotiated with Princeton's president over lunch.

"Eliot was interested in getting stuff done more than he was interested in using the pulpit," says Mieher, who later graduated from Harvard Business School. "Eliot's always been a policy guy. You look at politicians—do they like appearing in crowds or are they policy wonks? For Eliot, it's not a close call." Bill Taylor, another Princeton roommate who became one of Spitzer's closest friends, put it this way in 2005: "There really is a straight line between Eliot at Princeton and the Eliot we see today."

Indeed. Even then Spitzer could play hardball, attacking rivals and punishing critics in a rookie-league foreshadowing of his pugnacity in later life. When an underclass representative penned a scathing critique of the Spitzer-led student government ("every bit the farce the student body thinks it is"), he confronted the sophomore and told him, "You're going to be really sorry you did this!" He then stripped his critic of a committee chairmanship—and fired his girlfriend from her unpaid job as student-government secretary.

Spitzer majored in the university's Woodrow Wilson School of Public and International Affairs, home base for most student-government types.

Princeton's only selective undergraduate major—half the applying sopho-
mores didn't get in—the Wilson School came under attack as a bastion
of "elitism" in a *Princetonian* column written about that time by fellow
student N. Gregory Mankiw, who later became an eminent Harvard
economist and chairman of the Council of Economic Advisers for President George W. Bush.

Spitzer spent summers in Washington, working for a Bronx congressman and Ralph Nader—typical Princeton fare. After junior year, he set
up City Surveys, a small polling business, with a classmate named David
Grant, who had conducted polls for the *Princetonian* and later became a
college math professor. Spitzer wrote the questions and dealt with the
clients. "My job was to do the math," recalls Grant. "But he really wanted to understand how you calculated error and what the statistics were
behind it. You'd never have to explain anything to him twice. You'd tell
him, and he'd clock it." Spitzer also spent one vacation traveling the country alone, working as a day laborer, in a sort of self-study course on living
life without privilege. He mopped floors in Atlanta, where he stayed in a
thirty-dollar-a-week flophouse; he stacked fiberglass insulation in ware-
houses in New Orleans; he picked tomatoes in upstate New York, working alongside migrant farmworkers. He lived on his meager income, but
stashed away a credit card for emergencies. Spitzer has always had a
"searching, aggressive intellect," notes Mieher. "He was being a kind of
sponge of experience. He wanted to learn stuff."

While Spitzer took everything he was doing seriously, he didn't necessarily take *himself* seriously. He has a dry, self-deprecating sense of humor
that was not often evident in public—then or later. He played pranks on
friends. He challenged Mayer to a spaghetti-eating contest (and lost, despite eating six bowls). He organized a campus-wide toga party. He drank
beer, smoked pot, and dated girls—always *smart* girls. In his elected
campus role, he often sounded like a junior bureaucrat. In smaller groups,
he had a winning charm.

Before leaving Princeton, Spitzer experienced a brief radical episode.
When his term as student-government chairman was ending, a group of
students, taking aim at the sort of stick-up-the-butt campus politicos that
Spitzer personified, ran a prank slate for student office as members of the
"Antarctica Liberation Front" (ALF). They campaigned under a joke
platform of "jihad," proclaiming, "The continent of destiny must be
freed!" ALF collected 38 percent of the vote, and one of its candidates

actually won. During senior year, after the university administration had rejected yet another student-backed measure, Spitzer concluded that student government at Princeton, which he had defended so ferociously, really was a joke. Backed by a small group of friends (including Elena Kagan, a future U.S. solicitor general), Spitzer published a manifesto in the *Princetonian* calling for his own version of jihad: he wanted students to resign en masse from their positions on university advisory committees. The notion of student influence is "a dangerous myth," Spitzer wrote. "It is time to demand change. . . . We have been co-opted into endorsing a structure which denies our voices any significance. . . . We must abandon the farcical system that causes us to legitimize our own disenfranchisement."

Spitzer's friend Bill Taylor dramatically resigned his seat and stormed out of a public meeting a few weeks later. But no one else followed. The short-lived revolution was over. Spitzer later called the episode "a senior moment—a college senior moment." But he would leave Princeton with a measure of frustration. As graduation approached, Princeton sent out a senior-class questionnaire. Under the section asking for family biography, he scrawled, "None of your business."

———

There is another fixture in the published accounts of Eliot Spitzer's rise: the story of how he and his wife, Silda Wall, met cute during their third year at Harvard Law School. The setting was a group ski condo in Vermont, where Spitzer, just arriving from Cambridge, burst through the door at 5 A.M., only to discover a startled young woman drinking coffee, dressed in flannel piggy pajamas. "Who are you?" Wall demanded, thinking he was an intruder. "Who the hell are *you*?" Spitzer shot back; he'd paid for the condo.

A biography of Spitzer, published while he was still attorney general, added that Wall wasn't interested in dating anyone at the time because she had just emerged from an "intense but unhappy relationship"—yet she soon fell in love with Spitzer anyway. What this account didn't mention is that Wall's "intense but unhappy relationship" was a *marriage*—a brief, devastating experience that she was loath to talk about it. Indeed, when author Brooke Masters, a *Washington Post* reporter, found out about the marriage in 2005, Wall successfully pleaded with Masters not to write about it, explaining that she and Eliot hadn't even told their daughters. Wall's first marriage was never mentioned in print until November 2006, after Spitzer had been elected governor and *The New York Times* profiled the new first lady of the Empire State.

Growing up, Silda Alice Wall had ventured only gingerly beyond the realm of her personal experience. For this reason, nothing seemed more improbable than her relationship with Eliot Spitzer. He was a nonpracticing Jew, New York City, and rich; she was a churchgoing Southern Baptist, small-town North Carolina, and middle class. Silda came from Concord, a mill town of twenty thousand, twenty miles northeast of Charlotte, where her father ran the county hospital for a quarter century. This gave Bob Wall stature as a city father; he served as president of the Rotary Club, chaired the United Way campaign, and became a director of the local bank. Wall was the first in his own family to go to college, and later earned two graduate degrees. He'd worked briefly in the family's wholesale grocery business in the years before landing in Concord.

There was no high-powered debating society at the Walls' dinner table—just peaceful small talk featuring local gossip and high school football. Silda's mom, Trilby (the Walls had married in 1955 after meeting in choir at Guilford College), reasoned that her husband faced enough stress during the day. Besides, raising upsetting topics over supper was poor manners.

Born in December 1957, Silda was the eldest of three children. Her name was her parents' distillation of a German word for "Teutonic war maiden." But growing up, she was about as perfect as a daughter could be: smart and gracious, slender and lovely. At Concord Senior High, Silda was a cheerleader, performed in drama club, played the French horn in the marching band, took Latin, and made National Honor Society. She dated the same boy—the captain of the football team and a future podiatrist—from ninth grade through her first year of law school. She didn't smoke or drink. (She had her first glass of wine at Harvard.) She graduated sixth in her class, with a 96.64 average. When college time came, Wall never considered leaving the state. She decided on Meredith College, a small Baptist women's school that a beloved teacher had attended, back when girls there wore white gloves for dinner. Meredith dated back to 1899, when it opened as Baptist Female University. Meredith students, says one 1980s graduate, "were the kind of gals you'd want to bring home to your parents."

If Eliot was largely molded by Bernie Spitzer's exacting formula for achievement, Silda was deeply influenced by her mom—and her frustrations. Trilby Wall was the consummate homemaker, a smart woman who dedicated all her talents to husband, family, and community. Raised Methodist, she converted to the faith of her husband, and the Walls went twice a week to Concord's First Baptist Church, where Bob served as a deacon. Trilby never earned a regular paycheck. She painted on the side, worked occasionally as a substitute teacher, became a certified master gardener, and later co-founded the local farmers' market. Eventually, she gently rebelled, substituting "home administrator" for "homemaker" when asked her occupation, and announcing that, after thirty years, she was through cooking meals every evening.

Silda resolved to have her own career, in addition—of course—to raising a family. For a time, she had contemplated art restoration. Then, eager to find a job where she could support a family on her own, she began considering law. But having never known a female attorney in Concord, she was thinking only about becoming a paralegal, until the attorney for her dad's hospital urged her to apply to law school. She did. A *summa cum laude* graduate of Meredith, Wall was admitted to Harvard, becoming the first Meredith alum to go there. She set out for a career in international law.

Then romance intervened. Midway through her first year at Harvard, Wall began dating classmate Peter Spiro Stamos, a Stanford graduate. They maintained a long-distance relationship the following year, while Stamos pursued his doctorate in political science on a Rhodes Scholarship at Oxford. Raised near Los Angeles, Stamos, handsome and charismatic, came from a Greek family. He would later become a McKinsey consultant, start a business, and launch a private investment firm that now manages more than $5 billion in assets. But at the time, he had big ambitions to go into politics. Classmates jabbered that he was destined to become the first Greek American president.

They were married on June 26, 1982, after Silda's second year of law school. Both were twenty-four. The Saturday-evening wedding took place at the Walls' church, First Baptist, and, while the event was a little cross-cultural by Concord standards, everything seemed picture-perfect, a throwback to an earlier era. Silda wore her mother's wedding gown, pure silk taffeta with a scoop neckline adorned with Chantilly lace, and a pillbox hat covered with pearls. Stamos's two brothers served as best men. And three clergymen presided: the Walls' Baptist minister as well as Greek Orthodox priests from England and Charlotte. Greek pastries were served at the reception. Afterward, the happy couple flew off for a honeymoon on the picturesque Greek island of Corfu, in the Ionian Sea.

Not long after the honeymoon was over, it became clear that something was terribly wrong. After returning from Greece, Wall flew with her new husband to England, where they planned to live for a year while he worked toward his degree. Silda had an internship with Amnesty International and a part-time job with an Oxford law firm. But she soon returned in shock to North Carolina: Stamos wanted a divorce. It is not clear precisely what went wrong; neither would discuss it for this book. But according to legal papers, the couple separated just twenty-nine days after the wedding. Wall and Stamos made a few abortive attempts to work things out, but by December, they had given up. Stamos remained in England. Wall worked in Washington until she could return to Harvard in the fall. This was the most devastating experience of her young life—a deeply personal failure for a woman who had never failed at anything. In Silda Wall's world, divorce was simply unimaginable.

When she met Eliot Spitzer in Vermont in January 1984, Wall had been separated from her husband for eighteen months. Her divorce would not be final until May. In the meantime, friends say, she had sworn she'd never trust a man again. But Eliot was so accepting about what she was going through—he seemed refreshingly different from the partner who had caused her so much pain. He also pursued her ardently. She'd later describe Spitzer as "my knight in shining armor." Despite their divergent backgrounds, they were also an intellectual match. Spitzer even had an interest in international law; he'd considered enrolling in a special joint program between Harvard and the Fletcher School of Law and Diplomacy at Tufts.

At Harvard, Spitzer had written his way onto the prestigious law review, in a competition for those who didn't make the cut purely on their grades. He also worked as a research assistant for Harvard professor Alan Dershowitz, helping him overturn the attempted-murder conviction of Claus von Bülow. Spitzer was a cerebral sort; he'd even co-authored a journal article on arms control in space. Silda, happily, couldn't imagine him pursuing a life in politics.

After graduation, Eliot and Silda both jumped onto the legal fast track in New York. Eliot took a one-year clerkship working for federal district court judge Robert Sweet, then signed on with Paul, Weiss, Rifkind, Wharton & Garrison, a top corporate firm. Silda found a high-powered job as well, at Skadden, Arps, Slate, Meagher & Flom, where she worked brutal hours on mergers and acquisitions, billing 3,200 hours a year—an average of more than sixty-one hours every week. Their Saturday-night dates often consisted of takeout food in a Skadden conference room.

On October 17, 1987, Eliot and Silda married. There was no Jewish version of *My Big Fat Greek Wedding* this time. They wed outdoors at night at the Boathouse in New York's Central Park, with Judge Sweet performing the civil ceremony. About two hundred friends and family attended, listening to musicians performing Handel's *Water Music*. As Wall Street panicked over "Black Monday"—the biggest financial crisis anyone could imagine—Eliot and Silda honeymooned in the Loire Valley of France. Then they settled down together in an apartment on East Seventy-second Street, in one of Bernie Spitzer's buildings.

By this time, Spitzer's career had taken a major detour: he'd bailed out from Paul, Weiss after just eleven months and gone to work for legendary Manhattan district attorney Robert Morgenthau, whose office later became the model for the TV show *Law & Order*. This was an unusual career move: young Ivy-educated New York lawyers who wanted experience as prosecutors typically signed on at the more prestigious U.S. attorney's office for the Southern District, which handled white collar crime. But that office had a hiring freeze. And Spitzer, miserable practicing corporate law (and certainly not needing the money), wasn't willing to wait. He started work as an assistant DA on August 25, 1986, at a salary of $31,500. He was twenty-seven years old.

Spitzer's first assignment was in the career criminal program, a plum job for a rookie, helping prosecute murderers and rapists. He amused one of his new colleagues there by asking whether he needed to move his "portfolio" into a blind trust to avoid conflicts of interest. After less than a year, he moved into the rackets bureau. Spitzer was brash, with obvious talent but little experience. "He just had supreme confidence in his own ability," recalls Dan Castleman, one of his supervisors, who left his job as Morgenthau's top deputy in 2009, after nearly thirty years in the DA's office. Spitzer's cross-examination technique, for example, needed work, "but he didn't think so. If you suggested a line of questioning, he would bristle at it. His sense of humor was his saving grace—his ability to poke fun at himself."

By January 1988, Spitzer had begun working on the investigation that defined his tenure and occupied most of his six years as an assistant DA. This was the prosecution of Thomas and Joseph Gambino, sons of an infamous Mafia boss, whose crime family had been taken over after his death by John Gotti, the "Teflon Don." Seeking to end mob control over the trucking business in New York's Garment District, Spitzer had convinced Morgenthau to let him set up an elaborate undercover operation to gather evidence. One cop working with Spitzer posed as a gypsy trucker, wearing a wire; another went to work in the Gambinos' warehouse. When that wasn't enough, the lawmen set up a sting operation by establishing "Chrystie Fashions," their own Chinatown sewing contractor, complete with immigrant labor. They rigged their sweatshop's offices with tapped phones and surveillance cameras, all in the hope of capturing Gambino goons using muscle to demand its trucking business.

Finally, Spitzer's crew brazenly bugged the Gambinos' headquarters, by cutting off power to the entire block to disable alarms, then sending in State Police investigators dressed as utility repairmen to pick thirteen locks and plant a wire in a ceiling tile. Fourteen years later, Spitzer excitedly described the operation to *The New York Times* as "a great black-bag job. . . . We set up a trucking company, we ran the sweatshop, we had wiretaps, bugs. It was a blast. . . ."

After more than a year of investigation, the DA's office brought charges for both extortion and, more creatively, antitrust violations. The high-profile case went to trial in February 1992, with Spitzer—by then thirty-two and head of the rackets bureau—as lead prosecutor, facing a dream team of defense lawyers. The New York press covered the trial closely.

Three weeks in, the two sides struck an extraordinary deal. The Gambinos would plead guilty to a single antitrust charge, pay a $12 million fine, and agree to get out of the business—a process that would be supervised by an outside monitor. But the accused mobsters wouldn't have to spend a day in jail. Some veteran prosecutors were horrified. The traditional approach was to throw the wise guys behind bars—or die trying. But Spitzer and Morgenthau reasoned that parts of their case were proving weak in trial, and that if the Gambinos won acquittal (and perhaps even if they were convicted), nothing would change in the industry. Says Judd Burstein, one of the defense attorneys in the case: "He came up with a very creative and tough plea bargain, which in the end was much more effective than just getting convictions and sending people to jail."

In the evolution of Eliot Spitzer, the Gambino case was an important moment in three ways. First, it would serve as Spitzer's controversial template for the attorney general's office, producing the desired result of changing an industry virtually overnight, while allowing the bad guys to cut a deal and walk away. Second, it offered a hint of Spitzer's private fascination with the undercover op, of the adrenaline rush he got operating in the realm of cloak-and-dagger. And third, it incubated Spitzer's political ambitions.

Spitzer invariably struck those he encountered as both impatient and ambitious, acutely aware of how his actions might affect his future prospects. In forging the Gambino deal, for example, says Burstein, "part of what was going on was his concern about his own reputation for losing a case like that. He was a young prosecutor and saw this as a chance for glory. When he saw there might not be the glory, he was smart enough to switch tacks and come up with a different way of dealing with it." Having wrapped the signature case of his young career—memorialized in a lengthy *New York Times Magazine* story—Spitzer left the DA's office that fall, returning to private practice at Silda's old firm, Skadden, Arps.

Though he'd always been miserable working at a big firm, Spitzer insists that when he went to Skadden in 1992, he expected to stay there long enough to make partner, and eventually end up in business—most likely at Spitzer Engineering. Of the three Spitzer children, Eliot was the only one who had the slightest interest in guiding the family empire. But he also had a visceral discomfort with the idea of being seen as a caretaker accepting a sinecure. He wanted to build something of his own from scratch, just as his father had.

Lloyd Constantine always assumed that would be in politics. Back in law school, Spitzer had spent a summer interning in the New York attorney general's antitrust bureau, then located in the South Tower of the World Trade Center. That's where he met Constantine, twelve years older and chief of the division. A graduate of Williams College and Columbia Law, Constantine had spent eight years doing legal services work, representing the poor, before joining the AG's office. A football lineman in college, Constantine still viewed himself as an athlete; like Spitzer, he was a brash and competitive man. "Within fifteen minutes," says Constantine, "I had an impression of him being very smart and very aggressive. It was pretty clear to me this was a guy who really cared about the law and was interested in a political career." In the years that followed, Constantine proudly claimed the role of Spitzer's mentor, close friend, and frequent tennis combatant. "He was in a hurry," says Constantine. "I didn't see him doing anything other than a career in government and running for public office." As Constantine saw it, Spitzer was just treading water until he could see an opening. "I was saying, through all of this: 'When are you going to make your move?'"

This time, Spitzer lasted only eighteen months in private practice. In early 1994, he told his wife that he wanted to run for attorney general of New York State. Silda was shocked. After marrying six years earlier, the Spitzers had quickly started a family. Elyssa was now four, Sarabeth not yet two. And Silda was already pregnant with their third. They had just moved into a larger apartment, at 985 Fifth, also owned by Spitzer's dad. While Silda had left the killer grind of Skadden, Arps back in 1987, she was working part-time at Chase Manhattan Bank, practicing international law. Now Eliot was going to run for statewide office?

"I'll think about it, but are you nuts?" she told her husband. "I was very surprised by the timing," she recalled in a 2005 interview. Silda had never imagined Eliot would run for office—at least not before their children were grown. She had some unpleasant history with a partner bearing political ambitions. Indeed, had she known when she met Spitzer that he would pursue such a career, she told me, "I would have probably run the other way. . . . As a spouse, I'd rather not see him involved in politics and have to deal with that."

Silda was also unsure that her husband would make a good politician. Spitzer was a cerebral Ivy League intellectual—hardly a natural gladhander. Most people with his pedigree had a visceral repulsion for the grubby business of running for office. "I didn't know if he had the temperament for it—the retail politics side of it," she said. "I didn't know if he'd have the patience."

On a personal level, Eliot's ambition presented his wife with a painful choice. He felt driven to avoid his destiny at Spitzer Engineering—to do something important on his own. But his aspiration now put him on a collision course with hers. Much as Eliot wanted to avoid ending up in his father's business, Silda, just as desperately, wanted to escape her mother's role as a homemaker. She had worked hard to build a successful legal career. She had come so far—Fifth Avenue was a long way from Concord. If Eliot were to spend the next six months—and beyond—traveling across New York, she'd be the only constant presence in the lives of their young children. She'd almost certainly need to quit her job.

And yet: she loved him. And she felt certain he would do a great job if he could somehow actually win. And she believed in people following their dreams—even though allowing Eliot to pursue his would force Silda to sacrifice her own. When Eliot raised the idea, they spoke about it only briefly. He wasn't much for talking things over with his wife—even important family issues. So Silda slept on the problem. In the morning, she didn't even speak to Eliot. Instead she left a Post-it note for him on his desk. It read: GO FOR IT! Discussing all these events, eleven years later, Silda cheerfully acknowledged the dynamic of their marriage—and her husband's ambition: "If I said 'No, don't run,' I don't know if that would have made a difference."

And so, on May 18, 1994, Eliot Spitzer announced his candidacy for attorney general of New York. His wife gave birth to the Spitzers' third daughter, Jenna, five days later.

Chapter 2: Becoming a Pol

B Y ANY STANDARD OF POLITICAL CALCULATION, ELIOT SPITZER'S decision to run for attorney general in 1994 was a delusion. Just thirty-four, Spitzer was a complete unknown. He hadn't held any elected office higher than student-government chairman at Princeton. He had no political organization or base of support. He was also entering the race late—just four months before the Democratic primary—against three established party rivals. To even win a place on the ballot, he would need to collect thousands of petition signatures from around the state. In fact, Spitzer had just two significant assets: his brains and his father's cash.

If his candidacy flew in the face of any political sense—and the private needs of his wife and growing family—Spitzer reasoned that he was seizing a once-in-a-lifetime opportunity. The AG's job had come up for grabs when Bob Abrams, the popular Democratic incumbent, abruptly announced his resignation during his fourth term, after fifteen years in office. The state legislature, as was its wont, had filled the vacancy with one of its own, a Democratic assemblyman from the Bronx named Oliver Koppell. But Koppell would have only months to make an impression before needing to stand for election. This opening had drawn two other candidates into the primary: former state senator Karen Burstein and Brooklyn DA Charles Hynes.

On a courtesy call to his old boss, Manhattan DA Morgenthau, Spitzer was asked how he'd raise all the money he needed for such a race. "I'm going to *self-finance*," he explained. And so he did: Spitzer quickly hired a raft of political consultants, launched a nonstop ad blitz, and began massively outspending his opponents. "It's outrageous," declared Koppell, who accused Spitzer of trying to buy the election. "All he has is intelligence, which I'll concede, and enormous amounts of money."

This first campaign marked the beginning of a smart, idealistic, and naïve man's plunge into the unfamiliar world of politics—a realm where pragmatism, self-interest, and experience usually prevailed. As a creature of ideas, Spitzer held in his mind a crisp, theoretical picture of how the world should operate—a vision, often noble, that was frequently re-moved from actual reality. Spitzer's entire political career—his glorious successes, his humiliating failures, his angry frustrations—would reflect the tension between these two poles, his struggle to either bend, or adapt to, the imperfect shape of life on our planet.

Almost no one thought Spitzer could win in 1994. They figured the race was just a "starter campaign," intended to build a public profile for a future run in which he might actually stand a chance. Spitzer himself had gone through a period of equivocation about launching a statewide race: he'd actually commissioned a poll to explore the idea of running for Congress instead. But by the time he declared for AG, he appeared to believe that victory was really possible—that the power of his ideas, am-plified by the family bankroll, would somehow triumph. "I didn't know enough," said Spitzer later, "to realize how it was going to play out."

Beginning with this race, Spitzer and his supporters always portrayed him as the virtuous, reform-minded anti-politician, an intellectual and moral exemplar. In his quest to become attorney general, the campaign slogan was "Total Change," and friends unhesitatingly described him as the straightest arrow they knew. Michael Cherkasky, a former boss in the DA's office, put it this way to a reporter in 1994: "If we think about what we would want our son to be, Eliot Spitzer is that kind of guy."

This self-image—and a visceral distaste for the very nature of politics—dictated how he started playing the game. His personal wealth was not merely an asset but a political virtue; it meant he was beholden to no one. But his inexperience was painfully evident, in ways both big and small. Barbara Kloberdanz, a veteran New York hand who served as his deputy campaign manager, recalls his first meet-and-greet appearance at a Manhattan subway stop. Spitzer stood awkwardly alone near the entrance, holding out a campaign flyer and calling out, "Something to read!" A friend happened past and accosted him: "What are you *doing*, Eliot? You sound like a Jehovah's Witness!"

Spitzer's putative campaign manager was an odd character named John Zaubler, a self-described conservative Republican who claimed to have collected fifty thousand political buttons. The thirty-three-year-old Zaubler had worked in Ross Perot's campaign for president and had once been arrested for creating a disturbance on a plane in the Atlanta airport. He'd grown up in Riverdale, near the Spitzers, and his father was a player in the New York real estate world; Spitzer had hired him as a family favor. But campaign workers say he had trouble operating the office phones and played virtually no role in running things. (In 2009, Zaubler would be arrested and placed under psychiatric examination after being charged with making death threats against Supreme Court Justice Sonia Sotomayor and President Obama.)

Effectively, Spitzer served as his own campaign manager, placing his personal stamp on every decision. He insisted on the campaign headquarters opening at 8:30 A.M. sharp, the office being kept neat, and his paid staffers looking presentable—all oddities in a political race. He also made them obtain three forms of identification to document that the hundreds of temporary workers they hired to collect petition signatures were employable. Such proof was technically required, but campaigns typically never bothered with it. "I'm running for attorney general," the candidate declared. "We need to follow the letter of the law."

Through this early point in his life, Spitzer had succeeded at almost everything he'd done, and he dealt poorly with frustration and failure. To his staff, he displayed a short temper. Spitzer was most often set off by the inevitable campaign screwup, beyond his personal control. He'd fulminate profanely for a while, then quickly calm down. Years later, when someone around politics would complain about a temperamental boss, Kloberdanz says she would scoff: "Oh, please! I've been yelled at by *Eliot Spitzer*!"

Spitzer's chief political calling card was his experience as a mob-busting prosecutor. So he cast himself as a tough-on-crime centrist, trumpeting his support for the death penalty (unusual for a New York Democrat; even his wife was against it) and his willingness to lock up juvenile offenders as adults. Never mind that the attorney general's office had virtually nothing to do with street crime. Spitzer also displayed creativity, offering a proposal to stamp numbers on bullets for easier tracing. His approach won him endorsements from the *New York Post* and *Daily News*, which praised him as "brimming with energy and ideas."

On the campaign trail, however, Spitzer was a dud, utterly lacking the common touch. He was uncomfortable plunging into a crowd, and his speech maintained an intellectual distance. "I find it tremendously satisfying to have a substantive discussion," he rhapsodized to an Albany political reporter. "I love the substantive discussions." The reporter noted Spitzer's weighty position papers, writing, "You can run out of breath just reading Spitzer's basic campaign literature, assuming you don't get a hernia lifting it." When another journalist asked the candidates for their favorite member of the Beatles, Spitzer responded: "I don't know. My favorite composer is Brahms." Even friends were underwhelmed. Jim Cramer, a Harvard Law classmate who later became famous as the host of CNBC's *Mad Money*, was then running a Manhattan hedge fund. In an interview, Cramer later recalled inviting Spitzer to address his firm's brokers. "He came in, and gave this talk, and he's not polished, he's stumbling over the words. Genuine, but unimpressive. He was just not ready for prime time. He had no feel."

In this first race, naive in so many ways, Spitzer also displayed a capacity for deceit on two sensitive issues: who was advising his campaign and how he was paying for it. Behind the scenes, this earnest reformer was taking direction from an improbable guru: Dick Morris. Morris was then at the peak of his powers as a Svengali-like advisor to President Bill Clinton; he'd regularly step out of Spitzer strategy sessions to take calls from the White House. The two men had family history—Morris's father had been Bernie Spitzer's lawyer—and Eliot trusted him implicitly. A secretive and controversial figure, Morris usually advised Republicans, including Jesse Helms and Trent Lott. (In 1994 in New York, he was simultaneously working for a Republican candidate for governor.) White House chief of staff Leon Panetta later described Morris as a cynical manipulator who pandered to Clinton's "dark side." In the political world, everyone knew Morris as both brilliant and dangerous. Another Spitzer consultant put it this way: "Dick will have ten ideas: six will put you in jail; three are dumb. But one of 'em will take you to the promised land."

Because Morris was so radioactive—loathed by Democratic activists, as well as antithetical to Spitzer's outsider image—pains were taken to conceal his role. Kloberdanz says that before she met Morris—who had to approve her hiring—she was told she was going to meet "a high-powered political consultant whose name may not be mentioned." Although

Morris served as the campaign's top strategist, Spitzer's public disclosure reports made no disclosure of the hefty fees he received; the money was funneled to him through other consultants. "We had a financial arrangement with Dick that was countenanced by Eliot Spitzer," says Hank Sheinkopf, a veteran New York consultant who often worked with Morris and prepared the ads for Spitzer's first two campaigns. "Dick got a piece of the pie from me." This subterfuge wasn't illegal, however. New York State's porous disclosure laws (which Spitzer was promising to reform) didn't require naming consultants who operated as "subcontractors."

The precise source of Spitzer's lavish "self-financing"—was it coming from him or his father?—was the second murky realm of his first race, though it wouldn't explode as an issue until later. In 1994, the candidate was left merely to address the charge that he was a rich usurper trying to buy his way into high office. He responded that New York's problems were so grave he had a duty to act. ("If I wait my turn, by twenty years it will be too late.") And he acknowledged his appetite for tempting the odds. ("Maybe I'm just a high-stakes gambler; I roll the dice in a big way.")

Inevitably, it ended badly. Spitzer finished fourth in the primary, polling just 18.5 percent. He had spent about $30 a vote, a total of $3.9 million—ten times as much as the victor, Karen Burstein.

Spitzer, who had said publicly this might be his only run for office, did not, of course, retire from politics. Instead, he quickly signed on to travel the state making speeches for Mario Cuomo, who was seeking his fourth term that November against a little-known Republican state senator from Peekskill named George Pataki. But 1994 was not a Democratic year in New York. Pataki upset Cuomo, once viewed as a serious contender for president. And Burstein lost to Dennis Vacco, a former U.S. attorney from Buffalo, amid Republican whispers that the openly lesbian Democrat would pursue a homosexual "agenda."

With Burstein's defeat, Spitzer immediately began laying plans to run again for attorney general in 1998. Winning the job would be the focus of his life for the next four years. And this time, he would do everything differently.

———

"Losing," Eliot Spitzer would later tell me, "is hands down the best way to learn." Spitzer's frustration with the outcome of his first campaign prompted a rare moment of introspection. A decade afterward, he described his reaction to me this way: "I remember in 1994, after I lost, I . . . I don't want to say 'soul-search' . . . But I thought: *did you learn something? Can you change the outcome?*" In other words, after spending $4 million and finishing last, his first thought was about running again. He also wasn't much for hashing things out at home. "It's interesting to watch someone who's had a defeat," said Silda. "The thing about Eliot is, he's very settled in who he is. There was no 'Let's talk about it.' He goes on a long run, and he thinks, and he works through what he has to work through."

Spitzer, of course, couldn't yet declare his candidacy for a 1998 election. But he used the intervening time shrewdly, launching what amounted to a four-year campaign for attorney general. He began by establishing a flexible base of operations, joining a new boutique law firm, Constantine & Partners, led by his old friend Lloyd Constantine. Spitzer signed on, according to Constantine, with the explicit understanding that he could have as much time off as he needed to pursue his ambitions.

A second run also required some repositioning in the Spitzer household. After completing her maternity leave from Chase Manhattan, Silda had reluctantly given up her job. Eliot's political career, with its long days and statewide travel, had naturally generated conflict at home; Silda pointedly joked that her husband had run in 1994 to get out of late-night feedings for their new daughter. Now, even when Eliot was in New York, he rose at 5 A.M., left their Fifth Avenue apartment for a brisk three-mile run around the Central Park Reservoir, then returned to sit at the kitchen table, head buried in the *Times*, while his wife scrambled to dress and feed the three girls and get the older ones off to school. As Silda recalled it later: "His idea of being up with the kids in the morning was being awake reading the newspaper." Finally, she put her foot down: Eliot agreed to handle the morning duty after his run so Silda could sleep in. Politics even influenced the Spitzers' choice of a weekend retreat. They began leasing the guesthouse on an upstate farm in Pine Plains, New York—midway between Fifth Avenue and Albany.

In 1994, Spitzer had run his campaign almost entirely through the media. "You'd take off from LaGuardia and look down and think: *no amount of one-on-one conversation matters; it's just too vast.*" But after losing, he decided that was dead wrong. So in his second run, realizing that personal contact "really does add up," he traveled the far reaches of

New York in his Dodge minivan, appearing at county fairs and rubber-chicken dinners and learning how to glad-hand. In the 1994 campaign, he'd voiced contempt for the political establishment. Over the next four years, he assiduously courted party leaders, appearing on the doorstep of every Democratic county chairman. Before he even formally announced, he'd driven seventy thousand miles around New York. To tap into the party establishment, he hired John Marino, who had run Cuomo's campaigns and served as state Democratic chairman.

Spitzer backed his charm offensive by opening up the family checkbook. In the aftermath of Cuomo's defeat, the Democratic Party in New York was in shambles. Only one Democrat held statewide office, and the party was deep in debt. This made the Spitzer fortune an even more precious commodity, and the candidate-in-waiting spread it around. During the period leading up to the 1998 election, Spitzer, his parents, and his campaign handed out more than a hundred donations totaling $300,000 to party candidates and organizations—$50,000 in Buffalo alone. Spitzer wrote many of the checks about the same time local party officials endorsed him. Yet he denied any quid pro quo, insisting he was merely helping build grassroots organizations where the locals were already behind him. "Spitzer doesn't make the same mistake twice," said his ad consultant, Hank Sheinkopf. "He learned from the defeat in 1994 the value of hitting the bricks and meeting people. The guy you met in 1994 was kind of callow. Very smart—but he didn't have that lean and hungry look in his eyes. . . . Spitzer became a pol in the '98 race."

Even as he was laying a foundation behind the scenes, Spitzer worked to buttress his centrist credentials and remain in the public eye. Together with a registered Republican, he launched a New York branch of a non-profit legal group, called the Center for Community Interest, as a sort of counterpoint to the ACLU. Its stated goal was to defend law-abiding citizens against unreasonable "civil liberties demands." In 1997, New York's Republican governor, Pataki, even talked to him about taking a job in his administration as head of the state division of criminal justice. This showed that Spitzer's centrist strategy was working; he was a Democrat even a Republican could live with. Spitzer declined. He was keeping his eyes on the prize.

He became a fixture on the TV talk-show circuit, appearing as a legal commentator on such shows as *Geraldo*, CNN's *Burden of Proof*, and Fox News's *Hannity & Colmes*. For Eliot, even the screamfests were child's play, a gentle reprise of his upbringing at the family dinner table. He opined on everything from the JonBenét Ramsey murder to Lady Diana's death to the O. J. Simpson trial. But Spitzer was never more in demand than in early 1998, when he appeared on *ten* separate programs in a single week to talk about the story that had the entire nation buzzing: the Monica Lewinsky sex scandal. Spitzer lamented how a criminal investigation had turned into a political issue. Silda had her opinions on this subject as well. She later told a friend that she couldn't understand how Hillary Clinton, in the face of personal humiliation, had so resolutely stood by her man. If she were in Hillary's position, Silda remarked, she'd be gone.

On May 5, 1998, with his wife and three daughters at his side, Spitzer formally announced his second run for attorney general. Once again, he cast himself as a very different kind of candidate—one who operated under a better, higher ethical standard. Evoking the film *Mr. Smith Goes to Washington*, he declared that the AG should be "the voice of ethics, the voice of integrity"—a "Jimmy Stewart in Albany."

Some of Spitzer's behavior, however, wasn't exactly reminiscent of *Mr. Smith*. By the time he announced, Spitzer had already scored his first upset, winning a straw poll taken of all those upstate county leaders he'd courted. Spitzer was facing three Democratic primary opponents in 1998: Oliver Koppell, running again; Evan Davis, former counsel to Governor Cuomo; and a state senator from Manhattan named Catherine Abate, who had also served as New York City correction commissioner. Abate was an early favorite—the only woman in the field, Italian American, with strong labor support.

But a few days before Spitzer's announcement, Abate made headlines herself, and not in a good way: she'd been forced to acknowledge the possibility that her deceased father had been in the Mafia. Abate had abandoned her long-standing denials, according to a *New York Times* account, following what she described as a "whisper campaign" by Spitzer, whose staff had given reporters a twenty-year-old newspaper story identifying Joseph Abate as a capo in New Jersey's Lucchese crime family. Spitzer apologized to Abate, but told the *Times* his aides had merely been responding to requests from reporters.

Much of the primary focused on Spitzer's massively outspent opponents howling that he was trying to buy the election. Davis called his donations to local party organizations illegal "vote-buying"; Koppell and

Abate filed lawsuits, insisting Spitzer had failed to properly disclose where he was getting his money. But all the formal complaints went nowhere, even as Spitzer flooded the airwaves, buying the kind of name recognition his opponents couldn't afford.

After Spitzer won the primary in September, with 42 percent, things got really ugly. Although no elected New York attorney general had been ousted in decades, Dennis Vacco seemed a juicy target. A protégé of Republican U.S. senator Al D'Amato, Vacco had purged 140 experienced lawyers after taking office and replaced them with a raft of political hires. His staff's inept legal work had prompted several judges to publicly criticize the office. He'd withdrawn a policy barring job discrimination against gays. And he'd accepted campaign money from a car-leasing company that was under investigation by his office. Vacco wasted no time attacking Spitzer as a Manhattan liberal, and cranked up the charge that he was lying about his finances. Spitzer pushed back hard, casting Vacco as a troglodyte who had sullied the AG's office by failing to defend consumers and turning it into a "patronage pit." One Spitzer TV spot noted that Vacco's chief deputy had failed the bar exam seven times.

Spitzer was a vastly different candidate this time around. To be sure, he retained a measure of awkwardness on the campaign trail. ("Instead of kissing a baby's cheek," wrote *The New York Times*, "he was more inclined to hand the infant a campaign flier.") But he'd shed the manner and methods of a neophyte, and didn't hesitate firing back as the race descended into endless exchanges of political buckshot through press releases and thirty-second ads. Spitzer was running his campaign from inside the Manhattan offices of Global Strategy Group, one of his consultants, and he had retained a large, ungainly, and expensive brain trust. Yet he remained an impatient micro-manager. In Spitzer's dream organizational structure, he sat at the hub, with spokes extending outward to a large number of experts who could offer competing "smart opinions" to debate and choose from. His team included two polling analysts, two former state party chairmen, and a media consultant. Ignoring advice from all of them, Spitzer kept ordering up new TV spots, hyperactively changing the ad rotation to react to every new campaign development. By the time the race was over, Sheinkopf had cut ninety-six different ads.

Struggling to maintain order in all this, as campaign manager, was a low-key, rumpled Cornell graduate named Rich Baum. Baum, then twenty-nine, was a former small-town political whiz kid. He'd grown up in Middletown, New York, the only child in a family of German Jewish Hudson Valley dairy farmers. Active in Democratic politics from his teens, Baum had earned his history degree at twenty-one, won election to the Orange County legislature at twenty-four, then served four years as Democratic minority leader. Spitzer had met him during his upstate travels, and after Baum lost a bid for county executive, Spitzer had signed him on. Canny and self-effacing, Baum, who looked like a skinnier version of Jason Alexander, had a gift for quickly calculating the political implications of anything. He would become Spitzer's political right-hand man for the next decade.

But in 1998, Dick Morris was once again the dominant force in Spitzer's camp, and the candidate would go to even greater lengths this time to deny that he was playing any significant role. With good reason: if Morris was a controversial figure in 1994, in 1998 he was a pariah—and a laughingstock. Two years earlier, during the Democratic National Convention, he'd been forced to resign as chief strategist for Clinton's reelection after a supermarket tabloid unearthed the story of his relationship with a prostitute named Sherry Rowlands. The *Star*'s story included a photo of Morris (who was married) embracing Rowlands on the balcony of his Washington hotel suite, and her claim that, to impress her, he'd let her listen in on phone conversations with the president. There was also a salacious little detail Rowlands offered about how he liked to suck her toes. After a period in seclusion, Morris had gone to work as a pundit for Fox News and a columnist for the *New York Post*, and had supposedly retired from political consulting in the U.S. And, oh yes—Morris also owed more than a half million dollars in back taxes to the federal government.

Determined to win, Spitzer had no problem employing a valued advisor with such baggage—presuming, of course, that no one found out about it before Election Day. In June, a *Daily News* reporter got wind that Morris was advising Spitzer, but Morris blew off the issue by insisting his role amounted to nothing more than unpaid "kibitzing" between old friends. George Arzt, a media consultant for Spitzer, says the candidate instructed him to tell the *Daily News* that Morris was merely an "unpaid volunteer," but that he never did so because he knew it wasn't true. In fact, Morris had been intimately involved in the campaign from the start.

Says Spitzer's ad consultant Sheinkopf, in a statement affirmed by three other top advisors to Spitzer in 1998: "Dick was there every step of the way, for every moment, in full form and body."

There was, of course, no disclosure before the election of any payments to Morris. But after the ballots were cast, Spitzer, questioned by a *Daily News* reporter, revealed that he had decided to pay him. Morris would get $175,000. Spitzer explained it this way: "At the beginning . . . I said very frankly, 'Dick, I'm not going to pay you. You're an old friend, you have liabilities now, you are not somebody who can publicly be part of my campaign.'" But Morris just couldn't be denied, according to Spitzer. "He is an aggressive individual [and] if you open the door a little bit, he will push it wide open. . . . He began to play a larger role and . . . I thought he should be compensated."

The situation demonstrated Spitzer's willingness to publicly dissemble on issues that were personally awkward, as well as his devotion to long-standing relationships. "Maybe I'm a fool for this," Spitzer told me in 2008: "I actually believe loyalty matters." While Morris had "his personal life issues to deal with," Spitzer noted, "I'd always found him to be one of the smartest political minds out there." In addition to being a creative strategist, Morris played an important personal role with the candidate. Says one campaign strategist: "When Eliot wanted to do something crazy, Dick got on the phone and said 'no.'" In future years, this critical role would fall to others, with mixed results.

———

As the 1998 race headed into its final weeks, both sides stepped up the mudslinging. Spitzer exploited a tragic development, linking Vacco, who opposed abortion, to the murder of a Buffalo doctor who performed abortions and had been shot in the back inside his home by a sniper. Spitzer cited a six-year-old judicial ruling that had rebuked Vacco, while serving as U.S. attorney in Buffalo, for failing to enforce a court order barring anti-abortion protestors from blocking the entrance to the doctor's clinic; he also invoked Vacco's decision to disband an abortion-rights unit in the AG's office. At the time, police hadn't even publicly identified a suspect in the murder. Yet in a TV debate, Spitzer suggested Vacco had blood on his hands. "The horror that occurred the other night," he declared, "should weigh heavily on his conscience."

For both sides, some of the worst damage was self-inflicted. For

Spitzer, the problem was his explanation of how he'd funded his political career. He'd bankrolled his two races almost entirely through personal loans he'd made to his campaigns. By the end of the 1998 race, this debt would total $12.2 million ($3.9 million for 1994, $8.3 million for 1998). Ever since he entered politics, reporters and opponents had been asking him where he'd gotten all this money. And Spitzer, with increasing vehemence, had repeatedly denied that he was getting any help from his father. "The money is all my money," he told the *Post* editorial board in October 1998. "It always has been my money."

The problem is that it wasn't. While Spitzer had acknowledged borrowing most of the money he'd loaned to his campaigns from Morgan Guaranty Bank, he had also insisted that he was managing the debt on his own, using eight Manhattan co-op apartments that his father had given him as collateral. In fact, personal tax returns Spitzer had released showed his declared income couldn't support the payments on so much debt—that he must have received help from his family.

This was an important distinction. While there were no legal limits on how much the candidate spent on his own campaign, Bernie Spitzer's support in any one year was limited by law to $353,000. Vacco was pummeling Spitzer on the issue, branding him a liar with no regard for the law. As Spitzer continued to bob and weave, his poll numbers—which had shown him within range of Vacco—slid.

Spitzer's advisors had tried for weeks to get him to tell the truth, to put the issue behind them before it was too late. Sheinkopf says he'd even urged Spitzer to run a TV ad acknowledging his mistake and announcing that he'd return any tainted family money. But Spitzer had refused. Though it was a reality of his adult life, Spitzer had always hated the appearance of relying on "Daddy's money." And he felt fiercely protective of his father, whom Vacco was treating as a punching bag. During a parade appearance by both candidates, Spitzer had rushed up and gotten in Vacco's face, angrily telling him, "You leave my father out of this!"

With just one week before Election Day and the *Times* about to publish a big story on the issue, Spitzer came clean. He acknowledged that his father, at the end of 1994, had loaned him the money to pay off his $3.9 million bank debt, with sweetheart repayment terms. (He had made only occasional payments to his dad since.) That, in turn, had made it possible for him to take out *more* bank loans in 1998. Tax returns also revealed that Spitzer was receiving about $200,000 a year in "consulting fees" from his dad; Spitzer had begun receiving this money about the time he declared his candidacy in 1994. Was this a backdoor campaign subsidy? Spitzer denied it. He insisted the money was for managing his father's stock investments, that he'd worked hard to earn it, and that he'd assumed that responsibility after quitting his job at Skadden, Arps to run for attorney general.

In essence, the Spitzers had cooked up a scheme to allow Bernie to secretly finance his son's campaigns when Eliot wasn't able to do it directly. In 1998, Spitzer would belatedly explain his deceit as an attempt to protect his father's privacy, while insisting that his manipulations had broken no state election law. (His dad had loaned him the $3.9 million immediately *after* the 1994 campaign, when he was a private citizen.) Bernie Spitzer offered a less lawyerly defense, explaining years later that, "in my naïveté," he couldn't understand how there "could be any objection to a father lending money to a son who wants to enter the political world."

The Spitzers, of course, were hardly naïve; what they'd done and said had deliberately finessed both New York's porous campaign-finance rules and an array of awkward political considerations, while ignoring any higher standard of law or truth. Spitzer's handling of the matter would linger as an issue for the rest of his political career. "It was dumb," he acknowledged years later. "The way I handled the inquiries was dumb because, as I have learned since then, transparency was the right way to do things. By not being forthright on this, people drew inferences and I paid a price for that. Live and learn. . . . I've since learned that there is very little that's private."

———

By the time Spitzer's last-minute confession hit the press, there was a sense of desperation in his camp. One new poll showed Vacco with a thirteen-point lead, with just days to go. At a 2 A.M. meeting of the campaign brain trust, there was discussion of whether Spitzer should shut down his spending and give up, to save the money for another day. Spitzer refused. "When you're down by two touchdowns with five minutes to go, you don't just walk off the field," he later explained. "You're more likely to lose than win," Morris bluntly told the candidate. "But I've seen people come back from worse. If you double down, you can win. But it has to be all negative through the election."

Throughout the race, Spitzer had resisted running a relentlessly negative ad campaign. Encouraged by his wife, he'd insisted on a fast-changing mix of spots that also showcased his ideas and background. But now everything was on the line; his promising career in public service was almost over before it had started. Spitzer agreed without hesitation. Morris immediately banged out the script for two brutal new TV spots. They featured shadowy images of Vacco, with dark clouds behind him and ominous music. Baum dubbed them the "Apocalypse ads," and the campaign rushed them onto the air.

The *Times*, as expected, gave the Manhattan Democrat its endorsement. But it wasn't exactly a rallying cry. Describing the race as a choice between "two flawed candidates," the paper accused Spitzer of "dishonesty" and "evasions" about conduct "clearly designed to circumvent laws that would have limited his father's direct contributions to the campaign." It was endorsing Spitzer, the *Times* wrote, only because Vacco was "an even worse choice."

Luckily for Spitzer, Vacco had also committed a gaffe — or at least a remark that could be portrayed as one. In an interview with *Jewish Week*, a New York paper, he had declared that it was impossible to prove the effectiveness of capital punishment because researchers "don't stand outside a bodega" (a Hispanic grocery store) and "ask the bandito if he would have killed someone if there was no death penalty." Spitzer's aides heard about it even before the story was published, convinced *Jewish Week* to provide a transcript, then eagerly passed it around to the daily media, determined to generate as big a stink as possible.

Vacco, who had called a press conference to blast Spitzer for his campaign-finance confession, instead faced a grilling about his own remarks. The Republican insisted he'd never mentioned "banditos" during the *Jewish Week* interview, but it didn't matter. On the campaign's final Friday, Spitzer staged a noisy media event outside a Manhattan bodega. There, Hispanic leaders angrily accused Vacco of stereotyping Hispanics as criminals. When Vacco publicly grumbled that it was "curious" the issue had emerged just in time to divert attention from his opponent's problems, Spitzer accused Vacco of falsely "alleging a conspiracy" between a Jewish paper and a Jewish candidate. That claim (which was never actually made) was "defamatory" and "insulting" to the Jewish community, Spitzer thundered. As the campaign rolled into the final weekend, the "banditos" story dominated the coverage, instead of reports about Spitzer's deceptions. Says media advisor Arzt: "It stanched the hemorrhaging."

Election night 1998 began well for New York's Democrats. While Republican George Pataki had cruised to his second term, Congressman Charles Schumer had beaten Al D'Amato, the incumbent U.S. senator. But it was impossible, deep into the night, to say who had won the race for attorney general. Spitzer held a tiny margin with 200,000 absentee paper ballots still to be tallied.

As the counting and re-counting across the state dragged on into December, Spitzer clung to his lead, ultimately claiming an upset victory by just 25,186 votes, out of 4.3 million cast. It was New York's closest statewide race in forty years. Vacco refused to concede for forty-one days, bitterly alleging all manner of irregularities and fraud, long after the outcome was clear. *Dead people had voted! Criminals! Illegal immigrants!* All this was memorialized in a giant headline in the *New York Post*: VACCO: ALIENS STOLE MY ELECTION.

Eliot Spitzer was the sixty-third attorney general of New York.

Chapter 3: Eliot Time

A S ELIOT SPITZER LATER DESCRIBED IT, HE AWOKE ON HIS first day as attorney general of New York with an "epiphany"—the sudden realization that he could have an impact unlike anyone who had ever held the office. For nearly two decades, each new wave in American politics had drained power from Washington: the vilification of big government, starting with Ronald Reagan; the move toward "judicial restraint"; the embrace of deregulation; and the abiding belief that rollicking, unfettered capitalism was the path to prosperity for all. Under the banner of the "New Federalism," Uncle Sam had retreated across a vast expanse, ostensibly in the name of states' rights. As a liberal Democrat, Spitzer had opposed this trend. But as a newly minted attorney general, he sensed an opportunity to seize the day—to step large into a yawning power vacuum.

Itching to get started, Spitzer had taken the oath of office from a justice of the peace at his weekend home in Pine Plains just after midnight on January 1. At that moment, Spitzer didn't know precisely where he was going; he certainly hadn't the slightest thought of launching the Wall Street crusades that would make him a superstar. But he knew he didn't want to just put bad guys behind bars. He wanted to bring cases that would change the world.

Despite all the campaign noise about fighting crime, the attorney general's office had historically focused on consumer-protection issues, especially local fraud. It had limited regulatory duties, over New York charities and real estate. It also served as the state government's law firm, representing administrative agencies and even the governor in all types of litigation; this responsibility occupied more than half the office's six hundred lawyers. Beyond these formal obligations, the AG could pick and choose which issues to pursue, wearing his white hat as "the people's lawyer." Bill Clinton, who got his political start as AG of Arkansas before becoming a governor and president, told Spitzer at a fundraiser that it was "the best job I've ever had." As Clinton explained, after taking the podium, "When I was attorney general, I didn't have to hire people or fire them, appoint people or disappoint them, raise taxes or cut spending, and if I did anything unpopular, I could always blame the Constitution."

Spitzer envisioned his AG's office as a giant public-interest law firm, scouring the landscape for injustice and cooking up new ways to fight it. This vision of his franchise had almost no limits. The job "provides an opportunity to do more for society than any other position I can imagine," Spitzer declared in a breakfast speech to the New York City Bar Association, less than a month after taking office. "The jurisdiction of this office is so elastic, is so expansive, that it never snaps. There is virtually no problem that you read about in the newspapers that you cannot begin to address through creative public advocacy in this office."

This speech, unnoticed at the time, was an early signal of the new AG's ambitions. Spitzer began by hiring a high-powered group of top lieutenants, impressive recruits to an office traditionally viewed as a backwater. Reflecting Spitzer's taste for intellectual pedigree, virtually all his top appointees had Ivy League degrees, a point noted in a stream of press releases detailing their elite backgrounds ("Articles Editor, Yale Law Review"). Among the key players in the operation were the AG's dozen bureau chiefs, who presided over specialists in areas ranging from health-care to criminal fraud, antitrust to the Internet. They'd been drawn by Spitzer's vow "to turn them loose"—to let ideas for big cases bubble up.

Spitzer's first deputy was Michele Hirshman, a prosecutor he'd plucked from the U.S. attorney's office in Manhattan, where she ran the public-corruption unit. Hirshman would preside over the legal staff. Constantine ran the transition, but remained in private practice. Spitzer was assembling a meritocracy, a public repudiation of Vacco's partisan hires, surrounding himself with "super-smart" people—his intellectual equals—with whom he could debate the thorniest issues and hatch new ways to tackle them. He even hired a few lawyers without any assigned duties—"floaters"—just because they were so brainy he liked having them around.

Rich Baum served as chief of staff, charged with tending to the new AG's reputation and political future. His close partner in that task was communications director Darren Dopp. Dopp, then thirty-nine, was a ballplayer—a star shortstop during his college days at the State University of New York in Binghamton, his native turf—who loved the game of state politics. He'd spent seven years as a reporter, and covered Albany and politics for the Associated Press. Then Mario Cuomo had hired him as his traveling press secretary. Dopp became a favorite of the governor, who was a former minor league pitcher; they'd talk baseball together for hours and shoot hoops in the driveway of the governor's mansion with Cuomo's son Andrew, his most trusted aide. After Cuomo lost to Pataki in 1994, Dopp went to work for the majority leader of the state assembly until Spitzer's election. A self-described "spinmeister," Dopp was a genius at the care and feeding of reporters, passing them juicy nuggets in a conspiratorial whisper. Intensely loyal, he became a trusted sounding board for Spitzer—an easygoing "guy's guy" to the AG's intense intellectualism. Though the two men were the same age, Dopp routinely called Spitzer "boss," just as everyone in the Manhattan DA's office had addressed the revered Morgenthau. Soon Spitzer, who obsessed over his treatment in the press, was calling Dopp a dozen times a day for a three-minute fix on what reporters were buzzing about. *What have you heard? What are you seeing? Where are we? . . . What else? . . . What else? . . . What else? . . . Talk to you later!* To prepare for these rapid-fire calls, Dopp kept a running list of developments in a small notebook. He and Baum joked that Spitzer "was sucking the knowledge out of our brains, before he went back to working with people of his own intelligence."

It would be two years before Spitzer began taking aim at Wall Street. But it was only months before he moved to extend his reach, finding ways to tackle problems that typically fell under the purview of the federal government. Smokestack emissions from other states were producing acid-rain damage and smog in New York; Spitzer sued Midwestern utilities operating coal-fired power plants, under an obscure provision of the federal Clean Air Act. General Electric and the state had been fighting for decades over PCB contamination in the Hudson River; under a novel legal theory, Spitzer sued to force the company to pay for dredging, arguing that the toxic chemicals were damaging commerce by rendering parts of the river impossible to navigate.*

Spitzer relished sticking up for the little guy. He sued upscale restaurants for discrimination, forcing them to hire more female servers. He filed more lawsuits to make sure bathroom attendants and grocery-store deliverymen were paid the minimum wage. He sued New York City to block the auction of more than a hundred community gardens. Always, Spitzer made sure that the public was keenly aware of his activities. Dopp's team churned out more than two hundred press releases a year, including self-congratulatory ones marking both Spitzer's first hundred days in office ("A.G. Lauded for Quality of Hires, Early Activism") and the end of his first year ("Attorney General Commended for Staff Selections and Key Initiatives"). For major cases, the stage was set with judicious leaks to key reporters.

In his most ambitious—albeit unsuccessful—early initiative, Spitzer even tried to impose national handgun regulation. Gun control, of course, was considered a federal legislative issue, not the province of a single state attorney general. But the powerful gun lobby had blocked any action in Congress. So Spitzer cooked up his own scheme to establish national controls, making his first attempt to use what critics would later decry as "economic extortion."

His office's legal research had suggested that any lawsuit against the gun companies was a long shot. Cities and private lawyers had brought cases, but the industry hadn't lost one yet. So Spitzer tried to bluff the gunmakers into accepting controls. In a series of meetings, he warned them that New York was preparing to file the first state lawsuit against them; this would surely bury them in expensive litigation, just like the tobacco companies. And there was only one way out: they would need to accept a code of conduct, which included installing trigger locks, limiting retail purchases to one weapon a month, making guns more easily traceable, and halting sales through dealers with a history of selling to criminals.

---

* The acid-rain lawsuits led to relatively quick settlements with two utilities that included a commitment to cut emissions. The GE battle dragged on for another decade; the company would finally begin dredging the Hudson in 2009. Federal agencies ultimately played a major role in both sets of negotiations.

Andrew Cuomo, by then secretary of the U.S. Department of Housing and Urban Development, jumped in, and the Clinton White House threatened a federal lawsuit against the gunmakers. Cuomo was planning to run for governor of New York in 2002, and Spitzer viewed his move as a meddlesome play for headlines. The AG fired off an angry letter to the White House, accusing the feds of screwing up delicate efforts at reform by having "injected" themselves where they weren't needed—precisely the charge that would so often be leveled at him from Washington. Spitzer and Cuomo battled bitterly for primacy on the gun issue, setting the stage for years of testy relations.

Spitzer tried to turn up the pressure on his own, organizing a boycott by cities and states that vowed not to buy weapons from any manufacturer who didn't accept his code of conduct. "If you do not sign," he warned the gunmakers, "your bankruptcy lawyers will be knocking at your door." But the manufacturers didn't blink. They knew Spitzer—and even the feds—had limited leverage. Most gun companies were private, immune from Wall Street fallout. Unlike the tobacco industry, they retained a noisy public constituency. And Spitzer's boycott never took off. When New York finally sued, citing a 1907 law declaring that the carrying of an illegal handgun was a "public nuisance," the case was quickly thrown out.

Despite the occasional failure, Spitzer's creative aggressiveness had made a quick impression. *The New York Times*, which devoted more and more coverage to his "string of audacious actions," lavished editorial praise on the new attorney general. Governor Pataki bristled that Spitzer was getting too much credit—and with good reason. Spitzer was already looming as a political rival.

———

The freedom to call your shots made the AG's job a natural springboard to higher office. As a candidate in 1998, Spitzer had acknowledged this history, but offered the requisite denial of any higher ambitions. "The old joke is that 'AG' stands for 'aspiring governor,'" he told the editorial board of the *New York Post*. "It isn't so for me." But by 2000—less than two years after he'd squeaked into office—there was already media buzz that Spitzer would run for governor, perhaps as early as 2002. The AG's spinmeister had even begun encouraging this speculation, after first getting Spitzer's blessing.

"Why would I want to do that?" Spitzer asked, when Dopp proposed feeding the rumors—quietly, of course.

"Boss," Dopp replied, "there's no harm in being written about as a possible future governor. And it could come in handy later on."

Spitzer just smiled.

In fact, the AG *was* entertaining plans to run for governor, though not until 2006, after he'd completed two terms. He'd confided his intentions to Mark Weprin, a Queens assemblyman who had been one of his earliest supporters. He'd also decided to do things differently, starting with his campaign for reelection: he was getting out of the "self-financing" business.

Just two months after taking office, Spitzer had hired Cindy Darrison, who had raised money for U.S. senator Daniel Patrick Moynihan, to build a fundraising organization for his 2002 reelection campaign. Work began immediately, and Spitzer proved a money magnet. One of his earliest big donations, $5,000, came from the insurance giant AIG, which would later find itself dramatically at odds with the attorney general. Spitzer's decision to raise money from outside his family didn't affect the $12 million debt from his first two races, owed to his father and Morgan Guaranty. He'd promised to pay that off on his own, and would do so during his time as AG. About half the money would come from the sale, for $6.1 million, of those eight co-op apartments that his father had given him. The buyer? Bernard Spitzer. (The AG insisted his dad had paid the market price.)

In the meantime, Spitzer was honing his skills in the banalities of politics. Among the AG's personal correspondence was a note to the Long Island Antique Bottle Association. ("Thank you for the beautiful antique milk bottle. . . . As you know, milk is the quintessential consumer product and our office represents the People of this State in keeping it safe and reasonably priced. I have proudly displayed the bottle in my office.") During a steady diet of public appearances, Spitzer ventured out to Staten Island to speak for four minutes at an Israel Bonds dinner. In a memo, Avi Schick, an Orthodox Jew whom Spitzer had hired as a deputy AG, carefully prepped him on political correctness for the occasion. He should note that "this week we celebrate Jerusalem Day"; he should cite recent anti-Semitic attacks in Europe as "an unfortunate reminder" of why the Jewish people "needed the state of Israel 54 years ago, and why they still need it today." Also, "referring to Jerusalem as Israel's 'eternal, undivided capital' would be appropriate, and might be expected."

Spitzer, says Schick, was "this odd type of micro-manager." Just as he had during his campaigns, he wanted to remain central command, aware of everything. In a big case, "he would want an update every fifteen minutes." But "he'd let you do your own thing." And he *exuded* combativeness. When a state environmental lawyer took a new job in Washington, Spitzer sent him a note with the scribbled admonition "Keep EPA honest!" When his top healthcare lawyer sent an e-mail asking the AG if he had anything to add to his marching orders, Spitzer simply wrote back: "Go get 'em!"

Indeed, "Go get 'em" seemed to sum up Spitzer's approach. From the start, he seemed undaunted by the sensitivity of a target. After New York City police shot and killed an unarmed West African immigrant named Amadou Diallo, setting off a storm of protests, Spitzer began his own investigation into the department's "stop-and-frisk" practices. This saw him butt heads with the popular mayor, Rudy Giuliani, who had reflexively defended the police and resisted turning over records. Spitzer ultimately issued a report showing that police were far more likely to stop minorities than whites. After September 11—when Spitzer, from his Wall Street office, watched the twin towers burst into flames—he went after the Red Cross. Threatening litigation, he forced the group to abandon plans to use some of the $500 million it had received for blood drives and overhead, rather than giving it directly to 9/11 victims. Spitzer had also jawboned the Red Cross—and dozens of other charities—into cooperating with a central aid database he established, rejecting Giuliani's suggestion that he should run it instead. Red Cross president Bernadine Healy—who resigned at year-end—later told *The Wall Street Journal* that Spitzer had employed "Jekyll-and-Hyde tactics," alternating between "being utterly charming" and "manipulative and scary."

While Spitzer sometimes collaborated with other AGs willing to play a supporting role in his crusades, he blasted other efforts organized by his peers through the National Association of Attorneys General. One fight resulted from a proposed state-by-state allocation of billions from the tobacco-industry settlement, which predated his election. In a private letter, Spitzer ridiculed the AGs of Mississippi and Florida, charged with calculating the split, for being too generous with states that had entered the litigation late in the interest of "collegiality." He blasted their various payout recommendations as "patently absurd," "bizarre," and "lacking any principled basis."

On another occasion, he attacked his fellow AGs for accepting corporate donations to subsidize social events for family members at their conferences. One private letter from Spitzer accused the Kansas attorney general of lying and falsifying meeting minutes on the issue. This dispute erupted in December 2001, after Spitzer showed up late to an AGs' conference in California to oppose the group's plans to use $50 million in leftover tobacco money for staff training and a Washington building, instead of public health programs. Once there, Spitzer also complained that the AGs were compromising their integrity during the conference by accepting a free trip to Disneyland and allowing corporate sponsorship of the event's banquet. California AG Bill Lockyer, who was hosting the event, took this personally.

"You have a hell of a lot to say for someone who doesn't give enough of a fuck to show up except when you want to be disagreeable!" responded Lockyer, in an exchange later reported by *American Lawyer*. The two men yelled and cursed at each other while the other AGs looked on in shock. Then Spitzer finally proposed his own version of an out-of-court settlement: "You want to step outside, that's fine! I grew up in the *Bronx*!" Riverdale, of course, wasn't exactly Fort Apache. "No problem!" Lockyer shouted back. "I grew up in East L.A. Let's go!" The two middle-aged lawyers continued their discussion in private, trading only verbal blows. Spitzer lost the vote on the tobacco money, thirty to one.

―――

By 2002—the final year of Eliot Spitzer's first term in office—America had changed. The dot-com bubble had burst, generating pain and rage among small investors, many of whom had bet their savings on Wall Street. A string of corporate scandals, starting with Enron, had exposed the perils of deregulation. And the Republican regime of George W. Bush showed little inclination to do anything about it. The stage was perfectly set for someone—anyone—seeking to right the wrongs. The precise vehicle through which Eliot Spitzer would seize the moment—conflicts of interest in Wall Street research—was virtual happenstance.

The point man on the investigation, thirty-nine-year-old Eric Dinallo, head of the AG's investor-protection bureau, did not start out as a

Spitzer favorite. He hadn't gone to an Ivy League school or worked as a federal prosecutor. He'd come instead from the Manhattan DA's office, where he'd helped investigate A.R. Baron, an obscure New York broker-age firm that had swindled investors. Just as the AG's office had histori-cally limited itself to state issues, its investor-protection bureau had modest ambitions, like targeting boiler-room fraudsters hyping penny stocks. During Spitzer's early tenure as AG, the hot cases in his office involved pollution and guns, not Wall Street.

At the end of his second year on the job, Dinallo had included "inves-tigation of investment banking firm analysts" on the to-do list he'd sub-mitted to Spitzer—but it ranked second. He'd begun pursuing the problem in earnest after reading that Merrill Lynch had paid $400,000 to settle a complaint brought by a Queens pediatrician who claimed to have lost his daughters' college money by following the investment advice of Henry Blodget, Merrill's star Internet analyst. Merrill, of course, was a jugger-naut, a $45 billion business that made more than $3.8 billion in annual profit. The largest of Wall Street's investment banks, it also advised more small investors than anyone else, with twenty thousand brokers manag-ing two million accounts.

Blodget was a failed writer, a graduate of Exeter and Yale who'd shuffled through a string of low-level jobs, including fact-checker for the National Audubon Society. His luck had turned at thirty-two, when, after landing as an analyst at CIBC Oppenheimer, he audaciously predicted that an unprofitable Internet bookseller named Amazon.com, already valued at an eye-popping $240 a share, would soon hit $400. After Am-azon topped $400 within a month, Blodget became a media darling, and Merrill hired him in early 1999. In 2001, he earned $12 million.

Research analysts had played a big part in inflating the bubble. Inter-net companies were impossibly complex, with business models no one understood in an industry that, just a few years back, didn't even exist. Almost no dot-coms were actually making money; their progress was instead measured in the form of dubious new metrics like "eyeballs" and "page views." Yet their stocks kept spiraling upward, and everyone want-ed a piece of the action. Analysts translated this strange new world for investors, usually in a way that boiled down to a single word: *buy*. Blodget's celebrity soon rivaled even that of Morgan Stanley's Mary Meeker, known as "Queen of the Net." He appeared on CNBC and CNN regularly, telling naïve investors what stocks to snatch up. CEOs reveled in his research reports, which continued to tout their stocks even after they'd headed south.

When Spitzer's investigators sifted through the thirty thousand e-mails they'd subpoenaed, they found stunning proof of what insiders on Wall Street had long suspected: analysts were hyping stocks to boost their firms' investment-banking profits. While publicly touting shaky companies to investors, Blodget was internally describing them as a "dog," "crap," and a "piece of shit." InfoSpace, an important banking client, remained on Merrill's "Favored 15" list of top buys—widely circulated to average investors—even while Blodget told Merrill colleagues it was a "powder keg." The e-mails left no doubt about the analysts' motivation. "What's so interesting about GoTo except banking fees????" one fund manager asked Blodget, about a faltering dot-com for which he'd just issued a "long-term buy" rating. "Nothin," Blodget wrote back.

In theory, analyst research was supposed to be independent of banking considerations, to provide objective financial advice to the firm's Main Street clients. In practice, Blodget was a critical part of Merrill's "deal team," helping the bankers pitch CEOs for lucrative underwriting work. Hiring Merrill bought a company bullish research reports from Blodget— it was simply part of the package. And the Internet analysts eagerly claimed credit: in an internal memo reviewing their activities for a twelve-month period ending in November 2000, they bragged of helping bag banking deals that made Merrill $115 million.

When dot-com stocks began plunging, the analysts privately questioned their pandering to banking clients. "I don't want to be whore for f-ing mgmt," one of Blodget's research colleagues e-mailed him. "We are losing people money and I don't like it." At one point Blodget wrote that he was thinking of actually starting to call stocks "like we see them, no matter what the ancillary business consequences are." But, of course, that didn't happen. During the three years he worked at Merrill, the firm's Internet analysts never slapped a "sell" or "reduce" rating on a single stock. At the end of 2001, Blodget resigned, as part of a multimillion-dollar severance package that included a non-disclosure agreement and Merrill's commitment to cover his legal fees.

By March 2002, after his team had spent more than a year on the case, Dinallo had assembled critical mass—enough for the sort of juicy case against a big target that Spitzer always said he wanted. At every step of the way, the AG had urged Dinallo to push deeper and further, and the shocking e-mails had grabbed his attention. Now, Spitzer was ready to confront the company.

Merrill didn't exactly roll over. It hired a team from Skadden, Arps (where Spitzer had once worked), as well as Bob Morvillo, a feisty criminal defense specialist who would later represent Martha Stewart. In a series of private meetings, Merrill and its lawyers deployed all the usual tactics that might prove fruitful in a big white-collar case brought by, say, the SEC. First they tried denial (Spitzer was taking the e-mails out of context). Then they argued "horizontal equity" (everyone's doing it— why pick on us?). Then they offered a hint of intimidation ("Merrill has powerful friends," Morvillo told Spitzer). Finally they tried pulling strings, albeit clumsily, hiring former mayor Giuliani, the 9/11 icon, to plead the firm's case with the AG personally; in the previous four years, Giuliani had refused to even return Spitzer's calls.

Spitzer wouldn't budge. Branding Merrill's behavior "indefensible," he wasn't interested in hearing explanations. Instead, he laid out what Merrill would have to do to avoid prosecution, possibly even criminal prosecution. Spitzer wanted Merrill to pay a fine—a big fine—as acknowledgment that its offense was serious. Even more, he wanted to reinvent how Merrill provided research, to give investors truly independent advice by separating the analysts from investment banking. Merrill was willing to strike a deal, but on one condition: Spitzer would need to bury the damning e-mails.

Again, Spitzer wouldn't budge. This was a critical decision, making everything that came later possible. While prosecutors routinely seal embarrassing evidence as part of a pretrial settlement, Spitzer wasn't simply trying to extract a pound of flesh from Merrill Lynch. As Merrill's lawyers eagerly pointed out, the sleazy practices he'd found existed across Wall Street. Spitzer's goal was to go after the conflicts at *all* the banks. And he knew that nothing would accomplish that—and vaporize all of Wall Street's excuses for its behavior—like a public airing of the appalling evidence. Spitzer's merciless refusal to entomb the evidence from his investigations separated him from other prosecutors.

On Monday, April 8, 2002, Spitzer unsheathed his secret weapon: the Martin Act. Originally passed in 1921, this obscure New York law gave the AG unmatched powers to investigate and prosecute securities fraud committed by any business that operated in the state. Under the Martin Act, New York's AG could bring civil or criminal charges against either companies or individuals—and he didn't even need to prove that his targets had intentionally deceived or actually damaged anyone. It was a violation of the Martin Act to merely omit material information. Pre-dating even federal securities laws, the Martin Act was a blunt tool from an earlier age, allowing prosecution of virtually any kind of financial scheme. Its core was the simple principle of right and wrong, rendering the usual rules-based corporate defenses impotent. There was nothing like it in America. Yet no previous AG had explored its power to reach beyond hypesters in Queens. This AG would, wielding it in each of his big Wall Street cases. A legal writer later dubbed it "the Sword of Spitzer"—the "legal equivalent of King Arthur's Excalibur."

The Martin Act, which Dinallo had studied intimately, provided the basis for Spitzer's entire investigation of Merrill Lynch. On this day, without warning his target, the AG used it to quietly obtain a court order from a state judge in his chambers, requiring Merrill to immediately dis-close conflicts of interest in its research reports while he continued his investigation. Order in hand, Spitzer then presided over a packed press conference, where he decried "a shocking betrayal of trust by one of Wall Street's most trusted names." He simultaneously released an affidavit excerpting the most shocking e-mails. A 181-page collection of internal Merrill documents was publicly filed in court.

Caught off guard by Spitzer's move—they had overestimated the young AG's patience—Merrill executives yelped, declaring themselves "outraged." In a statement, they insisted there was "no basis" for his al-legations, which revealed "a fundamental lack of understanding of how securities research works." The e-mails had been taken out of context; Spitzer's conclusions were "just plain wrong."

A few years later, when he was being celebrated for a string of tri-umphs against mammoth targets, this first foray against Merrill would be remembered as a certain victory, masterminded by an unblinking cru-sader. But at the time, Spitzer privately entertained misgivings. He was going after Wall Street's biggest firm, in an industry that was New York's most important employer. Despite his brash persona of certitude, Spitzer always craved rapid public validation of what he was doing; it's one rea-son why he reveled in favorable press. On this occasion, Spitzer had called Charles Schumer, the New York Democrat who served on the Senate Banking Committee, and asked him to stand by his side during the press conference where he unveiled his move against Merrill Lynch. "The first forty-eight hours are so important," Spitzer said later. "I wanted reinforcement from the establishment that this was okay." Notoriously cozy with Wall Street, Schumer had refused. "No. These are *New York* jobs," Spitzer says Schumer told him. On the morning of the Merrill announcement, Spitzer had breakfast with his new political consultant from Chicago, David Axelrod, who would become famous for his work with a young Illinois politician named Barack Obama. "I'm about to file a very big case," Spitzer told Axelrod. "It's either the best idea I've ever had—or the worst."

In public, however, Spitzer betrayed no doubts, telling the press that this was just the "small first step" in a campaign against pervasive conflicts on Wall Street. Merrill's behavior "jeopardizes the integrity of the marketplace," Spitzer declared. "The case must be a catalyst for reform throughout the entire industry." Spitzer insisted he'd moved against Merrill only after settlement talks had proved "futile"; he announced that he'd already begun investigations of other firms.

Less than two months later—warp speed, by government standards—Spitzer had the validation he'd wanted: Merrill Lynch had agreed to settle. Since the AG's shocking revelations, the firm had become a whipping boy in the press, and its stock had dropped 19 percent, wiping out $8.8 billion in market value. At Merrill's annual meeting in late April, CEO David Komansky—publicly contemptuous of Spitzer's evidence just a few weeks earlier—apologized for the "very distressing" e-mails that had come to light.

Spitzer had his own motivation to strike a deal. The SEC had been slow to join the fight, Dinallo's investor-protection bureau had just a dozen lawyers, and he knew he couldn't simultaneously investigate and prosecute all the banks alone. Spitzer had an entire industry to reform, and he didn't want to get bogged down in a war of attrition against his first target. A quick settlement would show that he could produce results and set everything else in motion.

The agreement was announced on May 21. Merrill would pay a fine of $100 million—a number big enough to make an impression. The firm would take specific steps to end the influence of banking on research, and expand its disclosures to investors. A special monitor would oversee compliance. And Merrill would offer a statement of "contrition"—

a symbolic humbling Spitzer would insist on in his settlements. (The SEC routinely allowed settling targets to "neither admit nor deny" its allegations.)

Spitzer's war on Wall Street had placed him at odds with federal and industry regulators, to whom he'd given no advance notice of his plans. Nonetheless, the SEC had been well aware of conflicts involving research, which had long been an open secret on Wall Street. In 2001, its compliance staff, without thinking to examine e-mails, had explicitly discussed the issue in an internal report; the enforcement staff had even begun to investigate a few firms. But under new SEC chairman Harvey Pitt, a veteran securities defense lawyer who had promised a "gentler" hand with the industry, the agency had said nothing publicly, instead encouraging the banks to fix the problem themselves. Says Columbia law professor Harvey Goldschmid, an SEC commissioner at the time: "In the summer of 2001, the commission knew as much about what was going on as Eliot did. The commission didn't do anything. Eliot did the tough work with Merrill and others. I don't think the corrections on Wall Street would have happened without his driving force."

This was precisely the reason why the banks were so aghast at Spitzer's actions: their *real* regulators had known all about this, and done nothing. Now Spitzer's revelations had rendered the entire analyst system indefensible. And as they began to comb through their own documents in response to subpoenas, the other big firms realized, to their growing horror, that they had the exact same problem as Merrill.

———

The New York AG had forced the embarrassed SEC to join his crusade, but Pitt and Spitzer just didn't get along. Both men were intellectual smarty-pants—the smartest guys in the room—and, although ostensibly on the same side of the table, they came from different planets on the issue of regulation, both ideologically and temperamentally. When the two men first met on the issue in Washington, Pitt later told Spitzer biographer Brooke Masters, he came away thinking, "He's not as smart as he thinks he is because nobody could be that smart." Pitt had privately told the New York AG that, while he was free to prosecute fraud, rule making to reshape an industry—Spitzer's ultimate goal—remained the exclusive province of Washington. Spitzer, for his part, had publicly described the SEC as "asleep at the switch," and viewed Pitt as an industry toady. But he knew he needed help. The federal agency had vastly greater resources, including nine hundred enforcement lawyers. So now they were thrown together, in a sort of shotgun marriage, along with regulators from the National Association of Securities Dealers, the New York Stock Exchange, and other states.

Mediating this awkward relationship was Dick Grasso, the diminutive, chrome-domed chairman of the NYSE, who was worried about the impact the scandal was having on the financial markets. Eager to see the matter resolved quickly, Grasso convened the wary regulators, like feuding heads of the Five Families, at Tiro a Segno, a private Italian club in the West Village with a shooting range in the basement. Says Dinallo: "He had an innate instinct for when the tempers were about to flare, and he solved it with food and red wine." Ultimately, they agreed to work together, dividing up the investigation of the big banks.

Cooperation notwithstanding, Spitzer was determined to remain the preeminent player, deciding what showcase targets and fresh problems to attack, then shaping the solutions. He was happy to let the SEC and others follow behind, doing the long, hard grunt work involved in prosecuting a string of similar cases. But he wanted to lead the way, to stamp his personal brand indelibly on the scandal and keep his name in the headlines. Says Dinallo: "Eliot and I both had the instinct that we could not be perceived as a one-trick pony after Merrill Lynch."

In September, exploiting records largely unearthed by other regulators, Spitzer filed a new lawsuit, broadening his attack on conflicts to include "spinning." This was the practice of giving CEOs special shares of hot IPOs—initial public stock offerings—that could be sold for a tidy profit right after they started trading. Spitzer named five telecom executives, including WorldCom's Bernie Ebbers, charging that they were offered the shares as "an integral part of a fraudulent scheme to win new investment-banking business." Ebbers alone had made more than $11 million from flipping shares in twenty-one IPOs.* The spinning suit had emerged from scrutiny of documents from Salomon Smith Barney, part of Citigroup, where telecom analyst Jack Grubman had held sway. The Salomon e-mails documented precisely the same research conflict Spitzer had found at Merrill.

---

* Spitzer's suit sought disgorgement of $28 million in profits from the executives. All five eventually settled, paying a total of $10.7 million.

At $20 million a year, Grubman was the most extravagantly paid research analyst ever, and he personified Wall Street's ethical cluelessness. Until confronted by *BusinessWeek* a few years earlier, he'd falsely claimed to have graduated from MIT. He'd also famously told a reporter, "What used to be a conflict is now a synergy." Once a magnet for banking business, which he eagerly courted with bullish research reports, he'd become a target of investor loathing after refusing to downgrade telecoms even as their prices plunged. For years, Grubman never issued a "sell" rating, and his private e-mails were every bit as blunt as Blodget's in explaining why. "Most of our banking clients are going to zero and you know I wanted to downgrade them months ago but I got a huge pushback from investment banking," he wrote in 2001. On another occasion, he publicly reaffirmed the "buy" rating for an underwriting client on the same day that he privately described the company as a "pig."

But the most remarkable tale in the e-mails, which became public later, emerged from Grubman's often-sexual exchanges with a female fund analyst, in which he wrote that he'd upgraded AT&T's rating after Citigroup chairman Sandy Weill—who also served on the AT&T board—asked him to take a "fresh look" at the company. Weill was a billionaire, a titan of Wall Street. In the e-mails, Grubman confided that he'd actually upgraded the stock to enlist Weill's help in getting his twins admitted to the exclusive preschool at New York's 92nd Street Y. After Grubman boosted AT&T from a "hold" to a "buy," AT&T selected Salomon as lead underwriter for a major stock offering. Weill, meanwhile, had spoken to a friend on the Y board, and Grubman's twins were admitted. Later, at Weill's suggestion, Citi made a $1 million donation to the Y; the head of Citi's charitable foundation understood this was a "thank you" for the admission of Grubman's children. Thus spun the unvirtuous circle of life in upscale Manhattan.

Grubman had finally left Citigroup in August 2002, reportedly receiving $19.5 million through his separation agreement, as well as $13 million in deferred pay.

———

Five days before Christmas of 2002, Eliot Spitzer stood in the boardroom of the New York Stock Exchange with Grasso to announce a $1.435 billion "global settlement" of the research scandal with Wall Street's ten biggest investment banks. The agreement, Grasso declared, would end "one of the darkest chapters in the history of modern finance." Its center-piece was a package of reforms giving Spitzer most of what he wanted. Banks would sever all ties between analysts and investment bankers, ban spinning of hot IPOs, and fund independent research for investors—though figuring out precisely how to do that would take months. The biggest payment, $400 million in fines, investor restitution, and funding for third-party research, would come from Citigroup. Merrill would pay $200 million, including its earlier $100 million, as would Credit Suisse First Boston, where regulators also uncovered damning e-mails. Then Morgan Stanley ($125 million) and Goldman Sachs ($110 million), followed by Bear Stearns, Deutsche Bank, JPMorgan Chase, Lehman Brothers, and UBS Warburg, each of which would pay $80 million.

Those in attendance at the press conference included leaders from the four agencies that had played the biggest part in hammering out the deal: the New York AG, the SEC, the NYSE, and the National Association of Securities Dealers, as well as other state regulators. But Harvey Pitt was absent. The wrong man for an era of public outrage over Wall Street greed and corporate scandal, Pitt had resigned as SEC chairman the previous month.

The deal had been reached after months of tricky negotiations, marked by media leaks and infighting. The banks had squabbled over where their respective fines—chicken feed for firms that made billions a year—would rank them in the pecking order of transgressors. The federal regulators worried that the agreement was too harsh, the state regulators that it was too soft. Everyone was acutely sensitive to the niceties of blame and credit. It was all taking too long, not happening in what Spitzer's staff had come to call "Eliot time." Ultimately it was Spitzer, determined to wrap things up by year-end, who orchestrated the closing play in the scandal, just as he had executed its opening gambit. Two days before the press conference, the AG had dramatically summoned lawyers for the banks to his office, told them they should be "ashamed" of how they had treated investors, and said that it was time to stop acting "like a bunch of children in a sandbox." They would have twenty-four hours to sign off on the global settlement. If they refused, he would sue them, and the AG's office would be burrowing through their e-mails for five years. "Any questions?" Spitzer asked. Acutely aware of what had happened to Merrill Lynch, everyone capitulated.

Spitzer had engaged in considerable saber rattling along the way—at one point telling the media, in a scary phrase that would become one of his favorites, that Merrill's behavior "bordered on criminal." Yet no firm or individual involved in the research scandal would face criminal charges. While Spitzer would regularly wield criminal prosecution as a threat during his investigations, it was usually just a bludgeon. He viewed his power to criminally indict a big company as a weapon of mass destruction, too horrific to deploy except in the most extreme circumstances of corporate perfidy and defiance. He regarded the feds' criminal prosecution of Arthur Andersen in the Enron scandal—a death sentence for the accounting firm—as a serious mistake.

Spitzer maintained a lower barrier for charging individuals, and Dinallo had presented the argument for indicting the analysts, telling Spitzer, "This is the most damning evidence you'll ever see in a white-collar case." But in the research scandal, Spitzer regarded even its worst actors—Blodget and Grubman—as mere players in a corrupt ecosystem. *That* was his real target. So Grubman would be banned from the industry for life and cough up $15 million in fines and restitution. Blodget, also banned for life, would pay $4 million. As for billionaire Sandy Weill, he'd been given a pass as part of the deal with Citigroup. Spitzer says he had concluded he lacked the evidence to charge him anyway. As would often happen in Spitzer's cases, the biggest fish escaped the harshest punishment.

The New York attorney general would bring no more lawsuits in the Wall Street research scandal. But when final settlement papers were signed, his office released thousands of additional incriminating analyst e-mails, lest anyone forget what all this had been about.

———

As the research case was winding its way toward resolution, Spitzer, with a certain righteous glee, stuck a fork in the eye of his targets. The occasion was a black-tie banquet in late November at the Ritz-Carlton Hotel in Manhattan, sponsored by *Institutional Investor* magazine to celebrate members of its prestigious "All-American Research Team"—the analysts judged the best in the business. Spitzer, improbably, was the keynote speaker. He spoke after the award winners were called to the podium, one by one, to loud applause.

"It's wonderful to be here this evening, because I really want to put faces to all those e-mails," Spitzer began. The joke prompted a few titters. But the rest of his remarks did not. Spitzer proceeded to inform the honored guests, in front of their spouses and children, that they really deserved no praise. He told them he'd commissioned his own research, which showed that the analyst all-stars, touted by their firms in investing magazines, had done a *mediocre* job of picking stocks—no better than the average analyst. They were guilty of "lackluster performances," Spitzer declared, part of an industry dispensing "dishonest" advice to mom-and-pop investors.

Two Spitzer deputies were in attendance that evening: deputy AG Avi Schick, who had drafted the speech, and chief of staff Rich Baum. Baum admired his boss's willingness to not only walk into the lion's den, but to stick his head between its teeth. "A lot of shitty things go on because no one's ever willing to say things like that," he said later. At the same time, he knew how obnoxious it would surely seem, and fretted that his excitable boss might get into an altercation with a furious analyst afterward. Says Baum: "I wanted to make sure he didn't confront someone, and give them the big 'fuck you.'"

During a break just before the speech, after sitting among the happy, unsuspecting honorees, Schick had urged his boss to soften his remarks. Spitzer had refused. "If it was the right speech back at the office," the AG told him, "it's the right speech to give now." When Spitzer finally finished excoriating the "industry-wide failure," the stunned room fell silent. A few diners, muttering and cursing their guest speaker, had already walked out. At Schick's table, a perfectly coiffed female analyst from Houston turned to him. "Are you with Spitzer?" she demanded. "Well, you're a flaming asshole too!"

Chapter 4: Wild Kingdom

IN APRIL 2002, LLOYD CONSTANTINE HOSTED A CAMPAIGN fundraiser at his West Side apartment for his old buddy Eliot Spitzer. With the beaming attorney general looking on, Constantine tapped a glass to quiet his seventy guests, chattering over sushi prepared by Rupert Murdoch's personal chef.

"I know what you're thinking," Constantine began. *What are we doing here? Why does Eliot need our money?* Spitzer was facing only token opposition for a second term; he would win by 1.5 million votes. "What Eliot will tell you is that he's in the fight of his life. That's total *bullshit!*" Chuckles rippled through the room. Constantine continued: "*I will tell you the truth. We're in it for . . . the long haul.*" He let the words hang in the air. "And if you don't know what *the long haul* is, we will refund your money, and we will validate your parking."

By the time he'd unveiled his landmark assault on Wall Street conflicts of interest, Spitzer was not only a shoo-in for reelection, but a hot prospect for higher office. Facing Spitzer in 2002 was such a hopeless cause that the Republicans fielded an unknown former state court of claims judge named Dora Irizarry as a sacrificial lamb. After her dutiful slaughter, the White House would reward her with an appointment to the federal bench. Albany was already presumed to be Spitzer's next stop.

Spitzer publicly denied hatching any plans. But virtually every step he took in the 2002 campaign helped boost his prospects for becoming governor of New York in 2006. He'd gathered chits with black voters through an early endorsement of gubernatorial candidate Carl McCall, an African American who won the Democratic nomination but inevitably got crushed by Pataki. He'd built a formidable fundraising operation. He'd spent $2 million on TV ads, created by Axelrod, to boost his image as "the people's lawyer." And he'd once again spread his bankroll around New York, giving generously to other Democrats and party organizations.

As the Election Day cakewalk approached, Bernie Spitzer acknowledged the ultimate ambition of those backing his son "for the long haul." "Would I like him to become President?" pondered Bernard, during an interview with the *New York Observer*, a local weekly. "Of course. I'd love to spend the night in the Lincoln Bedroom." And would Eliot like to become president? "I think he would. It's his very nature."

The research scandal had ignited a remarkable love affair with the mainstream media that would burn, largely unabated, until Spitzer left the attorney general's office. In September 2002, *Fortune* magazine had placed him on its cover, as "The Enforcer." In October, *60 Minutes* memorably anointed him "the Sheriff of Wall Street." *Reader's Digest* called him "America's Best Public Servant." And in December, *Time* magazine named him "Crusader of the Year" (he'd just missed out on Man of the Year honors), gushing. "There has not been such an affirmation of what's right since Moses and the Ten Commandments." For this election, Spitzer's beloved *Times* gave him its enthusiastic endorsement, "as a savvy and responsible champion of the public interest."

On Wall Street, there was quite the opposite reaction. The brokerage firms had watched Spitzer, virtually overnight, effectively become a national regulator of the financial markets. This horrifying prospect had moved them—and their friends in Washington—to try to rein Spitzer in through legislation preempting state regulators; they'd much rather have dealt with the somnolent SEC than the madman in New York. Spitzer's public comments fanned their fears, conjuring up the image of a wild-eyed freedom fighter who might strike anywhere. The SEC, Spitzer declared in a PBS interview, was "akin to a World War I type of army that digs its trenches and marches forward ten feet at a time." But at the New York AG's office, he said, "we feel as though we're fighting a guerrilla war. Every day, we're saying . . . Where can we dive in? . . . What is the biggest problem that isn't being attacked?"

After failing to hobble Spitzer in Congress—in an era of corporate scandal, he'd simply become too popular—some businesses began trying to adapt. In mid-2003, Morgan Stanley hired Eric Dinallo as the firm's chief regulatory officer, presumably hoping his presence would avoid any future Spitzer assaults. But surely the research case had been a once-in-a-lifetime event. It seemed inconceivable that Spitzer could generate such tumult again.

———

Of course, he *would* do it again (and again), uncovering outrages that would rapidly upend two more giant industries. Both scandals would follow the strategy Spitzer had forged during the research case. *Step one*: broadly investigate a gray area of odorous—but long-accepted—industry practice. *Step two*: expose an example so grotesque that it rendered the accepted practice indefensible. *Step three*: leverage the resulting uproar to swiftly exact reform of the entire industry, including gray-area behavior.

Mutual funds were his next target. David D. Brown IV, a new arrival at the AG's investor-protection bureau, via Harvard Law and Goldman Sachs, had zeroed in on the $7 trillion industry in Spitzerian fashion—by reading a tedious academic study in the *Journal of Corporation Law*. The article concluded that the mutual fund industry was bilking small investors by charging them twice as much in advisory fees as institutional customers. According to the study, this discrepancy added up to about $9 billion a year—and it wasn't right, Brown told Spitzer. He thought he could cook up a way to tackle the problem with a lawsuit.

A cerebral, slender man with a buzz cut and rimless glasses, Brown was a born-again do-gooder. At forty-four, after two decades in corporate law, he'd left a $500,000-a-year job at Goldman to join Spitzer's "band of brothers," as he put it, for $92,000 a year. He'd been deeply influenced by September 11—and Spitzer's first term—to quit his life as a "corporate dweeb." At Goldman, Brown had been on the other side of the table, responding to the AG's subpoenas during the research investigation. Initially dismissive, he'd soon realized that Goldman, which had always considered itself a cut above, had the same appalling conflicts of interest as everyone else.

If Brown began his mutual fund investigation like a policy wonk, he soon kicked it into high gear like a criminal prosecutor—with a hot tip from an industry informant. The tip came from Noreen Harrington, a former Goldman Sachs trader who had worked for Eddie Stern, the thirty-eight-year-old son of a high-profile Manhattan billionaire. Eddie's dad, Leonard, had accumulated a fortune building the Hartz Mountain pet supply empire, then multiplied it developing industrial real estate in the swampy New Jersey Meadowlands. After a $30 million gift, NYU had renamed its business school in his honor. Eddie, who managed the family's Wall Street investments, had launched a hedge fund in 1998 called Canary Capital, which maintained a truly remarkable track record even after the bull market ended. In 2000, for instance, when the S&P 500 dropped 9 percent, Canary returned almost 50 percent; in 2001, while the S&P fell another 13 percent, Canary gained close to 29 percent. Stern's secret, according to Harrington? Market timing mutual funds.

Market timing was the practice of whipping money in and out of funds, usually in a matter of days, to profit from pricing inefficiencies. But there was a problem with this strategy: under the rules in place at most mutual fund firms, it was forbidden. And for good reason: it cost average buy-and-hold investors money. As a result, most fund prospectuses contained language bluntly declaring timers unwelcome; they warned that they had the right to boot any customer making more than a specified number of in-and-out trades in a year—usually just four.

Nonetheless, as Brown soon discovered, dozens of big-name mutual fund complexes actually *welcomed* market timing—secretly, by select investors. *Janus. Putnam. Alliance. Strong. MFS. Franklin Templeton. Invesco. Pimco.* Indeed, the practice was so widespread that it had developed its own shadowy subculture—a kind of alternative mutual fund universe—that included not only hedge funds like Canary, but small brokerage firms and sleazy middlemen who arranged timing deals with fund insiders. Market timing was the open secret in the unfolding mutual fund scandal.

And there was more: late trading—a practice that was flatly illegal. Late trading didn't just improve the odds for timers; it virtually guaranteed them. Mutual fund prices were set once a day, based on the value of the fund's stock holdings at the 4 P.M. market close. Late trading allowed Canary (and, as it turned out, many others) to buy and sell fund shares at the current day's price *after* the 4 P.M. cutoff time, even though such orders were supposed to be filled at the next day's price. This meant that a timer could observe post-closing developments on a Monday that were sure to boost shares on Tuesday—a big earnings surprise, for example— then buy a mutual fund at the cheaper Monday price predating the news.

Then they'd dump the shares on Tuesday, pocketing the gain. Spitzer likened this to "betting on a horse race after the horses have crossed the finish line." This was the grotesque behavior in the fund scandal.

Harrington, who had quit working at Canary, tipped Spitzer's investigators about both of these practices. Firing off subpoenas, Brown soon began reeling in witnesses and e-mails. Within a month, the AG's office was negotiating a deal with Stern. As it turned out, Canary—with $800 million in assets—had engaged in both market timing and late trading on a massive scale. That made Stern one of the worst offenders, a natural target for criminal prosecution. But Spitzer, as ever, was after the industry, not just one big fish. He also wanted quick public validation, not a protracted legal fight, as well as a star witness to guide him through this murky world. So Stern got a sweet deal. He paid just $40 million in restitution and fines (a fraction of the profits he'd actually made) and was barred from managing non-family money for ten years. Neither Stern nor any of his family or clients would face criminal charges; he didn't even have to admit wrongdoing. Stern was even allowed to invest in mutual funds—as long as he held them for at least a year.

What he helped Spitzer uncover, in return, was truly shocking—the biggest scandal in the history of the mutual fund industry. Pioneered two decades earlier by a Massachusetts CPA operating from an office above his garage, market timing had evolved into a sophisticated gambit in which hedge funds slung around billions. Skillful timers could make fat profits by jumping into a fund, then leaping back into cash. And unlike trading stocks, it was commission-free. But it all depended on getting fund companies—which were publicly cracking down on timers—to let them in.

Why would the fund companies do this? To boost their bottom line, which depended on how much money they managed. So investors like Canary were granted "timing capacity"—permission to trade a predetermined amount in and out of specific mutual funds—and exempted from stiff short-term redemption charges. In return, the timers plunked down "sticky assets," a second, predetermined sum that sat quietly in a money market account—or perhaps a hedge fund run by the same firm—generating management fees. With the end of the bull market, fund firms were especially desperate for assets.

Internal e-mails exposed how executives of mutual fund firms furtively cut these deals, at odds with both their policies and often with their own fund managers. The problem was that the large sums rushing in and out forced a portfolio manager to keep extra cash on hand to pay the exiting timer, hurting the fund's performance. Market timing also generated extra costs from trading and capital gains, further reducing returns. One study calculated that timing cost long-term shareholders as much as $5 billion a year.

Stern had learned this game in the early 1990s from a former college math professor who went on to run *Perfect 10*, a soft-core porn magazine. By the time Harrington blew the whistle, Canary had struck "capacity" deals with thirty big-name firms. Alliance Capital, for example, granted Stern $110 million in rapid-trading privileges, after he'd agreed to park another $55 million in Alliance-run hedge funds. All told, Alliance held more than $600 million in "approved" timing money; the firm employed a "market timing supervisor" and even generated an internal "top ten timers list." Janus had ten timing agreements. When an employee there complained about timers in 2003, Janus International CEO Richard Garland e-mailed back. "I have no interest in building a business around market timers, but at the same time I do not want to turn away $10-$20m!"

At Invesco—described as a "timer-friendly complex" by the firm's own chief compliance officer—Canary made 141 exchanges in the Dynamics fund during a two-year period, generating $50 million in profits while long-term investors were getting crushed. An Invesco executive, whose official job description involved *catching* timers, wrote, "If done correctly, this kind of business can be very profitable." Fund managers there were less enthusiastic. Market timing "is killing the legitimate shareholders," one complained. Wrote another, speaking of Canary: "They came in two days ago . . . with $180 million, and left yesterday. . . . They are day-trading our funds, and in my case I know they are costing our legitimate shareholders significant performance. I had to buy into a strong early rally yesterday, and now I'm negative cash this morning because of these bastards, and I have to sell into a weak market." Indeed, after the scandal broke, half of eighty-eight mutual fund companies questioned by the SEC admitted cutting deals with market timers, while a quarter of thirty-four brokers surveyed acknowledged that they'd helped customers engage in late trading. At some fund companies, portfolio managers and executives were even timing their own mutual funds.

Spitzer launched his first legal attack in September 2003, just three months after Harrington had called his office. This was remarkably fast. As Harrington would later joke, it usually took the government longer to fill a pothole. The complaint blew the whistle on four timing-friendly firms, but highlighted Canary's late trading, especially in Bank of America's Nations Funds. BofA had not only allowed Canary to time its own mutual funds; it had helped finance Canary's activities with a $300 million credit line, and allowed it to peek at confidential fund holdings. Most egregiously, it had set up an electronic terminal in Canary's offices to help Stern late-trade mutual funds until 6:30 P.M.—two and a half hours after the market closed.

The fund scandal was every bit as outrageous as the research conflicts, with its own elements of duplicity and customer betrayal. "The full extent of this complicated fraud is not yet known," Spitzer told reporters. "But one thing is clear: the mutual fund industry operates on a double standard." Once again, the SEC, which Spitzer had informed just minutes before his press conference, appeared clueless; it had a whole *division* charged with inspecting mutual funds. But this time, the feds rushed to Spitzer's side to join the investigation. No one could doubt he really had the goods. "God bless Eliot Spitzer," the SEC's mortified enforcement chief, Steve Cutler, told the press, a day after the AG filed suit. "He got a tip and pursued it."

As the scandal mushroomed, fund companies, brokerage firms, clearinghouses, and market timers all became joint investigative targets. Many rushed to make public confessions, hoping to blunt the damage. Scores of fund executives, compliance officers, brokers, and portfolio managers lost their jobs; several would be banned for life from the industry. Spitzer, who had been criticized for putting no one behind bars in the analyst investigation, also brought criminal cases under the Martin Act, ultimately winning ten criminal guilty pleas for late trading, fraud, and destroying evidence.

But the AG was unable to extract a guilty plea from the lone criminal target in the Canary case: Bank of America broker Ted Sihpol. Sihpol, thirty-six, was the point man in the bank's unholy relationship with Eddie Stern. Initially, Canary would submit "proposed" trades by fax early enough for Sihpol to time-stamp them before the 4 P.M. deadline. Then, after 4 P.M., if Canary decided to cancel any "orders," the brokers simply tossed the trading ticket. The electronic terminal used for late trading, which BofA installed a few months later, allowed Canary to bypass the brokers altogether.

Sihpol's bosses had also known all about these arrangements. One e-mail, written to the bank's head of asset management, offered "accolades" to everyone involved in providing "access to [BofA mutual funds] for market timing activities" and establishing "this profitable relationship." Yet Sihpol, married to a former BofA compliance officer, was the only one facing criminal charges. Accused of larceny and securities fraud, he faced up to twenty-five years. He'd already been fired and was looking at a lifetime ban from the securities industry on SEC charges. After going to court to force BofA to foot the mammoth legal bill for his defense, Sihpol dug in to fight. Cast by his lawyers as a low-level scapegoat—why weren't Stern and the bank's top brass facing jail time?—Sihpol would eventually emerge victorious after his criminal trial, becoming a hero to Spitzer's enemies. He later settled with the SEC for $200,000 and a five-year ban from the industry, and became a Realtor.

But the fund firms fell like dominoes. Much of the grunt work on the ensuing civil settlements—about twenty in all—would fall to the SEC, though the federal and state regulators were usually working in tandem. That, of course, didn't stop Spitzer from taking potshots. When the SEC reached its own settlement with Putnam without immediately announcing a fine, Spitzer told *The Washington Post* that he "wouldn't let them handle a house closing." In private, according to a Spitzer deputy, the AG spoke to SEC enforcement chief Cutler "like an animal." With rare exception, the federal regulators hated the attorney general; they viewed him as a reckless headline grabber who raced to file hot cases poaching on their turf. But it was hard to deny his impact. With a tiny staff and with remarkable speed, he was pulling off reforms that would have taken the SEC years.

As Spitzer moved toward his first settlement with a mutual fund firm, he returned to the issue that had drawn him to the industry in the first place: high fees for small investors. In November 2003, Alliance agreed to pay $250 million in fines and restitution and to chop fees by about 20 percent—around $350 million over five years. The fee cuts, which Spitzer usually insisted on in his subsequent settlements, prompted sharp criticism that he had overreached. After all, his investigation had focused on trading abuses, not excessive fees. As UCLA securities law professor Stephen Bainbridge put it: "It's as though you got busted for pot possession, and the DA said you had to give up snowboarding." The SEC, saying regulators had no business setting fees, refused to participate in this part of Spitzer's fund settlements.

Spitzer acknowledged that his remedy was "a stretch," even while offering intellectual and legal justification: both problems reflected a breach of fiduciary duty on the part of mutual fund directors, who lacked independence. But in truth, that was little more than a fig leaf for Spitzer's trademark form of rough justice. What he'd uncovered was horrible, it provided him with exquisite leverage, and he was determined to exploit it to make the world a better place. Lloyd Constantine put it this way: "If you went over the line, he's going to prosecute you. He doesn't care whether he found a mountain or a molehill. He wants to *level* it. If he's uncovered five grams of venality and that gives him the hook to change things, *fine*. He uses that as an opportunity to clean house."

By the time it was all over, the mutual fund scandal had produced fines, restitution, and fee reductions totaling an eye-popping $3.6 billion. Many of Spitzer's settlements also required more independent mutual fund boards. An academic study suggests all this had helped lower fees across the industry by about 6 percent, saving investors another $1.5 billion per year. Spitzer had done one more thing that helped mom-and-pop investors: he'd put market timers out of business.

––––––

"Where will Eliot Spitzer strike next?" asked *BusinessWeek* as the fund investigation began winding down, reflecting the AG's growing reputation as a corporate bogeyman. The answer: insurance—an even larger financial enterprise than mutual funds, and one that was notoriously underregulated. *Sleazy industry practice*: in return for steering their clients' business to particular underwriters, corporate insurance-brokerage firms were getting "bonuses" that amounted to kickbacks. *Scandalous behavior*: the brokers were rigging bids.

This case also began with a tip—an anonymous two-page, single-spaced letter that landed, on April 5, 2004, on the desk of David Brown. Brown, who had succeeded Dinallo as chief of Spitzer's investor-protection bureau, was busy putting the finishing touches on another big settlement in the mutual fund scandal. He knew nothing about insurance. But the letter's detailed explanation of "contingent" commissions at industry giant Marsh & McLennan grabbed his attention ("Marsh is receiving major income for directing business to preferred providers . . . i.e. the bigger the incentive [they pay Marsh], the more business they get"). By then, Brown was well schooled in the Spitzer method: act first and study up later. Two days later, he sent Marsh a broadly drafted subpoena. Then he began learning about what he had already begun investigating.

The hammer fell just six months later, on October 14, when Spitzer sued Marsh, the world's largest insurance broker, backed by almost one hundred pages of exhibits. Four insurance underwriters—AIG, ACE, the Hartford, and Munich-American RiskPartners—were also named as participants in the scheme. Two AIG executives simultaneously pled guilty to criminal charges. Once again, Spitzer had exposed the venal underbelly of an industry, operating right under regulators' noses. Once again, he had done it with his targets' own words: smoking-gun e-mails that showed Marsh betraying its clients.

While companies hired brokers to find the best insurance policy at the best price, the brokers, incredibly enough, were also being paid by the insurers. These "contingent commissions" were only vaguely disclosed to customers as a payment for unspecified "services." But they presented a clear conflict of interest: while Marsh's marketing materials insisted that "our guiding principle is to consider our client's best interest in place-ments," its internal e-mails told a different story. "We need to place our business in 2004 with those that have superior financials, broad coverage, and pay us the most," wrote one Marsh executive. Indeed, the messages showed how Marsh directed business to the insurers with which it had struck the most lucrative commission deals, even ranking underwriters by the profitability of the agreements. "I will give you a clear direction on who [we] are steering business to and who we are steering business from," a Marsh managing director advised colleagues.

Even worse, Spitzer exposed a broad pattern of bid rigging, orches-trated by Marsh with the collaboration of the giant insurance companies. Shocking e-mails showed how Marsh had made sure that no one underbid its chosen underwriter for a piece of business. One such case involved casualty coverage for Fortune Brands, a big conglomerate that sells Jim Beam whiskey and Titleist golf balls. E-mails show ACE was prepared to offer the policy for $990,000, but agreed to revise its bid *upward* to $1.1 million, at Marsh's direction. "Original quote $990,000 . . . ," an ACE executive explained to a colleague. "We were more competitive than AIG in price and terms. [Marsh] requested we increase premium to $1.1M to be less competitive so AIG does not loose [*sic*] the business." On another occasion, a Marsh broker e-mailed an executive at CNA Insurance: "I want to present a CNA program that is reasonably competitive but will not be a winner." When CNA refused to submit a phony bid, Marsh made one up and submitted it in the company's name anyway.

Marsh brokers demanded that insurers submit such phony, inflated bids—known as "B quotes"—to give its clients the illusion that they were getting competitive prices. ACE, for example, was warned to keep playing ball if it wanted more insurance business from the broker's clients. "I do not want to hear that you are not doing 'B' quotes or we will not bind anything," a Marsh senior vice president e-mailed an ACE VP. A manager with one insurer, Munich-American RiskPartners, privately complained that such practices were "repugnant" and "basically dishonest. . . . It comes awfully close to collusion or price fixing."

Taking the charade a step further, Marsh even asked insurers to show up for client presentations where the outcome was pre-determined. In March 2001, a Marsh broker e-mailed Munich to send a "live body. Anyone from New York office would do . . . perhaps you can send someone from your janitorial staff." The Munich manager was not amused: "WE DON'T HAVE THE STAFF TO ATTEND MEETINGS JUST FOR THE SAKE OF BEING A 'BODY.' WHILE YOU MAY NEED 'A LIVE BODY,' WE NEED 'A LIVE OPPORTUNITY.' WE'LL TAKE A PASS."

When Spitzer unveiled his investigations into Wall Street research conflicts and mutual funds, reform had required months of painstaking negotiations. This time, it happened literally overnight. Spitzer had filed suit on a Thursday, sending insurance stocks reeling. On Friday, Marsh announced it would stop accepting all backdoor payments from insurers, which in 2003 had amounted to $845 million—more than half the company's profits. Aon and Willis Holdings, Marsh's biggest rivals (the three controlled nearly 80 percent of the brokerage market), soon followed suit. With a single court filing, Spitzer had ended a long-standing, lucrative—and sleazy—industry practice.

There was, however, an even more dramatic display of Spitzer's growing unilateral power—and his willingness to use it. Marsh's dismissive response throughout the investigation infuriated Spitzer. At one point, the company's lawyers suggested that the AG just didn't really understand the insurance business. That might be true, Spitzer told them. "But I *do* understand bid rigging." At his press conference after suing Marsh, Spitzer delivered a blunt message to the company's directors: there would be no settlement with his office if they didn't fire their CEO. "The leadership of that company is not a leadership I will talk to," he declared. "It is not a leadership I will negotiate with."

Marsh's CEO was fifty-three-year-old Jeffrey Greenberg, a member of the insurance industry's royal family. Jeffrey was the eldest son of the legendary Hank Greenberg, the chairman and CEO of AIG, the world's largest insurance company. Jeffrey's younger brother, Evan, was CEO of ACE. Marsh had prospered during Jeffrey's five-year tenure, and the Greenbergs were notoriously iron-willed. But Spitzer's lawsuit—and his words—had prompted a run on Marsh shares: in four trading days, its stock had plunged by nearly 50 percent, wiping out $11.5 billion in market value.

Desperate to halt the bleeding—and end fears of a criminal indictment—the Marsh board fired its CEO just eleven days after the AG filed suit. Looking for an executive that Spitzer *would* deal with, the directors then replaced Greenberg with Michael Cherkasky, the AG's old friend from the Manhattan DA's office. Cherkasky knew little about insurance but had leveraged his relationship with Spitzer to leapfrog rivals for the job from his spot as head of Kroll, Marsh's private-investigation subsidiary. Spitzer responded with a public statement that criminal prosecution of the company was now "unnecessary."

Marsh settled with Spitzer four months later, agreeing to apologize for "shameful" conduct, pay customers $850 million in restitution, and ban contingent fees and bid rigging. Aon and Willis Group Holdings, the other big brokers, and several major underwriters also settled. By the time it was all over, twenty insurance executives had pled guilty to criminal charges.

Watching all this from the eye of the storm, Brown marveled at his boss's clout, especially over public companies. "I admired him tremendously as a muscular populist liberal who wasn't afraid to confront business institutions by punching them in the nose. The MO was to keep things under wraps, announce them in a big way, then work with the press. You lay out all the appalling facts, and they're dead, because they're in the market. That's all you have to do. When he really had the facts on somebody, it was like something out of *Wild Kingdom*."

Spitzer understood the power of a lawsuit, as both a legal and public-relations document. His complaints told a story, with a keen eye for what would generate the most outrage. They invariably led with the most scandalous conduct, and often included details that offered the ugly flavor of his targets' behavior, even when it wasn't essential to their legal claims. Spitzer also knew how to cast a complex matter in simple, populist terms. Conflicts of interest in Wall Street research? "The largest consumer scam ever." Permitting market timing in mutual funds? Like a casino that "allowed favored gamblers to use loaded dice."

One of the things that drove Spitzer's enemies batty was just how gleefully he went about his business, exploiting his leverage to the hilt, moralizing about right and wrong, and peppering his public appearances with in-your-face remarks. "The way he practices law is a kind of physical sport," Constantine explained in 2005, while his friend was still attorney general. "He enjoys the power, and he likes to win. This is not Solomon exercising his judgment with a heavy heart. This is a young, strong, jubilant male in triumph. There are hubristic moments."

———

"They got the wrong fucking guy!" Ken Langone, a sixty-eight-year-old investment banker, told me in his Park Avenue office. It was mid-2004. Langone's adult son, sporting a Mohawk haircut, was sitting in on this off-color tirade, directed against Eliot Spitzer and the Wall Street CEOs who had served with his dad on the board of the New York Stock Exchange. "I'm nuts, I'm rich, and boy, do I love a fight!" Langone declared. "I'm going to make them shit in their pants!"

If the usual playbook for political ascent in America was to make powerful friends, Eliot Spitzer's signature was making powerful enemies. Just a month after launching his insurance investigation, he added two big names to the blue-chip list of Spitzer haters by suing Dick Grasso and Langone. To be sure, this was not a conflict "the people's lawyer" needed to launch. No everyday citizens had been cheated; even total victory would recover not a penny for the public till. It would also require a tough, expensive war of attrition with two proud, rich men—on behalf of a few thousand of Wall Street's wealthy.

The issue? Dick Grasso's money.

Grasso, of course, was Spitzer's old ally in settling the research analysts' scandal. He had lost his job as chairman and CEO of the NYSE in

September 2003, in the outcry over news that he had enjoyed a $140 million payday. The exchange board, which approved the payment, had turned around and fired Grasso just days later, after word of his massive windfall got out. The board then brought in John Reed, the former chairman of Citigroup, to replace Grasso on an interim basis (he was paid $1 a year).

In a rare interview about the case, Reed said his first move was to find out if Grasso had already cashed his mammoth paycheck—he says he was prepared to stop payment if it hadn't gone through. He then commissioned a detailed private report, which concluded—not surprisingly—that Grasso's compensation had been "far beyond reasonable levels," with pension benefits that were at least *four* times what was reasonable. Reed thought the situation was "actionable," the result of "stupidities" and a "comedy of errors" by the board, but far too awkward for the exchange to handle itself. So he asked the SEC and the New York attorney general to pursue the matter instead. In February, Grasso rejected Reed's formal demand to return $120 million. The SEC, after looking into the matter for a few months, decided it had no jurisdiction. In May 2004, Spitzer filed suit.

Spitzer embraced the Grasso affair as a vehicle to weigh in on a raging issue right in his populist sweet spot: greedy CEOs and their outrageous pay. And, as Spitzer noted years later, "This was the only case where we really had jurisdiction." To be sure, by any conceivable standard, Grasso's compensation—more than $30 million for 2001 alone—*was* outrageous. The exchange, which had just fifteen hundred employees and $1.1 billion in revenues, wasn't really a business; it was a not-for-profit corporation, a sort of public utility for trading that also operated as a regulator. SEC chairman William Donaldson, by comparison, was paid $175,000. Donaldson had preceded Grasso as NYSE chairman, serving until 1995, and never made more than $2 million—about what Reed thought the job was worth. But even if you were looking to pay Grasso like a CEO of one of the biggest financial companies that traded on the exchange—say, Citigroup or American Express—Grasso had been grossly overpaid. All this had resulted from a deeply dysfunctional governance process: the NYSE was overseen by an oversize, inattentive, celebrity board, handpicked by Grasso himself, and dominated by CEOs whose businesses he regulated.

Spitzer had filed suit under New York's not-for-profit corporation law, which requires that compensation be "reasonable" and "commensurate with services rendered." He demanded the return of more than $100 million in "excess" compensation. As defendants, the AG named not only Grasso, but his friend and admirer Langone, who had chaired the compensation committee. Spitzer accused them of duping their fellow board members—a group of financial sophisticates that included future Treasury Secretary Hank Paulson, then CEO of Goldman Sachs.

It would be hard to imagine two tougher men to crack. A short, scrappy college dropout from Queens—friends called him "Punky"—Grasso had worked at the exchange for thirty-six years, after starting out as an $81-a-week clerk. Before becoming a symbol for corporate greed, he had been a 9/11 hero, credited with getting the exchange up and running just six days after the attacks on the nearby World Trade Center. With his shaved head and raspy voice, he ran the place with an iron fist—it became known as "the House of Grasso." The little man's bark was venomous; one subordinate who endured a Grasso tongue-lashing stumbled out of his office and promptly collapsed. Grasso ran the place as his fiefdom and lived like a pasha—he charged the exchange for everything from his personal eyeglasses to flowers for his favorite restaurant hostesses. By the time he was fired, he owned three homes and ten cars, and traveled in private jets with armed bodyguards. Even his personal assistant made $240,000 a year. But during his eight years in the top job, almost no one disputed Grasso's performance running the exchange.

Langone was a big, blustery, profane man, the son of a Long Island plumber and a master of the corporate boardroom. After earning his MBA in night school, he'd helped Ross Perot take Electronic Data Systems public, launched Invemed Associates, a small investment-banking firm that he still runs, and co-founded Home Depot. Worth an estimated $1.2 billion, Langone was famously generous with both New York charities and CEOs, known for ensuring that they didn't go home "with an empty pail." While critics understandably branded Langone a "serial overcompensator," his philosophy was unapologetic: if a CEO isn't performing, he should be fired, but "you can't pay a great manager enough money." Langone thought Grasso was flat-out irreplaceable—"the embodiment of capitalism," he called him. What were the financial limits of this philosophy? "I suppose that if we gave Grasso a billion dollars, we might have overpaid him," Langone told me in 2004.

So it shouldn't have come as a surprise that after Grasso named

Langone to chair the comp committee, his take-home quickly multiplied. During the four years Langone held the job, Grasso's annual pay and bonus totaled a stunning $80.7 million. But that didn't even include his *real* jackpot: an array of outrageously generous retirement programs. By 2003, this windfall had swollen to $139,465,000. In the old days, that wouldn't have been a problem; in its two-hundred-year history, the exchange had never publicly disclosed how much its boss was paid. But in the corporate-governance debate prompted by Enron, keeping this all secret was simply impossible. Nervous that a future board might blanch at paying him so much, Grasso, then just fifty-seven, negotiated to take his accrued retirement out immediately as a lump sum, as part of a four-year contract extension. As if that weren't enough, Grasso was supposed to receive another $48 million in "retirement" money by 2007, in addition to his bonus and salary. When the news got out, a firestorm erupted—GRASSO'S JACKPOT, screamed the *New York Post*—and he was fired instead.

Ugly as all these facts were, the situation made for an even uglier lawsuit. In addition to insisting that it was simply excessive, Spitzer was alleging that Grasso and Langone had misled the other directors about the CEO's pay. There was indeed evidence that Langone had handed out incomplete information and failed to highlight how Grasso's retirement was mushrooming. NYSE staff and consultants had also prepared separate sets of compensation charts, with certain columns totaling millions missing from the versions given to the board. But the directors, inattentive as they were, clearly knew that Grasso was getting paid a king's ransom and had approved it anyway. The board also included the biggest names on Wall Street—in this case, those Spitzer was portraying as misled were neither unsophisticated nor naïve.

There was one more problem: at the time of Grasso's payout, Langone had stepped down as chairman of the comp committee. His successor was former state comptroller Carl McCall, whom Spitzer had endorsed in 2002 for governor. McCall had supported the payout too. Why wasn't *he* getting sued? Was the attorney general playing politics? Finally, while Paulson and several other NYSE directors professed shock at how much Grasso made, some insisted they knew about every penny. Reed, outraged at the board's inattentiveness, thought Spitzer should sue the entire comp committee.

In a private letter hand-delivered months before the suit was filed,

Grasso's pugnacious Washington lawyer, Brendan Sullivan, told the AG that the facts "cry out" for him to drop the matter. Sullivan had a reputation for never settling a case. "Please don't let your Office be used, or better said *abused*, by those who want to engage in a political witch-hunt," he wrote. "If your Office wants to enter the long-running debate about compensation levels in Corporate America, do so *prospectively*. This would be the worst test case any litigant could embark upon." Grasso's compensation had been approved by a board of "financial geniuses," Sullivan added. "Neither the law nor the facts permit carefully considered and meticulously structured contracts to be tossed out the window because someone comes along and concludes, in hindsight, that they might have done something differently."

Baum, Spitzer's chief of staff, also thought that going after Grasso's pay was a mistake. While bringing suit was right on the merits and would generate plenty of press, Baum told his boss, it was clearly a political quagmire. "Why are we pissing off all these people in a tough case? You're just jumping into a pit with every important person in the world, and you have to tar all of them to get from here to there. You have to prove that all these guys are idiots."

Spitzer says he did everything he could to try to settle the matter before bringing suit. "He wanted a psychological win," says Reed. The AG made a pilgrimage to the office of Marty Lipton, a powerfully connected New York corporate lawyer who had informally advised both Grasso and the NYSE board. He recalls pleading with Lipton to orchestrate a face-saving compromise, in which Grasso would return some of what he'd received—perhaps $50 million. "Come up with a number that Dick can give back to the board," Spitzer recalls telling Lipton. "The board can give it to a charity—I don't care what they do with it." But he couldn't simply drop the matter: "We have a principle to have to stand up for—*too much is too much*. I think it's compelling." Spitzer says Lipton warned him that there would be no easy resolution if he went to court, and the battle would be damaging for everyone. "Don't bring this lawsuit," he says Lipton told him. "You're destroying your chance to be the first Jewish president."

When the suit was finally filed, Grasso and Langone fought back ferociously, just as everyone had predicted. Grasso countersued the exchange and attacked both Spitzer and the NYSE board on the editorial page of *The Wall Street Journal*. Both men called the affair a private business dispute—none of Spitzer's business—and denied that they'd misled anyone. This wasn't a fight over money, they insisted—it was about *honor*. Both vowed to fight to the death. "If Grasso gives back a fucking nickel, I'll never talk to him again," Langone told me. He was ready for war: *"Bring it on, baby!"*

Spitzer offered his own trash talk, telling a reporter Langone's remarks were "grotesque" and declaring that he was "ready to rumble." He'd also told former General Electric CEO Jack Welch—a Langone friend—that he was so angry at the counterattacks he was going to "put a spike through Langone's heart." (To which Langone responded: "It better be made out of steel, because if it's wood, it's going to break!")

These were not exactly the words of a sober, deliberate prosecutor. In private, however, Spitzer was still seeking a way out, dispatching emissaries to explore settlement terms. He even sidled up to Langone at a black-tie charity dinner, telling him: "You and I are both aggressive people. In another life, we could have been friends." Langone's response? The precise words were: "Not likely," before Langone turned his back. But Spitzer recalls it this way: "He just about ripped my head off."

With no resolution in sight, the AG vowed to prevail in court, even while minimizing the matter, telling me at the time that he had more important issues on his agenda than "the silliness over one guy's pay." The Grasso case would drag on in court for years, with the two sides deposing sixty-one witnesses and exchanging more than a million pages of documents. In the intervening period, Grasso himself would largely remain out of the spotlight. Ken Langone would wage a holy war.

"Politics," a Washington consultant once remarked, "is show business for ugly people." By the end of 2004, Eliot Spitzer had become his trade's equivalent of Brad Pitt. The fury of a few fat cats on Wall Street was a badge of honor. From a second-tier office in a single state, Spitzer had transformed himself into the most powerful public official in America outside of Washington. A profile in *The Atlantic Monthly* pronounced him "the Democratic Party's future," casting him as a man driven to fight evil. The piece likened interviewing Spitzer about what he did to "sitting down with Bruce Wayne, Batman's alter ego, and asking him why he dresses like a bat and lurks in the corners of Gotham each night."

Under attack by Democratic rivals as a captive of special interests, presidential candidate John Kerry had tapped the New York attorney general to vouch for his "absolute integrity" at a press conference in Albuquerque, New Mexico. Suddenly, people were jamming Spitzer's speeches to hear him talk about "fiduciary duty." They stopped him on the street, shouting: "Give 'em hell, Eliot!" They even asked for his autograph. Recalls Spitzer: "There was a moment where I couldn't walk through an airport, whether in Chicago or San Francisco—wherever it was—without people wanting to talk about what I was doing." Although Spitzer was just forty-five and presumably in midcareer, *Washington Post* reporter Brooke Masters was already preparing to write his biography. Titled *Spoiling for a Fight: The Rise of Eliot Spitzer,* the book would liken the attorney general to his hero, Teddy Roosevelt.

All this was soon followed by the ultimate confirmation of Spitzer's status as a politician who had crossed over to celebrity—a profile in *Vanity Fair.* "We feel he is doing important work, and would like to bring his message to a national audience," the magazine's articles editor had written Spitzer's press office, in requesting "an exclusive regarding other profiles" in national magazines. "As New Yorkers we are great fans of Mr. Spitzer, and we'd like to introduce him to the rest of the country." When the 7,500-word story was published, with Arnold Schwarzenegger bestriding the magazine's cover, editor Graydon Carter sent the AG an early copy, conveying "my compliments, my admiration, and my very best wishes."

At the 2004 Democratic Convention, in Boston, Spitzer had spent much of his time in private meetings with big national party fundraisers, from Hollywood producer Rob Reiner to Texas lobbyist Ben Barnes. He was among a select group of insiders invited by Washington power broker Vernon Jordan to a private luncheon at the Four Seasons with Barack Obama, whose keynote address had also placed him on the national stage. Already, there was chatter about what role Eliot Spitzer might play in a Kerry administration: *chairman of the SEC? Attorney general? Supreme Court justice?* But none of this was to be. There would be no Kerry administration, and Spitzer wasn't pursuing a path to Washington—not directly, at least. He was aiming for Albany in 2006 instead.

That ambition put him on a collision course with U.S. Senator Chuck Schumer, another smart, press-friendly Jewish New York City Democrat with razor-sharp elbows and a ton of campaign money in the bank. Spitzer and Schumer, who was nine years older, had some personal history. Spitzer had almost left the DA's office to go to work for Schumer when he was a congressman; Spitzer's sister, Emily, had dated Schumer while at Harvard. Now Schumer was mulling a run for governor too, and clearly wanted Spitzer to stand down until he'd made up his mind. He viewed Spitzer as his junior, a sort of political kid brother.

A primary fight between the two men would be a very expensive bloodbath—the Democrats' worst nightmare. And, after commissioning a poll, Baum told Spitzer he might well lose. While the AG did better among general-election voters, Schumer was more popular among Democrats. Undaunted, Spitzer quietly commissioned opposition research on Schumer, and kept working to lock up support among county leaders. Schumer was annoyed—"He's crowding me," he privately complained. But when a key job opened up in the Senate Democratic leadership, he decided to stay in Washington instead.

The election was two years away. Pataki was clearly not going to run for a fourth term, and there was no one else on the landscape who worried the attorney general. On November 14, 2004—the day Schumer announced that he was staying in the Senate—Spitzer, for the first time, felt certain: *"I'm going to be governor."*

Chapter 5: Irwin

ELIOT SPITZER'S ANNOUNCEMENT OF HIS CANDIDACY FOR governor was a mere formality. He confirmed what everyone knew in December 2004, just three weeks after Schumer pulled out. This was extraordinarily early for a 2006 election, but Spitzer wanted to build a sense of inevitability, to scare off other candidates. He was also eager to keep his political ambitions from overshadowing everything he did. So on this occasion, he *didn't* hold a press conference, instead making it official in calls to a handful of reporters.

By this time, the darling of the mainstream press had become the bête noire of the conservative establishment. The *Wall Street Journal* editorial page attacked Spitzer regularly as an autocratic, anti-business meddler—the "Lord High Executioner." *National Review* branded him "the most destructive politician in America." Thomas Donohue, president of the U.S. Chamber of Commerce, took the extraordinary step of attacking the New York attorney general at a Washington press conference. Complaining that Spitzer acted as "investigator, prosecutor, judge, jury, and executioner," he called his approach "the most egregious and unacceptable form of intimidation that we've seen in this country in modern times."

But rough justice made great politics. In the aftermath of Kerry's thrashing, there was talk about the attorney general as the leader of a new political movement—"Spitzerism," the *Times Magazine* called it. Its premise was a populist appeal to the growing "investor class"—the 50 percent of American families with money in the stock market—and its hook was the theme of Spitzer's cases: *Wall Street is taking you to the cleaners.* Spitzer even offered a manifesto for this crusade, in an essay in *The New Republic* on how Democrats could reclaim the allegiance of middle America. He placed his own actions squarely in this context—not as an attack on capitalism, but as an attempt to reestablish "a level playing field," in the name of simple fairness. "We did not investigate Wall Street because we were troubled by large institutions making a lot of money," he wrote. "We took action to stop a blatant fraud that was ripping off small investors." Already viewed as presidential material, Spitzer aimed to make New York a showcase for the virtues of activist government—a stark alternative to the prevailing ideology in Washington.

It was unclear whether all this really had the makings of a national movement. But it was certainly working for Spitzer himself, in ways that made his political handlers drool. Polling showed that the AG was unlike virtually any other Democrat in a critical way: voters thought he was *tough.* And the howls from business targets only reinforced that image. In New York, Spitzer had numbers unprecedented for a Democrat. He was more popular with men than women; his approval ratings (above 60 percent) were almost as high among Republicans as Democrats; and he polled almost as well in conservative upstate as in liberal New York City. "He had everything," says Jefrey Pollock, Spitzer's pollster. "*Reforming watchdog for the public interest . . . went after big business . . . put people in jail.* Good Lord, he had a fabulous profile! All he had to do was be a successful governor. If he could run New York and tame the beast that was Albany, maybe he *could* go fix Washington."

The statehouse was a springboard for national ambitions. Four New York governors had become president: Martin Van Buren, Grover Cleveland, Teddy Roosevelt, and FDR. Four more, including Thomas Dewey and Al Smith, had won their party's presidential nomination. Nelson Rockefeller had served as vice president; Charles Evans Hughes had gone on to become chief justice of the U.S. Supreme Court. Whoever held the job was instantly a presidential prospect.

But this path to Washington was also treacherous. Albany had consumed the ambitions of many gifted politicians—most recently, Mario Cuomo. State government in New York was a quagmire. Success—if it was even possible—would require skills Spitzer hadn't needed to deploy often as attorney general: horse trading, patience, and deference to the egos and agendas of other powerful men. He was already a national figure, and had the luxury of picking his fights. As governor, he'd be forced to deal with pedestrian issues and people, and be tested in ways he couldn't imagine. It would surely be a worthy proving ground. But just as surely, it wouldn't be easy.

Spitzer seemed to recognize the peril. I interviewed him in 2005 for a *Fortune* magazine profile. It was before the gubernatorial race had begun in earnest, but Pataki wasn't running again and the polls showed Spitzer far ahead of everyone else. He already knew he'd be governor—"unless I screw it up"—and spoke about how things would be different. "To a certain extent as AG, I live in a binary world. I look at facts and make determinations about right and wrong, legal and illegal, then make decisions that flow from those facts about pursuing cases. A governor is much more in the world of making triage decisions where limited resources are used for many important and compelling causes. Those decisions necessarily leave one a little dissatisfied—they're more in the form of compromises."

He'd even thought about life after Albany. Spitzer seemed to have perspective on where he'd been and where he was going; he was more reflective than I'd seen him during a half dozen conversations since he became attorney general. If elected governor, Spitzer told me, he would serve just two four-year terms. "After a certain period of time, you've exhausted your creativity." And then? "Work on my backhand." Did he think he could become president? "I am smart enough to know it would be extremely stupid to talk about," he correctly responded. Spitzer also knew that whatever happened would depend on what he did, not what he'd done. "The reality is that if I'm elected governor, I start with a clean slate. After three years as governor, no one will care about whether I was good, bad, or mediocre as attorney general."

Spitzer told me he loved his life in elected office. "You're fighting fights that are interesting and important—*nothing* can hold a candle to this." But he was wary of what politics might do to him. You begin to believe your own rhetoric, he explained; you begin to believe all the nice things people say about you. "Too many years in this," said Spitzer, "can alter you in ways that aren't healthy."

———

In the tight circle of Eliot Spitzer's enemies, his formal declaration for higher office had opened a new front for counterattack. They could not only challenge his arguments and legal tactics in the press and courtroom;

they could work to derail him politically. This effort would soon gain a fierce and relentless new ally.

At the age of seventy-nine, Maurice "Hank" Greenberg was arguably the most powerful businessman on the planet. He had run American International Group for thirty-eight years, building the company into a global leviathan worth $157 billion. By 2005, AIG operated in 130 countries with 92,000 employees, supplementing its enormous insurance income with fat profits from exotic sidelines such as aircraft leasing and derivatives trading. Greenberg was famously brutal with competitors, employees, analysts, customers—even members of AIG's board, who would occasionally pose probing questions, only to have Greenberg dismiss them as "stupid." He ran roughshod over state regulators, too. Delaware officials who crossed him found private investigators from Kroll knocking on doors in their neighborhoods, asking questions.

The company Greenberg had assembled seemed calculated to defy oversight. Its organization chart contained so many hundreds of far-flung subsidiaries, listed in such tiny type, that it was best read with a magnifying glass. Years later, after AIG had collapsed, threatening the entire global financial system, an executive brought in to sort it all out put it this way: "The best businesses are run by people who kick their tires every day. We don't even know where the tires are." But in 2005, all this was viewed as part of Greenberg's genius, evidence of how much smarter and tougher he was than anyone else—everything was in his head. He got away with it because he produced spectacular results. AIG's profits just kept rising, defying every historical pattern in a notoriously cyclical business.

Spitzer had started investigating the insurer as part of his Marsh investigation, which prompted the firing of Hank's son Jeffrey Greenberg; two AIG employees had pled guilty to bid-rigging charges. But the feds were already after the company. The SEC had accused AIG of accounting fraud in 2003, for using a product called "finite insurance" to manipulate an Indiana corporation's financial statements. AIG paid $10 million to settle; the agency had doubled the fine because the company had withheld incriminating documents. AIG was also in trouble with both the SEC and the Justice Department on a second matter: its Enron-like use of off-balance-sheet entities to help a Pittsburgh business dress up its financial statements. Once again, AIG was uncooperative, blowing up a tentative settlement at the last minute and issuing press releases declaring government threats of legal action "unwarranted." After AIG's shocked board ordered Greenberg to settle, the deal was finally signed in November 2004, with the Department of Justice granting an AIG subsidiary deferred prosecution on criminal fraud charges. Greenberg's behavior had raised the price tag by $20 million, to a fine of $126 million.

On February 9, 2005, Greenberg proudly announced a record year for AIG, with profits of more than $11 billion. Then, asked on the investor conference call about the "relatively hostile regulatory environment," Greenberg pronounced the government crackdown of recent years excessive. "When you begin to look at foot faults and make them into a murder charge, then you have gone too far," he said.

At that point, Spitzer's probe of insurance bid rigging was far from over. And there was more. Unbeknownst to Greenberg, just one day earlier, attorneys for General Re, a reinsurance company owned by Warren Buffett's Berkshire Hathaway, had met secretly with prosecutors from both the SEC and Spitzer's office to describe a shady deal their company had made with AIG. Cooked up by Greenberg himself in a phone call to Gen Re's CEO, the transaction boosted AIG's insurance reserves by $500 million; Greenberg initiated the deal after analysts complained that AIG's insurance reserves were too low, prompting a drop in company shares. Regulators later concluded that the transaction was a "sham."

And so it was that on the very day Greenberg railed about "foot faults"—only hours after his dismissive comments—Spitzer's investigators sent AIG a detailed subpoena for information about the Gen Re deal. That evening, Spitzer was the dinner speaker at the offices of Goldman Sachs, where the firm was conducting a compliance program. "Hank Greenberg should be very, very careful talking about foot faults," Spitzer warned ominously, departing from his prepared remarks. "Too many foot faults and you can lose the match. But more importantly, these *aren't* just foot faults."

Eager to lead the way—the SEC and Justice were already preparing their own demands for documents about the Gen Re deal—Spitzer turned the knife two days later, with a subpoena for Greenberg's deposition. This was an extremely unusual move—prosecutors usually work their way *up* the corporate chain of command. But Spitzer wanted fast results, and Greenberg had been directly involved.

This backed the wily CEO into a corner. After AIG's first scuffle with the SEC, the company's board had proclaimed that any employee who didn't cooperate with regulators would be fired. But Greenberg's newly hired criminal lawyers were now telling him to take the Fifth (he ultimately would)—and Spitzer refused to put off his deposition for more than a few days, until March 17.

On Sunday, March 13, AIG's independent directors gathered at the Midtown law offices of their attorney, Richard Beattie, a former Marine Corps jet pilot and frequent advisor to *Fortune 500* companies. Beattie had gotten a sobering private assessment of the AG's investigation directly from Spitzer the day before, during a long walk through Central Park. Now he passed on what he had heard to the directors, who had already begun looking for a way to ease their CEO into retirement.

The directors met for more than eight hours, during which time Greenberg periodically called in from a yacht (called *Serendipity II*) and AIG's jet to berate them: "*You're going to destroy the company! . . . If I have to go, the stock is going to tank! . . . This company's being run by a bunch of lawyers who couldn't even spell the word 'insurance'!*" With that, Beattie quietly scribbled out INSURANCE on a sheet of paper and passed it around the room. Did Greenberg intend to take the Fifth? He wouldn't rule it out. The directors had another big issue: PricewaterhouseCoopers, AIG's audit firm, had concluded it couldn't certify the company's financial statements as long as Greenberg remained in charge. With that, says Beattie, "the ballgame was over." After dark, the board finally demanded Greenberg's resignation as CEO. He would be permitted to remain as non-executive chairman.

The months that followed would produce more fireworks. Greenberg was forced out as chairman after his lawyers entered an AIG building in Bermuda over Easter weekend and removed eighty-two boxes of documents potentially subject to subpoena. The incident prompted Spitzer to threaten obstruction-of-justice charges against the company; the documents were soon secured. A few weeks later—before he was even finished investigating—Spitzer took to national television, telling ABC's George Stephanopoulos he had "overwhelming" evidence that AIG had crafted deals "for the purpose of deceiving the market. We call that fraud. It is deceptive, it is wrong. It is illegal." During the interview, Spitzer stopped just short of saying Greenberg had broken the law. But he pointedly added that AIG "was a black box run with an iron fist by a CEO who did not tell the public the truth. That is the problem."

In late May, Spitzer sued for fraud, alleging that Greenberg and AIG had engaged in all manner of sleight of hand—not to keep the company afloat (as at Enron) but to cover up the slightest blemish in its performance and to burnish results. Underwriting disasters had been disguised; reserves fraudulently inflated; states had also been shorted on workers' compensation payments. When all else failed, Spitzer charged, AIG had simply made numbers up, with the CFO dictating hundreds of millions in bogus adjustments to a subordinate, who jotted them down in a spiral notebook.

AIG's earnings restatement—which Spitzer had rushed to beat—came five days later, validating his claims. The company's new management shaved $3.9 billion from reported profits since 2000, and confessed that AIG had suffered from "control deficiencies, including the ability of certain former members of senior management to circumvent internal controls over financial reporting." AIG ultimately settled all its outstanding disputes with the SEC, the Justice Department, and Spitzer for a staggering $1.64 billion—the biggest civil penalty ever. Greenberg refused to settle, remaining a defendant in Spitzer's civil suit. The phony reinsurance deal led to criminal pleas by two Gen Re executives; five others, including AIG's former head of reinsurance, were later convicted in federal court, where Greenberg was named an unindicted co-conspirator.*

Greenberg gave no quarter in defending his actions. Still in control of C. V. Starr and SICO, two private sister companies that held AIG stock worth billions, he decamped to the offices of his personal attorney, David Boies. From there, Greenberg established a sort of CEOship-in-exile, launching a legal and PR war with his enemies that would continue for years, even as AIG nightmarishly imploded, tanked by risky derivatives ventures that had begun while he was in charge.

---

* Greenberg was never charged with a crime. Federal prosecutors say Spitzer hampered their efforts to charge him in the Gen Re investigation by prematurely granting immunity to a high-level AIG deputy in his civil inquiry. Spitzer, in turn, notes that the feds insisted he defer to them in probing allegations that Greenberg sought to manipulate AIG's stock price, then never brought a case. On this subject, the AG's files contain an unusually blunt November 21, 2005, letter from Manhattan U.S. Attorney Michael Garcia, "deeply concerned" that the AG planned to add such charges to his civil suit "despite our repeated request." If Spitzer did so, Garcia warned, he would be "compelled" to seek a stay of the AG's case "to protect our [criminal] investigation." Wrote Garcia: "It is hard to see how the public interest would be served by creating such a situation."

Throughout it all, there was no one Greenberg blamed more for his woes than the attorney general of New York: It was Spitzer who had ousted his son from Marsh; Spitzer who had forced the AIG board to fire him; Spitzer who'd branded him a criminal on national television; Spitzer who had pressured the company to recant five years of perfectly sound financial statements. But for Spitzer, Hank Greenberg bitterly insisted, he would *still* be at the helm of AIG, running the ship in his inimitable manner, and none of the epic calamities that ensued would have ever occurred.

———

It should come as no surprise that Greenberg and Ken Langone were friends. So it was natural that the two billionaires would discuss what to do about Eliot Spitzer. Both men had made it perfectly—and publicly— clear how they felt about the attorney general. Furious at his treatment in the Grasso case, Langone had declared a jihad against him. Though he tried to place his motivation on more high-minded ground than simple revenge, that invariably came across as an afterthought. "One way or another," Langone proclaimed in late 2005, "Spitzer is going to pay for what he's done to me and the havoc he's caused in the New York business climate." This particular remark appeared in *New York* magazine, in an article written by CNBC's Charles Gasparino, a journalist with long-standing ties to the billionaire. The story was headlined TARGET: SPITZER. In it, Gasparino reported that Langone was telling friends he could raise as much as $30 million for Nassau County Executive Tom Suozzi, a likely Spitzer primary opponent—or might fund an independent campaign to Swift-boat the AG.

Greenberg was just as bitter. In December 2005, months after he had left AIG, Spitzer whacked him again, releasing a report alleging that he had bilked an AIG-related charity through a string of self-dealing transactions thirty-five years earlier. No charges were filed in the matter. "I have no idea what the hell that man's problem is," Greenberg fumed to one reporter. "He doesn't care what the facts are," he told another. "The agenda is to demonize me." Greenberg said he would consider joining Langone in backing Spitzer's opponents.

In fact, the two moguls were already working against the attorney general in quieter ways. Republicans, of course, had been digging for dirt on Spitzer ever since he first ran against Dennis Vacco. Opposition research was part of the political game, routinely practiced by both parties.

By the fall of 2004—before Spitzer even declared for governor—one of those engaged in such muckraking was a veteran New York elections attorney named Larry Mandelker, who served as outside counsel to the Republican state committee. But Mandelker wasn't doing this work for the Republicans. He was doing it for Ken Langone.

One memo Mandelker prepared detailed a possible line of attack: the AG's handling of a lawsuit against Wal-Mart for selling toy guns without required safety markings to distinguish them from real weapons. Spitzer had settled his case for $200,000—far less, per gun sold, than New York City had settled for in a similar matter. Why had the AG let Wal-Mart off so light? "We should examine," Mandelker wrote, "whether executives from Wal-Mart have either contributed or raised money for any of Mr. Spitzer's campaigns, the New York State Democratic Committee, or any other organizations of the State or National Democratic Party."

On October 19, Mandelker faxed this memo—one of several—along with five pages of supporting documents, to representatives of the man funding his work. According to the fax cover sheet, the material went to Jim McCarthy, the aggressive Washington PR strategist working for Langone in his war with Spitzer, and Thomas Fedorek, who ran the private-investigations practice for the New York office of a firm called Citigate Global Intelligence. Fedorek had previously worked at Kroll. In the space for "our client," the fax cover sheet listed a single name: "Langone."

Mandelker and Fedorek wouldn't discuss the matter with me. In a series of conversations, McCarthy told me that Langone's investigative work—which remained secret—was confined exclusively to the AG's public record, and neither explored his personal life nor involved any surveillance. McCarthy said the effort lasted about six months, but refused to disclose how much money Langone had spent. Finally, according to McCarthy, the Langone camp had used this research exclusively for its own purposes: gathering ammunition for Langone's speeches lambasting Spitzer and McCarthy's attempts to fuel criticism of the AG in the press. McCarthy said nothing was turned over to any campaign or political committee. (Such assistance would have required public disclosure.) He also says Greenberg had nothing to do with Langone's 2004 research efforts, though both McCarthy and Mandelker had done work for AIG while Greenberg was CEO.

Greenberg, however, was engaged in his own efforts. The fallen AIG chief had a reputation for employing stealthy tactics; President Reagan had even considered him for the number-two job at the CIA. After he got crosswise with Spitzer, he began taking steps to strike back. While Greenberg was still at AIG, one of his top deputies met with the top executive of a Washington PR firm, asking him to explore what they could do to "trash" the attorney general. This effort never got off the ground; Greenberg, who went through publicists like disposable razors, fired the firm first. A year later, after Greenberg had been forced out of AIG, he retained a Cambridge, Massachusetts, consulting firm called eSapience to deploy a massive rehabilitation program, later described in a lawsuit and "highly confidential" internal documents. Aimed at changing "the public conversation" about Greenberg, the plan included hiring a ghostwriter to prepare Greenberg's autobiography and inventing two scholarly sounding think tanks to host seminars where he would be the keynote speaker. Another element of this master plan, according to the eSapience lawsuit: "securing" a *New York Times* journalist to write a critical story about Spitzer's case against Greenberg. After seven months, Greenberg fired eSapience, which sued him for $2 million in unpaid bills.

With Greenberg's encouragement, prominent figures—some of them Democrats—had sprung to his public defense. Bob Kerrey, a former Democratic senator and president of the New School, in New York, criticized Spitzer in the *Times* for trying Greenberg in the press. (It was perhaps not entirely coincidence that a Greenberg-controlled foundation had given the university $10 million, its largest foundation grant ever.) Mario Cuomo, meanwhile, was collaborating in a campaign to sign on prominent New Yorkers for Greenberg testimonials.

It was easy for the attorney general to dismiss previous counterattacks as the meaningless howls of his deserving targets. But Spitzer had been taken aback by Greenberg's ability to enlist respected advocates, by the scope of his influence. "It was shocking how far his reach was," says Baum.

One day, the AG had stopped by to chew it all over with Dopp. "You know, boss, it's been a hell of a run," Spitzer's PR man told him. "But if we ever so much as stumble, they'll be merciless. A single misstep and they'll stomp us in the nuts."

"I know," Spitzer replied. "That's why we can't have any missteps.

I'm sure they've got people watching everything we do. And I'm sure that's been going on for a while."

———

Increasingly, as he plied his trade, Eliot Spitzer's temper loomed as a problem. For years, it had seemed a powerful weapon, one that he deployed carefully. Blunt talk could settle a case by putting the fear of God in his targets. "In private, if you use it tactically, it can be a good thing," Spitzer told me in 2005. "It's got to be something that's used, rather than something that overtakes reason. I've tried to keep my most egregious flare-ups to the privacy of my bedroom at home."

Still, there had been occasional episodes making the attorney general seem less like a man speaking truth to power than simply a hothead. Most of these incidents had been easy enough for Dopp and Baum to swat away. Vowing to drive a spike through Ken Langone's heart? *A hearsay account from a hallway conversation.* Threatening to "go outside" with the California attorney general? *Boys will be boys.* In truth, his closest aides knew better. Spitzer, for example, had made the comment about Langone on the floor of the 2004 Democratic National Convention, and delightedly informed Baum about it immediately afterward. ("I just told Jack Welch I'm going to put a spike in Langone's heart!") For every incident that briefly became a media kerfuffle, there were a dozen more where Baum and Dopp had watched their boss erupt, and reined him in. For Spitzer's top deputies, his temper was an ongoing management issue—as much of an open secret as research conflicts were on Wall Street. They privately joked about the periodic emergence of Eliot's raging evil twin— "Irwin," they called him.

From the beginning, Spitzer's crusades had always relied on a sense of moral authority for their power. This was good battling evil, right versus wrong, an incorruptible man with a perfectly square jaw going after the craven and dastardly. Spitzer regularly sprinkled his public comments with the language of righteous condemnation—the behavior he had uncovered was "repugnant," "avaricious," "disgusting." Indeed, it was the malevolent cast of Spitzer's targets that made his wide-ranging solutions and rough tactics seem defensible, even necessary.

Bank of America chief Ken Lewis, for example, had visited the AG in mid-2003, just as his institution was about to be branded for its part in the late-trading scandal. "It was one of the most unpleasant meetings I've ever been through," Lewis said later. "It was a tongue-lashing, a total whipping." At the time, Spitzer offered no apologies for dishing out such treatment. "He deserved it," the AG explained. "They thought they could say 'sorry' and everything would be okay. He needed to hear that what they had acquiesced in and participated in had been horrendous."

In truth, there was a part of Spitzer that liked being feared. He regularly made jokes to Wall Street groups reminding them that anyone in the room could end up as his next target. Spitzer seemed to view himself as an avenging angel, adding public shaming and private humiliation to the customary punishments for wrongdoing and inadequate contrition. He insisted that even the harshest attacks were never personal, though his well-heeled targets often felt as though they'd been mugged. A bully? Spitzer scoffed: "Bullies pick on *little* people." Indeed, the stature of the AG's victims had always provided a measure of comfort to his staff. "I never saw Eliot kick a person when he was down," says Baum. "He only kicked people when they were up."

As Spitzer looked back on his big cases, his only major regret was that he had not been *rougher* on top executives, by pursuing criminal charges against them. For all his belief in the ultimate goal of systemic change, Spitzer had come to conclude that nothing really deterred white-collar fraud like throwing a few millionaires in the slammer.

John Whitehead wasn't a malevolent target. He was one of Wall Street's most respected elder statesmen, a measured eighty-three-year-old with snowy hair and Midwestern manners. A Harvard MBA and D-Day veteran, Whitehead had worked for thirty-eight years at Goldman Sachs, the last eight as co-chairman of the firm. Then he'd served five years as deputy secretary of state under President Reagan. In 2001, Governor Pataki had named him chairman of the Lower Manhattan Redevelopment Corporation, charged with revitalizing the area around Ground Zero. Charities had showered him with awards for his philanthropy and nonprofit work. All in all, it was hard to imagine a more sympathetic victim of "Irwin."

The problem, it turned out, was that Whitehead was also an old friend of Greenberg, and one of the many prominent surrogates he had enlisted in his rehabilitation campaign. A moderate Republican, Whitehead had generally admired Spitzer's efforts to clean up Wall Street; he'd even called the AG during the research investigation to volunteer a bit of counsel, as "an old Wall Streeter." But Spitzer's treatment of Greenberg was a different matter. In the spring of 2005, Whitehead submitted a six-hundred-word op-ed column on the subject to *The New York Times*; the paper declined to run it. He then sent it to a friendlier forum: *The Wall Street Journal*, which published the piece on April 22.

Titled MR. SPITZER HAS GONE TOO FAR, Whitehead's column tracked the Greenberg line of attack: the AG had accused Greenberg of fraud on national television; he had unfairly singled him out for common industry practices that, at worst, constituted minor offenses; he was responsible for Greenberg's ouster; he had targeted Greenberg because the AIG chief had "antagonized" him; and all this was terrible for the city's business climate, still struggling to recover from 9/11. Why had "one of America's best CEOs" been treated so harshly? Whitehead speculated in print that it was the result of Greenberg's opposition to tort reform. All told, Whitehead concluded, the attorney general's actions were "beginning to do more harm than good."

This hardly constituted a vicious attack, but when Spitzer read it, he immediately tried to reach Whitehead. The two men were both traveling that Friday. Spitzer was heading to Philadelphia for a speech and fundraiser, Whitehead jetting to Texas with his fiancée for a big weekend at an old friend's ranch. They didn't connect until the afternoon, when both men were in cars, being driven to their destinations.

Where did you get your information? Spitzer demanded. He wasn't opposed to tort reform! *Where did you get your information about the AIG case?* Whitehead allowed that he'd discussed these matters with Hank. With that, according to Whitehead's later account, Spitzer exploded. Was there *anyone* who wouldn't do Greenberg's bidding? "Mr. Whitehead," he told the former Goldman Sachs chairman, "it's now a war between us, and you've fired the first shot. I will be coming after you. You will pay the price. This is only the beginning, and you will pay dearly for what you have done. You will wish you had never written that letter."

Whitehead was shocked, at both the words and the tone—the attorney general of New York was *screaming* at him. His fiancée, sitting next to him in the car, could even hear it. Whitehead said he tried to get a word in, but Spitzer hung up before he could respond. The entire conversation lasted about two minutes. When Whitehead arrived at his friend's East

Texas ranch a short time later, he and his fiancée immediately retreated to a quiet room, where they wrote down what they had heard. Says Whitehead: "I thought it might be useful if we had a street fight on the subject." After returning to New York, he sent the notes to his lawyer, and asked him to put them in his safe. For eight months, there was no public discussion of the angry tone of this conversation—just a few brief press mentions that the AG, concerned that Greenberg was orchestrating a campaign of false media attacks, had complained to Whitehead about his column.

That December, Spitzer had opened a new front in his war with Greenberg with his report accusing the ex-CEO of self-dealing in AIG transactions dating back to the 1960s. A week later, Whitehead's byline appeared on the editorial page of the *Journal* again. In a 374-word column, Whitehead said he was writing to "set the record straight" in response to media rumors about his phone conversation with Spitzer. Whitehead then recounted the exchange, including Spitzer's threats. Lest there be any doubt, Whitehead also described how he had "written it all down right away, so I would be sure to remember it exactly as he said it." And then he added: "I was astounded. No one had ever talked to me like that before. It was a little scary."

Once again, Spitzer and his team worked to dismiss the episode. After conferring with his boss—who insisted he hadn't threatened Whitehead—Dopp told reporters that Whitehead's account was "a complete fabrication." The two men had merely engaged in a "spirited conversation." In unattributable "background" e-mails to reporters, Dopp ridiculed Whitehead's claims as "bogus" and "nutty," and insisted it was all part of "an orchestrated political attack" by Greenberg and his Republican friends, who had already pounced on the episode to call for a criminal investigation of the attorney general. "This is what the GOP will do for the next 10 months," Dopp wrote. "They will try again and again to undermine Mr. Spitzer's strength, which is his well-earned reputation for integrity." The attorney general had added his own denial. "I don't make threats," he told a reporter. "I disagree with people."

As the AG saw it, Whitehead—impeccable reputation notwithstanding—was shilling shamelessly for a bad man who had done bad things. All that didn't change a central fact: everything Whitehead had claimed about his conversation with Spitzer was true. Kristie Stiles, Spitzer's young national fundraiser, had been with him in the car on the day he spoke with Whitehead and had watched it all unfold. Shocked, she called Ryan Toohey, the AG's campaign manager, to tell him about it afterward. Eliot's eyes had suddenly narrowed to slits before he let loose: *You'll wish you had never crossed me!* "Eliot really lost it in the car," Stiles reported. "It was like *Gunsmoke!*" Whitehead's account was verbatim.

This incident was distinctly different from Spitzer trading trash talk with Langone. Whitehead wasn't the target of a fraud case. He was above the fray—an elderly gentleman, two years older than Spitzer's father. He might foolishly be doing Greenberg's bidding, but no one thought he was a liar. After a few weeks, Spitzer tried to smooth things over, inviting Whitehead to meet for coffee to clear the air. Nuts, Whitehead responded. "Since you continue to be unwilling to concede the accuracy of my report of our phone call, I see no point of our meeting for coffee," he e-mailed back. "Those words, every one of them, are what you said."

———

"Hi, Governor!" called a greeter outside the Pearl River Hilton in upstate Rockland County, where Spitzer had just arrived to speak at an evening fundraiser for a local Democrat. It was still 2005. "Not yet!" Spitzer replied, with a smile.

A waiting aide asked the candidate if he'd like a "ginger ale"—code among his staff for Scotch and water. *Later.* Spitzer instead set about working the ballroom—slapping backs, squeezing shoulders, giving hugs. He had become a far more skilled politician, with a genuine interest in the game as yet another intellectual exercise to master. "Politics isn't chess—it's checkers," he scoffed. Spitzer still wasn't the sort to feel your pain—on the stump, he was rarely personal and always cerebral. But in assuming the role of the populist warrior, bashing Republicans and greedy moguls, he was able to get some blood boiling.

When he took the podium that night in Rockland County, Spitzer's rhetoric, as usual, soared far above local concerns. The Hurricane Katrina debacle had just unfolded. Spitzer blasted the federal response, as the inevitable result of the GOP's disdain for government. "What we are seeing out of Washington is the destruction of the social fabric. When you see a government so inept, so destructive, you have to stand back and ask, 'Why?' We have been living through an era where the leadership of the other party has denigrated the very notion of government."

The next night, Spitzer's destination was the primary victory party for Fernando Ferrer, the Bronx Democrat who had just won the nomination to face Mike Bloomberg, New York City's unbeatable billionaire mayor. Spitzer had backed Ferrer's candidacy early, shrewdly winning points with Hispanics, yet another key statewide constituency. An inveterate front-seat driver, Spitzer, as always, sat next to the bodyguard piloting his government-issue Crown Victoria, telling him which route to take downtown.

Spitzer worked his phone on the way, counseling Ferrer's advisors to bring the candidate out to claim victory during prime time. "Don't make the Howard Dean mistake; don't play to the people in the room! Play to the TV audience!" When we got there, Spitzer jumped onstage. "We want a *real* Democrat to be the mayor of New York!" he shouted into the microphone. "We do not need a *fake* Democrat! When the Democratic Party is united, in the *state* of New York, in the *city* of New York, in the *boroughs* of New York, we . . . will . . . not . . . be . . . *defeated*!" It wasn't exactly poetry, but the crowd roared nonetheless. A bearded Hasidic rabbi, the Reverend Al Sharpton, and a union leader followed Spitzer onto the stage.

Back in the car afterward, Spitzer worked his BlackBerry. Silda had been sending him text messages with election results. It was close to midnight. He called home to check in, as he did regularly whenever I was with him. "All right, babe," he told her. "I'll be home in fifteen minutes. . . . Okay, babe. *Love you*."

———

After twelve years, Silda Wall was warming to the role of political wife. She shook hands, hosted fundraisers, and even made speeches. On the campaign trail, she was gracious and charming, perfectly at home in a black Baptist church or chatting up a Long Island housewife. In deference to convention, she'd even started using Spitzer as her last name.

Silda and their three daughters softened Eliot's rough edges in ways he never could—even his jokes were about lawsuits. At holiday season, the family sent out hundreds of small jars of homemade jam. An annual holiday card followed, often featuring a family photograph taken by Pam Fox. Pam and George Fox were close family friends who vacationed regularly with the Spitzers. George ran a hedge fund called Titan Advisors; Pam had once worked with Silda at Skadden, Arps.

Eliot's marriage to a Southern Baptist from North Carolina had also produced an improbable broadening, in the form of a fascination with NASCAR; Silda's brother was chief engineer for Hendrick Motorsports. "There's an adrenaline to it," Spitzer explained. "On one level, it's as close to the Roman Colosseum as we get these days. You never know when mayhem will break out." This had political benefits, too. It made the Jewish, Scotch-sipping Manhattan lawyer seem more accessible to the beer-drinking upstaters who flocked to the Watkins Glen raceway.

Since giving up her legal career, Silda had spent much of her time working with the Children for Children Foundation. She had launched the nonprofit in 1996, spurred by her revulsion at extravagant Manhattan birthday celebrations. Its original intention was to encourage kids to donate some of their haul to the less fortunate. Over time, it had vastly outgrown its crumbs-from-the-rich origins, involving thousands of children in an array of programs from serving hot meals in homeless shelters to running book drives. The budget grew exponentially as well, to $1.5 million, fueled by an annual gala, foundation grants, and corporate sponsors (some presumably hoping to ingratiate themselves with her husband). After a decade running the show, Silda had stepped down as board chair and begun spending much of her time on the campaign trail.

Silda was a little taken aback by the vitriol that had been directed at her husband. But life had been good during Eliot's years as attorney general. While his government salary peaked at $145,285, their family real estate holdings provided more than $1 million in yearly income. They lived in Bernard Spitzer's Fifth Avenue building, with their three daughters and two dogs. The girls attended Horace Mann, Eliot's alma mater; like almost everyone in their circle with kids, they employed a nanny to help out. Eliot worked long hours, rarely going to bed before midnight and rising each morning at 5:15 for his run. But he didn't spend many nights away from home, and until deep into the campaign for governor, he usually kept weekends free for family trips to their rented farmhouse in Pine Plains.

To be sure, there was sacrifice. Silda had less of her husband; the girls had less of their father. But Eliot seemed happy. He was accomplishing great things, leading the important, interesting life he wanted, and making the world a better place. It was good for all of them.

Chapter 6: "Daddy, Please Don't Hit Me Anymore"

IN THE CITY OF NEW YORK, EXPENSIVE PROSTITUTION RINGS were one of those open secrets Eliot Spitzer liked to talk about, like research analyst conflicts on Wall Street. They were hidden in plain view, and sometimes not hidden at all. *New York* magazine, the glossy chronicler of the city's upscale lifestyle, had for years filled its back pages—and bank account—with ads for escort services. In 2004, one of its best such advertisers was a flashy prostitution ring called NY Confidential. It was run by a paroled Ecstasy smuggler named Jason Itzler, who strutted around Manhattan wearing a fur coat and a T-shirt reading, I AM YOUR GIRLFRIEND'S PIMP. Surrounded by his posse, Itzler made conspicuous appearances at hot downtown nightspots like Cipriani, where he dished out steel business cards boasting that his service provided "Rocket Fuel for Winners."

For about a year, no one bothered to bust him. Itzler, who was thirty-seven and got his start in the phone-sex business, operated out of a huge drug-filled party loft in Tribeca, where his clients ran the gamut from Manhattan lawyers to wiseguys from New Jersey. But according to Itzler, about 60 percent of his clientele worked on Wall Street; they told him they needed the outlet because they had high levels of stress and testosterone. Itzler charged them about $1,000 an hour, grossing as much as $450,000 a month. He even accepted credit card payments, which showed up on customers' statements as charges incurred at the fictitious "Gotham Steak." Checks from Gotham Steak were also used to pay for Itzler's

$6,000-a-week display ads in *New York,* touting "24/7" availability of "over 75 girls!"—the magazine didn't ask questions. The escorts, in turn, were paid from an account opened in the name of another front company, Tribeca Models. The memo line on the prostitutes' checks read "independent contractor."

Like many twenty-first-century enterprises, the upscale escort business had migrated shrewdly onto the Internet. Itzler's website was sophisticated and brazen, displaying the unclothed charms of his call girls and even offering drop-down menus for setting up a date online ("Which one of our beautiful women would you like to see?"). But most appointments were made the old-fashioned way—by phone with hooker bookers. Bookers also served as the escorts' handlers, briefing them on the logistics and payment arrangements for each appointment, and checking in with them before and after. The bookers got a 10 percent commission. The balance was split between the escort and the house.

Many customers became regulars, known in the industry as "hobbyists." The industry even had its own online version of *Consumer Reports*: TheEroticReview.com, which invited explicit critiques of individual women, with separate sections for "appearance" (tattoos, silicone, breast size), "services offered," and "juicy details" ("whether or not you enjoyed it in graphic emotional and sexual terms"). Another website, Eros.com, served as an online shopping mall for escorts and for new job opportunities in the industry. It even provided a sort of *Good Housekeeping* seal of approval, to assure johns that the women depicted on an escort service's website were "Eros-verified"—actually available for hire—rather than part of a bait-and-switch.

Among the prostitutes at NY Confidential was a starry-eyed young woman from New Jersey, just nineteen, whom Itzler had recruited into the business after meeting her at a trendy hotel bar where she worked as a hostess. The girl, who had dreams of becoming a singer, identified herself as Ashley Alexandra Youmans; she would later become known as Ashley Dupré. Itzler billed her on his website as Victoria, "NY Confidential's newest seductress," and she quickly began taking home several thousand dollars a week. But Itzler's prize escort was "Natalia"—his petite girlfriend, Natalie McLennan, who commanded as much as $2,000 an hour (two-hour minimum), despite a nasty cocaine habit. Itzler boasted that Natalia was the best-rated escort *ever* in the storied history of TheEroticReview.com.

As Itzler saw it, he had a terrific product to promote, and hyping it on his website and in ads just wasn't enough. He cut a deal with a pair of lowbrow filmmakers who began shooting video inside the loft for a proposed reality show called *Inside New York Confidential*. Itzler even went along to pitch the idea to executives at VH1. He talked about trying to franchise the NY Confidential "brand" in other cities.

All this was, of course, illegal—and busting a prostitution ring had always been a headline grabber for the tabloids. But in New York, law-enforcement agencies had bigger crimes to tackle. The feds—the FBI and the U.S. attorney's office—virtually never pursued prostitution rings. State agencies had only intermittent interest. Attorney General Eliot Spitzer, however, had brought two conspicuous prostitution cases, both in 2004.

First, he charged the owners of a New York travel agency with promoting prostitution, for allegedly organizing "sex tours" to Southeast Asia. When his jurisdiction was challenged—why was the AG of New York trying to prosecute sex acts in the Philippines?—Spitzer's office, in a court filing, asserted the state's need to prevent the spread of disease: "No matter where the prostitution activity may be contemplated, New York surely has an interest in protecting its citizens from sexually transmitted infections from those who travel abroad to engage in sex with prostitutes and then return to New York." (The case was ultimately dismissed.)

Later that year, the AG's office arrested eighteen people involved in what a press release called a "massive" enterprise based on Staten Island. They'd operated escort services named Personal Touch and Gentlemen's Delight that dispatched call girls throughout the city. "This was a sophisticated and lucrative operation with a multi-tiered management structure," Spitzer said in a statement announcing the bust. "It was, however, nothing more than a prostitution ring, and now its owners and operators will be held accountable." The proprietor of the enterprise, which charged $250 an hour, ended up serving two years in prison.

Inevitably, the task of cracking down on high-dollar operations like NY Confidential fell to local cops and prosecutors. In Manhattan, DA Robert Morgenthau, Spitzer's old boss, reluctantly accepted it as part of his franchise, though he preferred devoting his investigative resources to white-collar crime. "It's not a priority matter for us," Morgenthau told me in an interview. "But if you're going to be prosecuting street prostitutes, you shouldn't let the high-end ones go." Ultimately, the prosecution of New York City's pricey escort services was driven by a crusading Irish cop named Myles Mahady. A detective on the Manhattan South vice squad, Mahady viewed all forms of prostitution as an odious social scourge. He had no patience for the notion that it was a victimless crime; he'd seen too many desperate women victimized in human trafficking. Mahady regarded the pimps as social parasites who had gone unpunished for too long. The upscale operators? "They're a better-dressed parasite." Mahady also favored Spitzer-style public shaming for johns. He applauded those jurisdictions that posted their names and photographs online.

Typically, the operators of a busted upscale service got just a year or two in the slammer. The escorts almost never served time; they scattered and went back into business with another agency under a new name. Customers were never pursued. In this strange game of whack-a-pimp, it was inevitable that Mahady would bust Itzler, who had even bragged to a gossip reporter that the cops were "on my side."

Mahady's vice squad raided NY Confidential in January 2005. Itzler went off to jail, taking time out to proclaim himself to the media as "the king of all pimps." The evidence that police seized, which included the film shot for Itzler's proposed reality show, didn't leave much room for claims of innocence. "I'm a good criminal lawyer," says Barry Agulnick, who represented Itzler in the prostitution case. "But when there are sixty hours of videotape of a brothel in operation, it's sort of hard to plead not guilty and persuade a jury. The only thing I could have said was that it wasn't in 3-D." Natalie McLennan would pose for a splashy cover story in *New York* magazine, headlined NY'S #1 ESCORT REVEALS ALL, and make an appearance on the *Today* show before being arrested herself and returning to her native Canada. Bit players like Ashley would slip away, only to reappear later in a marquee role.

Despite all the publicity, NY Confidential actually remained in business for two months under new management: Paul Bergrin, Itzler's New Jersey lawyer in his Ecstasy-smuggling case, and Velina Stamova, a Bulgarian prostitute. Mahady eventually busted them, too, revealing more secrets. A former assistant U.S. attorney in Newark, Bergrin was charged with helping launder $800,000 in prostitution money for Itzler and falsely assuring parole authorities that the pimp was actually working twelve hours a day as a paralegal in his New Jersey law office. Bergrin also came under federal indictment, charged with (among other offenses) helping a drug gang murder the key government informant in a case against one of his clients.

Meanwhile, the paymaster at NY Confidential, a bodybuilding former banker named Clark Krimer—nicknamed "Superman"—had opened his own escort service, based in Brooklyn, where his prostitutes included his girlfriend, Ashley Youmans. After *his* arrest, Krimer became a witness in the DA's case against Bergrin. Stamova, the Bulgarian prostitute, became romantically involved with a scary gun freak named Suwei Chuang, who stashed a dead Maltese in his freezer and used dogs for basement target practice. When Stamova—who had become a police informant—finally blew the whistle on her boyfriend, Mahady arrested him, too.

In this sleazy, high-dollar world, driven by illicit relationships, greed, and betrayal, one case linked to another, forming an indelicate web. Says criminal attorney Marc Agnifilo, who represents some of its inhabitants: "It's like a John le Carré novel, except everything's happening in New York and everyone's a prostitute."

———

Even behind bars and dressed in a jumpsuit, the impresario of Emperors Club VIP seems the world's most improbable pimp. Mark Brener is a short, pasty, balding man in his sixties, who speaks with a thick Eastern European accent and has a sweaty upper lip. Yet he evangelizes with the serene certainty of a New Age guru, promoting a lifestyle combining diet, spirituality, and personal empowerment. It is an odd prescription from a man who'd made his living selling sex.

There is much about Brener that is odd, as a series of jailhouse conversations with him made clear. Brener is understated and polite, but reaches for control and bristles with arrogance. Seated on a plastic chair in the visiting area, noisy with inmates and their families, he soon informed me that he possessed a "transcendent" intelligence, making issues "clear as a drop of water"; he said he enjoyed our conversations because "everyone else in this room is stupid." At the outset of our second talk, Brener seized my hands and examined each one carefully, as though reading my palms. He instructed me to read his favorite books on spirituality, which included a volume titled *Toward a Meaningful Life*. On another visit, he demanded a second handshake, which he carefully appraised

("You have a strong hand"), and made a grimace after smelling my breath. "Because we are becoming friends, I need to tell you this," he said. "I think you may have a digestive system problem."

Brener had twice written his warden at the Metropolitan Correctional Center in Manhattan urging him to put the entire inmate population on a macrobiotic diet. One day, he called excitedly from prison, instructing me to immediately contact Apple CEO Steve Jobs, wizened from a battle with pancreatic cancer, to suggest a special diet for him, too. I told him that Jobs was a stubborn man who didn't listen to advice on personal matters, especially from journalists. Said Brener: "People change."

True enough. Brener's own life presented an extraordinary divide, marked by the death of his first wife. Before, he was a struggling tax advisor, a quiet, middle-aged family man. After, he was . . . a *pimp*. But as Brener saw it, the two passages had a parallel core, in the presence of the only two truly important women in his life: his beloved Eleonora, taken from him by disease; and Cecil Suwal, his college-age lover and partner in running the Emperors Club, taken from him by the FBI. "Do you know, my wife—I married her when she was twenty; she told me she had a crush on me when she was eighteen." And Cecil: "We were together when she was twenty—and *she* told me she had a crush on me when she was eighteen." The two women, born thirty-eight years apart, even had the same birthday: July 10. What did Brener make of this? Did he believe in reincarnation? "I don't go that far," Brener told me. But he did believe in fate.

In court, Suwal's lawyer would portray Brener as a Svengali and announce that his young client had severed all ties with him. But as he spoke to me about the young woman who'd helped him operate an international prostitution ring, Brener grew misty-eyed. He fervently believed that he had saved her life—and that they were meant to be together. When they both emerged from prison, Brener told me, he intended to offer her the "option" of becoming his partner once again.

————

If only Mark Brener had made it in America while operating a legal enterprise—instead of a brothel—he might be remembered as one of those heartwarming immigrant success stories. Brener was born in the Soviet Union in 1945, just five months after the Nazis' surrender, in the remote city now known as Orenburg, near Russia's border with Kazakhstan. The Breners, who had two sons, were Jewish and poor—in that place at that time, a terrible combination. When Brener was eleven, they moved to Poland, where his mother found work as the manager of a small factory. His father, suffering from strange outbursts, eventually abandoned the family.

It was in Krakow that Brener met the first love of his life, Eleonora, while both were attending university. She was a gifted linguistics scholar and pianist with an aptitude for new technology. They married while still in school, and had their only child, a son named Zvi (he now goes by Greg), in 1969. Later that year, they moved to Israel, where Brener became a civil servant, working for the country's internal revenue service. The Breners arrived in America in 1988, settling in Queens.

Shortly after arriving, he incorporated Mark Brener & Associates, setting himself up as a tax consultant; he'd passed a special licensing exam allowing him to represent U.S. taxpayers before the IRS. But Eleonora was always the family breadwinner. She worked for a big company as an information technology manager, a field dominated by men. Brener was a house husband who worked only intermittently, even after their son was grown. Murray Richman, his criminal defense lawyer, later put it this way: "All his life, he's been totally unsuccessful at everything he's done." Still, as long as they were together, things were fine. In 1994, Brener became a naturalized citizen, and they bought a townhouse in central New Jersey, in a tidy development not far from Princeton. Recalls Brener: "Life was great."

It was about one year later that Eleonora was diagnosed with terminal colon cancer. Told that his wife had just months to live, Brener says he convinced her to refuse chemotherapy and put her on a special diet. She lived longer than the doctors predicted. But inevitably, the cancer spread, and he took her overseas, in a desperate search for alternative cures. She died on September 19, 1997, in Mexico, at a controversial medical center near Tijuana that promotes "wholistic" care for cancer. They were both fifty-one at the time; they had been married for twenty-eight years. Says Brener: "It broke me—emotionally and financially."

Over the next six years, he spiraled downward. Renting out the New Jersey townhouse, he moved back to Queens, where he was trailed by bill collectors seeking tens of thousands for unpaid debts. In 2002, he hit his low point, facing court judgments from the New Jersey hospital that had treated his wife, American Express, Sears, and Citibank, to name just a few. His landlord went to court to evict him from his apartment for back rent. Brener pleaded for more time, explaining that he'd lost his job after the "disaster of September 11" and was living on $1,200 a month in unemployment and $670 a month in life insurance proceeds from his late wife. According to Richman, Brener sometimes prepared tax returns for people at storefronts in Queens. It was there that he stumbled across his financial salvation—one of his customers was a madam.

It's unclear precisely when Brener met Liang Hui Chen, a woman of about forty, but they were together by early 2003. They lived briefly in a small apartment building in Middle Village, Queens. The son of her landlord later told a *Times* reporter that she spoke of aspirations to become a schoolteacher. But there were strange doings at her apartment—men coming by for bulky envelopes in the middle of the night. In fact, Chen was running an Asian-themed prostitution ring. She had introduced Brener to the business; they began operating the service together and got married. Brener, who wouldn't discuss this period of his life during our meetings, told me he was "lonely" when he'd met her.

In 2003, their agency was called Emperor Special Escorts. Its garish website advertised such services as "sensual body rub"; its fifteen "exquisite" women were mostly Asian, ranging from "stewardesses" to "exotic dancers" to "the girls next door." Prices started at $250 an hour. A featured attraction was the "Emperor Special," which started at $450 an hour. The website described what would happen after the two women providing this service "discretely" arrived: "My girlfriend will start with professional relaxing massage that will prepare you for me. . . . After a while I will join and take over. . . . My soft fingers will go all over your body and both of us will tremble from unforgettable desire. . . . I will take you to the paradise."

By 2004, Brener and Chen had relocated to a one-bedroom co-op apartment in the twenty-nine-story Briarcliff building in Cliffside Park, New Jersey, just across the Hudson River from Manhattan. That July, using Chen's name, they registered the website address for a new escort service—Emperors Club VIP. Brener had experienced a brainstorm that would bring him fame and fortune: he was moving the business *upmarket*. No longer interested in hiring Asian prostitutes or charging just a few hundred bucks an hour, Brener had already begun advertising for models and college girls instead. It was one of those ads that had caught the eye of Cecil Suwal.

———

CC, as everyone called her, had always been audacious. Surely the drugs had something to do with it. But it was also clear that she was *different*. Suwal had grown up in Westchester before her parents divorced, then attended Blair Academy, a New Jersey boarding school. A tiny, doll-like girl with dark curls and porcelain skin, she was bright and brimming with personality. But she never fit in with her preppie classmates. She was street-smart and a bit of a loner.

In college, CC seemed perpetually wired—no surprise, since she was gobbling the amphetamine Adderall. Suwal was aiming at an advertising major, and had a strong interest in photography and website design—skills that would later serve her well. But she often seemed scattered, skipping on the surface of conversations, always seeking more drama. She soon got just that. After finishing her freshman year, she was back home in New York for the summer of 2003 when she answered Brener's ad in *The Village Voice* for college students willing to "model."

What did Cecil Suwal, then eighteen, do on her summer vacation? She worked as a prostitute. "I was like a bohemian in my first year in college," she explains. "I fell into it by chance. But for whatever reason, I felt comfortable there. A lot of the girls were young and we would hang out. We'd have a lot of extra money." Brener was then running the escort service with his second wife, Chen, who went by the name Rose. For business purposes, he had assumed her last name, introducing himself as "Alex Chen." By that point, Brener was starting to think about how to transition the operation beyond its low-rent roots, working to realize his lofty vision. But there was something holding him back: Brener's wife wanted to keep things the way they were. Says Suwal: "[She] really just couldn't see the picture."

After completing her sophomore year, Suwal spent a second summer working as an Emperor Special Escort, operating out of the agency's "incall" location in Lower Manhattan. She returned to college that fall, but her drug habit had grown worse. She was doing cocaine, amphetamines, and sometimes heroin. Her weight fell to ninety pounds. As Suwal recalls it, almost benignly, she was "taking the whole party scene to the next level," having "a little too much fun." Brener had visited her in Miami with thoughts of basing his upscale escort service there. He quickly decided he could make more in New York City. But he'd also been shocked at Suwal's condition. He told her that if she left school and moved in with him, he'd get her off drugs.

In the fall of 2004, she did just that. Brener and his second wife had recently split up. Suwal, thirty-nine years younger, became the born-again pimp's personal project. Brener told her what to eat. He dictated a regimen of vitamins and nutritional supplements. He lectured her on how to turn her life around. He checked constantly on her whereabouts. All this time, of course, she was working for him as an escort. As Suwal started to emerge from her haze, she told Brener she hadn't quit school to be a prostitute. She became a phone booker instead—and was soon both Brener's lover and his partner. "Mark was giving decent vibes," Suwal told me. "Despite the fact that he was a little mysterious, I was attracted to him from day one."

Suwal would help Brener, who had toiled away at his mom-and-pop business, make the great leap into the lucrative high-end niche in the marketplace. They commissioned a new website, placed a banner ad in the VIP section of Eros.com to draw upscale clients, and started hiring a new breed of call girl. In late 2004, Suwal opened up the first of two new bank accounts to launder the cash flow, using the names of shell companies: QAT Consulting Group Inc. (at North Fork Bank) and QAT International Inc. (at HSBC). When NY Confidential was busted up just a few weeks later, in January 2005, Brener figured it was the perfect time to make his move. "He saw the opening," says Shelley Everett, who had worked as a booker for both Itzler and Brener. "The big fish had gone down."

Later that month, Brener even had a sit-down with some old NY Confidential hands, including former paymaster Clark Krimer, with the thought of combining forces. Shelley Everett brokered the meeting, held at Krimer's Brooklyn apartment. They envisioned a synergistic "merger of equals": the NY Confidential team had flash and experience, and a raft of pretty escorts looking for a new employer; Brener had an existing business platform and wanted to expand. But the idea quickly fizzled—it was clear the two groups had different corporate cultures. So Brener decided to go it alone. He detailed his plans to Everett, who was skeptical about his intention to let Suwal help manage the business. She was too young, too wild, and too strung-out, she told him. "We're cleaning her up," Brener replied.

———

The stylish new website for Emperors Club VIP conjured up an altogether different fantasy world. There was no longer any talk of "body rubs" or escorts with backgrounds as exotic dancers. Instead, it promised "the most exclusive and discreet social introduction services" featuring "fashion models, pageant winners and exquisite students," meeting "our meticulous standards of beauty, intelligence and charm. . . . Each of our companions is a product of an exceptionally fine background and a success in her own right."

Individual escorts were rated on a scale of three to seven diamonds. A three-diamond girl went for $1,000 an hour, a seven-diamond for $3,100. The site offered artfully suggestive photographs and too-good-to-be-true profiles of each: the "model, dancer, actress, superstar" with "a masters of public relations"; the gorgeous entrepreneur who "created and sold an elegant Manhattan day spa while still in her twenties"; the "playfully bold yet sensually seductive" world-class dancer with a graduate degree and "breathtakingly beautiful blue eyes"; the piano-playing "classic beauty" with "astonishing intelligence." There was another change with the new Emperors Club: Brener now used the name "Michael," while Suwal went by "Katie."

Still just twenty-one, Suwal managed the growing stable. Among her tasks was dreaming up stage names for the new hires. Whenever she was stuck, Suwal would peruse a website for inspiration—BabyNames.com. *Simone. Chloe. Anais.* She'd help concoct an alluring persona for each, too. At least one girl was a "double," filling two roles: "Revlon supermodel" *and* sexy moonlighting "corporate professional." To sell the illusion that these were different women, the website displayed photos of her dressed in two different outfits and hairstyles, each with its own stage name and profile. When a john made a date, the booker would tell the girl which part she was to play.

Each of the new Emperors Club escorts had to sign a lengthy "contract" stating that she was doing nothing illegal. The fig leaf for escort services was that they received payment for providing companionship, not sex. The Emperors Club was merely bringing beautiful women together with lonely men; whatever they decided to do afterward, as consenting adults, was their own business. "These are wealthy guys and they're working hard," Brener would explain, through his thick accent. "They just want to call and know a pretty, smart girl is coming to their room. It's just hanging out—just hanging out, *right?*" Brener also instructed his call girls never to talk about what happened in the bedroom, lest they be overheard on police wiretaps. He later explained that he believed all this would avoid trouble with the cops—that he'd read a book about how to operate an escort service legally.

By industry standards, Brener and Suwal were rigorous in their employment screening. When Tammy Thomas, a single mother and veteran of the sex trade, responded to their ad for a phone booker in mid-2006, they interviewed her in the lobby of the Hyatt Hotel on Forty-second Street. After she passed muster on the first round, they provided her with a file on their escorts—photos, measurements, fake names, and profiles—gave her time to study up, then tested her a few nights later by making role-playing calls as johns. When Brener and Suwal finally hired her, Thomas even went through a probationary period of sorts. She started out working in the living room of their New Jersey apartment, staying all night to answer the phones so "Katie" and "Michael" could monitor her performance before turning in. Thomas was amused at the contrast between the Emperors Club's seven-diamond illusion and its tacky, zero-diamond reality. Brener's apartment, 12-L, looked like it had been furnished from a Salvation Army thrift store. Its decorations included a plastic Hanukkah menorah and a tiny Zen fountain. Brener and Suwal cooked on a portable gas burner in the kitchen. The bookshelf was filled with dusty old accounting texts and volumes on Eastern religion. Brener sometimes served Thomas a foul-tasting nutritional potion he'd prepared. ("This is going to make you feel so much better!") After diplomatically taking a couple of sips, she dumped it down the drain when he left the room.

After a month, Thomas had been allowed to work from home, giving her more time to spend with her son and attend PTA meetings at his school. She met with Brener and Suwal every two weeks or so to collect her pay. While many people involved in the sex trade had a taste for flashy cars, Brener and Suwal's pimpmobile was modest—a dented gray Honda minivan. On payday, they'd usually rendezvous with Thomas at the Barnes & Noble in nearby Edgewater, New Jersey, and sit in the Starbucks café to pore over the prostitutes' booking sheets. Then, after agreeing on the numbers, they'd adjourn to the parking lot and climb into the back of the minivan, where Brener would furtively hand over the cash, as well as a check for her share of any credit card payments. The escorts got paid the same way—in the back of the Honda minivan, usually parked on the streets of New York.

During these encounters, Thomas saw the strange dynamic between Brener and Suwal. "Katie" was smart and had a strong personality, but was remarkably submissive to "Michael." During one Barnes & Noble meeting, Suwal excitedly noticed a novel called *The Little Lady Agency in the Big Apple*, about a young British woman who runs a "girlfriend service" for helpless bachelors. Though she was helping run a business taking in thousands of dollars a week, she asked Brener for permission to buy the book. "He was definitely in control," says Thomas. "He told her how to behave, and she did so."

Suwal's old college friends, who saw her from time to time, were bewildered by her relationship with the strange old Russian dude. When a group of them came to New York City, he arrived for their dinner at a Midtown macrobiotic restaurant—with a gorgeous Eastern European woman in tow. Suwal introduced Brener as her business partner and boyfriend. "It seemed like this guy was trying to brainwash her," says Mehal Darji Rockefeller, a classmate at the University of Miami who socialized with Suwal and Brener in both Miami and New York. CC seemed at his beck and call. And she carried three cell phones that rang at all hours of the night. Over dinner, Brener boasted about his skills at hiding money and maneuvering nimbly around tax laws, and how that had proven useful in his business. But Suwal's friends had no idea what they did.

To be sure, Brener was old enough to be her grandfather. He dressed like a Steve Jobs wannabe: blue jeans, a black turtleneck, round wire-rimmed glasses, and thick platform heels. He stocked his bathroom with Rogaine. But there was much about the five-foot-five-inch former tax consultant that Suwal found compelling. Brener had "a very deep inner strength about him" and was "extremely intelligent," she says. "He's someone who is sort of tough to get to, but once you're there, it's really worth the chase. . . . We really clicked. We understood each other, and we brought out the best in each other."

There was clearly another element at work, too: for all her shocking, quite adult behavior, Suwal liked to play the little girl. She wore giant bows in her hair and kept a teddy bear in her bedroom. She had a fascination with the children's books about Eloise, the precocious six-year-old who lived on the top floor of the Plaza Hotel. Brener was a stern father figure—the sort of man she'd never known. And, she proudly told friends, he didn't need Viagra.

———

On the afternoon of September 21, 2005, the Cliffside Park Police Department received a call from a resident of the Briarcliff who was worried that a child was being abused. The man explained that he'd returned to his twelfth-floor condominium at about 1:30 A.M. the previous night. As he passed apartment 12-L, he told police, he heard what sounded like a little girl crying inside: *"Daddy, please don't hit me anymore! Please, Daddy, don't!"*

At about 3 P.M., two detectives arrived to question the occupants of the apartment. They spoke first to Brener, who appeared at the door in his bathrobe and identified himself as "Greg"—the name of his adult son. Perhaps his neighbor had heard him arguing with his girlfriend, Brener coolly suggested. But there had certainly been no physical violence and there were no children in the apartment. The detectives accepted the man's offer to look around. Suwal came out of the bedroom, also dressed in her robe. She looked quite young, Brener pointed out, and might easily have been mistaken for a teenager. "Mr. Brener also stated he appreciated that he has neighbors that would be concerned for a child's welfare," the police report noted. The detectives left shaking their heads. They concluded that the peculiar couple had been engaged in kinky sexual role-playing.

———

It was just a few months later when George Fox called for the first time. Suwal thought it was a prank. The caller ID on her cell showed that the originating number was blocked, and the nervous man on the other end was speaking in a whisper. *"Is anyone available?"* he asked. Suwal said she'd check and let him know, but the man refused to give his number; he said he'd call back instead. She didn't expect to ever hear from him again. When he did call back, one of the bookers finalized the arrangements. The Emperors Club had a new client.

By this point in her career in the escort business—it was early 2006—
Suwal had become accustomed to furtive calls. *Where will we meet?
How do I pay?* "People just show each other facets of themselves," she
later explained. "No one really shows 'This is me in all my glory.'" But
George Fox, she soon realized, had a special penchant for cloak-and-
dagger arrangements. This customer was "extremely paranoid," even by
the usual standards of important men employing expensive prostitutes.
"I remember thinking to myself," says Suwal, "he is just going to attract
a *situation.*"

Chapter 7: The Big Ugly

THERE IS NO DEADLIER SIN IN POLITICS THAN PRESUMPTION. But Eliot Spitzer's lead in the race for governor—against any opponent—was making the 2006 election look like a coronation. Spitzer's lone primary opponent was Nassau County Executive Tom Suozzi, a forty-three-year-old up-and-comer who oozed ambition. Catholic, handsome, and charming, Suozzi was the first Democrat to win the Nassau job in thirty years, and had credentials as a reformer: he'd cleaned up a financial disaster left behind by the Republicans and led a short-lived crusade to reform Albany. But Suozzi was an unknown beyond Long Island and running against a juggernaut. Romancing Langone hadn't paid off, either. Donations from the billionaire and his friends had totaled perhaps $800,000, a far cry from the promised millions. Polls showed Spitzer crushing Suozzi by sixty points.

The Republicans, meanwhile, were fighting themselves. Pataki and the state chairman favored a moderate, former Massachusetts governor William Weld. Although Weld had moved to New York, he faced criticism as a carpetbagger and dilettante. The party faithful preferred conservative John Faso, a former upstate assemblyman. Not that it mattered much—the polls showed the AG thrashing both.

In the meantime, Spitzer didn't hesitate to throw his weight around, most conspicuously on the issue of a running mate. In New York, Democrats vote separately during their primary to nominate a lieutenant governor, who then runs in November on a single line with the party's candidate for governor. In truth, it was a little hard to understand why anyone would want the job—whoever held it usually just disappeared. Under the state constitution, the lieutenant governor would move up if the governor died, resigned, or was impeached. But that had happened only eight times in New York's history. The lieutenant governor also had the power to break a tie vote in the state senate; that hadn't happened in decades. Mario Cuomo's first lieutenant governor was so bored he'd quit in the middle of his term.

About the only time anyone really cared about the lieutenant governor was during campaigns, when the job was used to balance the statewide ticket or to reward a key voting bloc. For the 2006 Democratic primary, Harlem's powerful clubhouse bosses, known as "the Gang of Four," had taken this issue into their own hands. All were black men in their seventies: Congressman Charles Rangel, former Manhattan borough president Percy Sutton, former New York City mayor David Dinkins, and former New York secretary of state Basil Paterson. For the lieutenant governor's job, they'd endorsed Leecia Eve, an African American attorney who'd worked for Hillary Clinton and was the daughter of a former Buffalo assemblyman. Percy Sutton was her godfather.

Spitzer had other ideas. As his party's presumptive nominee, he wasn't *about* to let anyone dictate his running mate. At the same time, he didn't want to offend black voters, about 14 percent of the electorate. So he came up with what seemed like an ingenious choice: David Paterson, the minority leader of the state senate and the *son* of Basil Paterson. Paterson, fifty-one, was bright, witty, well liked, and legally blind—which gave him a compelling personal story. He also had a reputation for being lazy, indecisive, and a womanizer. By lieutenant governor standards, all that made him plenty qualified. Spitzer sealed the deal by promising Paterson he'd get Hillary Clinton's U.S. Senate seat if she was elected president.

Spitzer had outfoxed the Harlem bosses, with a black candidate they *couldn't* oppose. "I thought it was clever," says Spitzer. "Not only did I succeed in choosing David, but I created the impression that I'd looked at them and said: 'No, I'm not going to do what you want.'" But as was often the case with Spitzer's victories, the episode left powerful people smarting. Rangel, clearly irritated, waxed sarcastic to the press: "When Eliot Spitzer, the world's smartest man, is telling me that he has picked his candidate and knows that his candidate can win, who am I to question the world's smartest man?" Eve dropped out of the race a few days later.

———

As with all rising political stars, those in Spitzer's orbit found their own lives bound ever more tightly to his career. During his eight years as Spitzer's chief of staff, Rich Baum had met and married Terri Gerstein, a Harvard-educated assistant AG in the labor bureau; they'd had two children. By 2006, Baum had completed his transformation from small-town officeholder to canny backroom operative—Spitzer's version of Karl Rove. He was rarely quoted by name and hated to have his picture taken. "I lurk in the shadows," Baum joked. Yet he'd emerged as the most powerful deputy to a man presumed to be the future governor of New York— and more. With increasing frequency, statewide political players dropped by the AG's downtown office to see him. Baum usually led them across the street to a wooden bench in the historic Trinity Church graveyard, where Alexander Hamilton was buried. "People are often angry when they talk to me," he explained. "Sitting in a cemetery gives them a little perspective."

Baum had grown amused by the endless string of feature articles about his boss, which invariably tapped familiar anecdotes: Eliot's Monopoly game with his dad; the debates at the family dinner table; how Silda and Eliot met in the ski house. "Every time a reporter comes and says, 'I want to write a profile,' it seems kind of boring and pointless," Baum told political writer Ben Smith in 2006. "They all come out the same. He is what he is. There's no guile, no secret agenda."

Early that year, Baum had left the AG's payroll to move over to the campaign, as "senior advisor." He set up shop in a small cubicle in a windowless area in the back of the campaign headquarters. Baum happily left the big office, the day-to-day operations, and the title of campaign manager to his friend Ryan Toohey.

Toohey, thirty-one, was the bad boy in Spitzer's world. He had started out as his personal aide—known in politics as the "body man"—driving him around the state during the 1998 campaign. Brash, smart, and charming, Toohey, who grew up in Buffalo, had politics in his blood. His grandmother had served for sixteen years as mayor of a small town near Niagara Falls. His dad had worked for the state assembly speaker, and his godfather was Joseph Crangle, a famous upstate political boss. Married for three years, Toohey was carrying on an affair with Spitzer's deputy campaign manager, who was also married; both couples later divorced. Shortly before Election Day, he would be arrested for drunk driving on a highway north of Buffalo, after his speeding Volvo rear-ended another car at 1:30 A.M. and rolled over. Miraculously, no one was hurt. But Toohey had kept it secret until a reporter called; Spitzer responded by announcing that he'd dock Toohey's pay. Toohey worked closely with Baum, serving as the campaign's political extrovert—the yin to Baum's yang.

Spitzer's chief outside consultant was again Global Strategy Group, run by Jef Pollock and Jon Silvan, who had worked for him since 1998. Dick Morris, Eliot's controversial old friend, offered private advice in occasional calls to Baum and Spitzer. But he was no longer calling the shots.

Dopp had remained in the AG's Albany office, where he continued to labor over Spitzer's performance, in all its forms. One important part of his job was assuring that his "principal" never looked foolish. That spring, Spitzer had accepted an invitation to throw out the ceremonial first ball at the season opener for the minor league Buffalo Bisons. When Spitzer was back in Albany, Dopp led him into a back hallway of the capitol to check out his technique. The attorney general had played varsity soccer and tennis in high school, but rarely touched a baseball. Dressed in his usual uniform—starched white shirt, tightly knotted tie, dark suit—Spitzer took off his coat and grabbed a glove. The AG's deputy press secretary, Paul Larrabee, assumed the catcher's position as Dopp presided over the practice. They were using tennis balls that day. Still, Spitzer threw hard—did he know any other way?—bouncing a pitch off the floor and striking Larrabee in the groin. "Does this happen a lot?" the AG asked, as his aide grimaced in pain. "Sure," said Dopp. "Not a problem." Spitzer wound up for another pitch. When it was over, Dopp dispatched a quick BlackBerry message to Baum: "Good news. Boss doesn't throw like a girl."

The Spitzer-Paterson campaign was humming, in ways that political organizations in competitive contests rarely do. By November, the campaign would collect nearly $40 million, with much of it coming from out of state. Spitzer's celebrity made him an easy sell in places like San Francisco and Hollywood, in small private gatherings with liberal activists and movie stars. "Outside New York, people thought he was this god," says Kristie Stiles, Spitzer's out-of-state fundraiser. "They'd tell him: 'Thank you for standing up for us!' They wanted to be part of it." In New York, he was showered with "smart money" from business interests eager to curry goodwill with the future governor. This group included former Republican senator Al D'Amato—political patron of Pataki and Vacco—who had become a lobbyist. D'Amato raised more than $1 million for Spitzer in small, discreet gatherings. Spitzer's fundraising had been so successful he literally faced an embarrassment of riches: he'd spoken often about the corrupting effect of money in politics, and was a staunch advocate of campaign-finance reform, including strict limits on contributions. He tackled this issue directly: as long as New York's porous rules remained in place, he explained, he wasn't about to "unilaterally disarm."

Spitzer was surrounded by true believers, both in the AG's office and in his campaign, and commanded enormous personal loyalty. Many considered him the best boss they'd ever had. He listened to their opinions; he worked harder than anyone; and they'd never seen his temper—at least not aimed in *their* direction. In 2002, campaign finance director Cindy Darrison, the architect of Spitzer's fundraising machine, had gone to China to adopt a baby girl, and Oxford Health Plans refused to insure the child until they returned to New York. "I told Eliot about this, and his eyes narrowed into slits and his jaw jutted out," Darrison recalled. After launching an investigation, Spitzer extracted a consent decree from Oxford that changed the policy for all international adoptions. Says Darrison: "I was weeping when I found out about this. You couldn't have done anything better for me."

Everyone wanted to go along with Eliot for the ride—wherever it might end up.

———

In truth, there wasn't really much that worried Spitzer's advisors in the 2006 campaign—not much, that is, besides his temper. Though polling showed it hadn't hurt him with voters, the Whitehead incident had put the problem in sharp relief. Their worst nightmare was that someone would capture Spitzer on tape, screaming at someone like a lunatic. In the meantime, Republicans were doing everything they could to turn his outbursts into an issue. A conservative website was even selling T-shirts reading, ELIOT SPITZER THREATENED MY LITTLE SISTER.

The solution to this problem came from the newest member of Spitzer's brain trust, a former Madison Avenue adman named Jimmy Siegel. Siegel, fifty-one, had just quit his job as creative director at BBDO, where he'd dreamed up witty ads for Pepsi and Tostitos while writing popular novels on the side. But what Siegel really wanted to do was sell candidates. A political junkie, he'd marched up to Spitzer at a Manhattan fundraiser in December 2005 and offered his services, free of charge. Toohey had reflexively blown him off, but he'd managed to slip a reel of his work to Silda. After Spitzer found his wife at home, in tears, watching thirty-second Visa spots, Siegel was in.

Siegel hatched an idea to "rebrand" the issue of Spitzer's temper. If their man talked tough, it wasn't because he was angry—he was *passionate*! Having a nasty temper was a problem. Displaying righteous passion—as Eliot had during his wars on Wall Street—was a *virtue*. Siegel even had a tagline for this nifty bit of political jujitsu: *Bring Some Passion Back to Albany.*

Among Spitzer's political handlers, there was some initial discomfort with "passion." "It just seems like *sex* to me," said campaign pollster Pollock; the connotation seemed "too hot." Conventional wisdom would be to put Spitzer in a Mr. Rogers sweater with dogs, wife, and kids. But Spitzer's research showed that New Yorkers, fed up with the mess in Albany, wanted "a bull in a china shop," according to Pollock. "Passion" was a way to give it to them, while defusing the "angry Eliot" issue. Siegel even filmed a spot that tackled the issue with humor. It showed Spitzer talking about how he'd arrived home to find one of his girls watching TV, and promptly sent her off to do her homework. "You know what, Dad?" he recalled his daughter telling him. "The Republicans are *right*—you *do* have a temper." In the end, it was never needed. For questions on the subject, Spitzer had prepared a stock response: "You can't change the world by whispering."

Siegel's lushly produced ads cast Spitzer as the Empire State's savior, and its citizens as characters out of *The Grapes of Wrath*. For every New Yorker "without a voice," he was the "one strong enough for all of us" . . . the one "willing to walk into the buzz saw of some very powerful interests and never back down" . . . the one who operated under "a simple rule":

> I never asked if a case was popular or unpopular. Never asked if it was big or small, hard or easy. I simply asked if it was right or wrong. In the end, it's not a bad rule.

This wasn't just another candidate. With stirring shots of Niagara Falls, the Statue of Liberty, and the twinkling lights of Manhattan, Spitzer was portrayed as a historic figure—a virtuous man bent on restoring a fallen state's greatness. And many in the campaign saw him just that way. "We really felt we were going to shake things up," said Siegel. "We had a guy who was one of those rare politicians who come along every thirty years." In a May 2006 video posted on the Internet, Siegel was positively giddy when asked at a party whether his man had any flaws. "As much as I've looked for a chink in the armor of Eliot Spitzer, unfortunately or fortunately, we can't find any," Siegel gushed. "The man is a great attorney general, will make a great governor, loves his wife, loves his kids, true blue, honest as the day is long—and a pleasure to work with."

With his massive lead in the polls, Spitzer set his sights on not just victory, but a record landslide. He fervently believed that Albany was a terrible place, where everything needed to change. He knew what had to be done. And with a big enough mandate from voters, he could deliver precisely that. Says Baum: "He wanted to be this transformational governor."

Dopp tried to ease his boss into an appreciation for the challenge of remaking Albany. He recalled Mario Cuomo's conclusion, after three terms, that only slow, incremental change was possible.

"Like hell it is!" Spitzer replied. "We're going to be different! We're going to turn the place upside down!" He'd push through new ethics and campaign-finance rules; launch an economic-development program for New York's depressed upstate; pass the state budget on time; cut taxes; fix New York's costly healthcare system; and boost education funding. To make all this happen, Spitzer publicly pledged to work eighteen hours a day.

In his campaign promises—and his ads—Spitzer eagerly upped the stakes with a second slogan that reflected his soaring, impossible expectations: *Day One, Everything Changes.*

———

After Tom Suozzi had spent $5 million and campaigned for months, the biggest question he'd raised was why he'd taken Spitzer on in the first place. A *New York* magazine profile, headlined TOM QUIXOTE, invoked a familiar adage: "The only way Spitzer loses is if he gets caught with a live boy or a dead girl." In fact, there were strange hints Suozzi believed something like that just might happen.

Though Suozzi remained a cipher in the polls, he was a pesky annoyance on the campaign trail, challenging the AG's credentials as a reformer and nipping at him as the favorite of the Democratic party "clubhouse." Spitzer's campaign wanted Suozzi to drop out before the September primary. Dopp was working this message through a back channel—Andrew Cuomo.

Mario's son was on the comeback trail in 2006, after his failed race for governor four years earlier and an embarrassing divorce from his wife, Kerry, Robert Kennedy's daughter. Andrew was running to succeed Spitzer as attorney general, facing three other Democrats for the nomination. The Cuomos had pull with Suozzi—long-standing political and personal ties. Tom had even dated one of the governor's daughters. Andrew hinted about a deal: his dad might be able to persuade Suozzi to drop out—or at least soften his attacks—*if* Spitzer would endorse Andrew. This, of course, wouldn't be a quid pro quo. But "there'd be no greater demonstration of friendship," Dopp says Andrew told him.

The Cuomos desperately wanted Spitzer's endorsement. The AG was so popular they thought it would lock up the nomination. But Spitzer just didn't like Cuomo. He hadn't forgotten how Andrew, while HUD secretary, had meddled in his gun-control initiative. And they came to the game from opposite poles: Eliot was a gifted prosecutor laboring to become a politician; Andrew was a gifted politician laboring to become a prosecutor. Spitzer didn't even view Cuomo as a *real* lawyer; he'd quit Morgenthau's office after just thirteen months and was a graduate of Albany Law School.

Spitzer really wanted to endorse Mark Green, a Harvard-educated former Naderite, even though he didn't stand a chance. Dopp and Baum worked to bring their boss around. "Andrew used to be a son of a bitch," Dopp told Spitzer. "But he's a changed man now." Spitzer didn't buy it, but he authorized Dopp to keep talking and provide informal help. Dopp says he spoke to Cuomo every day or two, trading campaign gossip and offering advice; he even arranged for Cuomo to get briefings about the AG's office from some of Spitzer's bureau chiefs. Still, both sides grew exasperated. Darren couldn't deliver Spitzer's endorsement; Andrew couldn't get Suozzi out of the race. Why didn't Tom just give up? He was fifty points behind!

According to Dopp, Cuomo confided to him that Suozzi believed the Spitzers had a skeleton in their closet—a "Big Ugly" from deep in their past. It had emerged from Suozzi's opposition research. Suozzi seemed to think it was a secret that could hand him the nomination. But he'd said he wasn't going to stoop to exposing it himself.

Baum and Dopp went to their boss. *What could Suozzi have?* The very notion of anything salacious involving Eliot seemed preposterous. Spitzer was ridiculously square. From time to time, Dopp made admiring comments about women while in his presence. ("Boss, get a load of *her*!") In eight years, Spitzer had joined in the banter only twice: agreeing that Donald Trump's third wife was indeed attractive, and allowing, after meeting the actress Penelope Cruz, that he could "understand" why people found her "dramatically alluring." Now Suozzi thought he had dirt on *Eliot*? "What did you do, boss—make a porno tape in college?" asked Dopp. Spitzer just chuckled.

Dopp says he also spoke to his old boss, Mario Cuomo, who was fuming at Spitzer's refusal to endorse his son. Then seventy-four, the former governor was a father figure to Dopp. He grew increasingly agitated during the conversation, bringing up various grievances and slights, insisting that Spitzer wasn't a man of "honor."

"You don't understand," Cuomo finally declared, his voice quavering with emotion. "He's *unfit* to be governor. He's a *bad man*."

Dopp was shocked. Why was Cuomo saying this? Was it because of how Eliot had financed his old campaigns?

"No, it's about more than that," Cuomo cryptically replied, according to Dopp. "*It's about the relationship between a man and a woman.*" He wouldn't go any further.

A few days later, Spitzer called to say he'd been thinking about the rumblings from the Suozzi camp, and had something he wanted to tell Dopp and Baum. The candidate's two closest aides began to fret: were they about to hear a confession?

They met on a Sunday. Eliot was visibly agitated. Months earlier, at the outset of the campaign, Spitzer had finally told them about Silda's brief first marriage. Could Suozzi now be thinking *Eliot* had caused the breakup? In fact, Spitzer told them, he and Silda had begun dating before her divorce was final. But they hadn't even met until long after she and Stamos had given up any hope of reconciliation. Stamos had even donated $10,000 to Spitzer's campaign. But his daughters didn't know anything about any of this, Spitzer fretted—was there a chance it would somehow get into the press?

Baum and Dopp reassured their boss. They didn't know what would become public. But in political terms, it all sounded harmless. They left the meeting scratching their heads.*

———

Even as Spitzer's influence grew, not everyone accepted his political judgment. On a busy day in Manhattan, he paused for a half hour to sit down in an empty hotel meeting room with a pot of coffee and Barack Obama. David Axelrod, the political consultant who had advised both men, once told the AG: "It's going to be an Obama-Spitzer ticket someday." Spitzer mused about their respective fortunes. Before his keynote address at the 2004 Democratic Convention, Obama was a state legislator no one had heard of, while the New Yorker was already a national figure. Now Spitzer was heading into the trenches of Albany, and the first-term Illinois senator was considering whether to seek the 2008 presidential nomination against Hillary Clinton, the heavy favorite. Spitzer advised Obama not to run. "There is no doubt in my mind you will be president someday," he told him. "But I think the better part of wisdom is to wait. It's good to get some seasoning—we're young. And the Clinton campaign is going to be tough to beat."

One of the constituencies Spitzer cared most deeply about was *The New York Times*. The paper's news pages were his favorite medium; its editorial approval was his most cherished affirmation. In this race, the *Times* stood staunchly behind "the supercharged Mr. Spitzer," just as it had during his eight years as attorney general. In its enthusiastic endorsement, the *Times* cheered for a victory "big enough to use as a cudgel," reasoning that Spitzer would need it. "As attorney general, he has been fearless and dogged in his pursuit of justice. We are eager to see what happens when he applies those attributes to Albany's immobile Legislature, which has a long, sad history in wearing would-be reformers down, waiting them out. Imposing change will take the kind of Herculean effort New Yorkers have come to expect from Eliot Spitzer."

———

* My account of this episode is based on interviews with Dopp, Baum, and Spitzer. Andrew Cuomo acknowledges having had back-channel discussions with Dopp during the 2006 campaign, but denies ever raising any issues involving personal impropriety. The Suozzi campaign, however, did explore rumors of skeletons in Spitzer's closet, one dating back to Princeton. None of the rumors were ever substantiated or made public.

But as Spitzer would soon discover, the paper held less sway in Albany than in Manhattan. After the election, Spitzer held a series of meetings with Governor Pataki to discuss the transition of power. The two men became friendly and, during these sessions, often engaged in political shoptalk. "If you do that, the *Times* editorial page is going to *kill* you," Spitzer warned Pataki at one point.

"Eliot," Pataki responded, "I haven't read the *Times* editorial page in eight years."

———

By late 2006, George Fox had become a familiar customer at the Emperors Club. His awkwardness on the phone had disappeared as he learned the ropes of patronizing prostitutes. But he remained unusually guarded. Tammy Thomas, the chatty booker, says she was struck by his refusal to engage in small talk: "I couldn't use my Midwestern charm on him." George Fox was equally direct with the escorts. "He practically attacked me when he walked in the door," one of them told Thomas after a session. "He was just *ready*."

To be sure, they were hookers, being paid a great deal of money for sex. But George Fox depersonalized the encounters in a way several of them found distasteful. He didn't bother with the comforting nicety of a little idle conversation; he was just using them to meet his needs. George Fox didn't have any interest in the vaunted "girlfriend experience" that many premium escort services touted. But the prostitutes he hired *did*. The way he treated them was simply . . . *dehumanizing*—not at all what they expected at the high end of their business. Two or three refused to see him again.

On one occasion, George Fox had booked an appointment in the late morning at the Mark Hotel, on the Upper East Side, just five minutes' walk from the Metropolitan Museum of Art. As usual, he paid the girl in cash—about $1,200 an hour. Not long after it was over, he called Thomas back, wanting to see a second escort. "Who else is around?" he asked. Thomas made the arrangements.

Then, late that afternoon, George Fox called again.

"You're going to think I'm crazy," he began. "But can you send somebody else right now?"

He wanted a *third* girl? The booker chuckled: "You must be Superman! The man of steel!" Thomas found him another girl. It wasn't even dark yet.

Tammy Thomas was a phone booker for an escort service, not a shrink. But she concluded that George Fox was a sex addict. "It was the sense of urgency I had from him," she says. Most customers requested a girl that they'd seen previously, or spotted on the agency's website. Or they described the type they liked—fashion model; girl next door; perhaps someone . . . *exotic*. Not George Fox. "He didn't care who it was; he just *wanted* them." And he wanted them right away. In truth, Thomas didn't particularly care for George Fox. But she was happy to have him as a customer. "I knew it was a booked date when he called. When you're in my business, that's a good thing."*

In the end, all the worst-case scenarios Baum and the rest of Spitzer's advisors had fretted about failed to materialize. No one had captured Eliot's evil twin li win on tape. Langone hadn't raised the threatened millions for Spitzer's opponents. Suozzi's mysterious "Big Ugly" never appeared.

In fact, the voting went just as the polls and pundits had predicted from the start. Spitzer won the primary with 81 percent of the vote; Suozzi didn't win a single county. The general election offered even less drama. John Faso had claimed the Republican nomination, after Weld dropped out. He criticized Spitzer for bullying CEOs; he promised to cut taxes; he questioned whether the Democrat could meet all his heady promises without spending too much. But Faso barely had enough money to run TV ads. On November 7, Spitzer administered a general-election beating unlike any before seen in a New York governor's race. He won 69.6 percent of the vote—a margin of 1.8 million ballots—and took fifty-nine of the state's sixty-two counties. In New York City, Spitzer rolled up a six-to-one margin. His landslide swept Democrats into every statewide

* Eliot Spitzer says this account of his seeing three prostitutes in a single day is simply "not true." But Suwal and Thomas both recall it with certainty—in Thomas's case, in considerable detail. "Angelina," one of the escorts who Thomas says she dispatched that day, also described this encounter with "George Fox," recalling that it took place at "an Upper East Side hotel."

office, the first time that had happened since 1938; Andrew Cuomo was the new attorney general. For virtually every Republican legislator in Albany, this was a nightmare to contemplate: their own districts had gone for the Democrat.

Eliot Spitzer, forty-seven, had claimed his historic mandate.

———

On the day of his big victory, New York's governor-elect purchased the first piece of property he had ever bought: the 160-acre farm, midway between Manhattan and Albany, that included the guest cottage his family had rented for years. Spitzer had waited to close on the $6.4 million deal to avoid looking presumptuous and to keep from reminding voters of just how rich he was. (He paid cash.) Spitzer envisioned the Pine Plains property as his refuge, his own version of Camp David.

The Spitzers had already resolved not to move into the Victorian governor's mansion, after giving the issue considerable thought. Silda had even met privately with Hillary Clinton to explore how to balance the role of political spouse with family concerns. While Eliot would travel to Albany as needed and spend some nights in the mansion, the Spitzer family would remain based in Manhattan, where the governor and his staff also had offices. They'd also try to rendezvous on weekends in Pine Plains. Silda would have an office, too, both in Manhattan and in the governor's wing on the second floor of the capitol, known as the executive chamber. This inevitably raised eyebrows—politicians' aides and reporters are always wary of a spouse's influence. No matter. No longer the reluctant partner, Silda was determined to treat her new position as first lady as a real job. After years of sacrifice for Eliot's career, this was her chance to make a difference, too. But it was clear it would cost some privacy: a *Times* profile after the election discussed her brief first marriage.

Spitzer's staff had made some decisions, too. With more than $6 million unspent after the election, Spitzer doled out "victory bonuses" totaling $1.3 million to forty-nine campaign aides. The biggest windfall went to Baum, who got $150,000. Toohey and Spitzer's top fundraiser, Cindy Darrison, got $100,000 each. Toohey would remain on the campaign payroll, as Spitzer's top outside political operative; he'd also begun a relationship with Liz Benjamin, an Albany newspaper reporter who wrote a closely followed political blog. Darrison, a single mother, planned to take a lucrative new job with D'Amato—until Spitzer told her that he'd bar anyone in the administration from dealing with his firm if she did. He'd happily accepted D'Amato's campaign money, but he wouldn't accept the PR hit from his fundraiser going to work for a lobbyist. Stunned, but with no recourse, Darrison instead took a job in the Midtown Manhattan office of North Fork Bank, where Spitzer, at Darrison's suggestion, had moved both his campaign and personal accounts.

As Spitzer picked the team charged with turning Albany upside down, many of the key faces were familiar. Baum, who headed the transition, would serve as secretary to the governor, a powerful job akin to the president's chief of staff. Dopp was named communications director. Marlene Turner, an attorney who had worked as the AG's scheduler, would serve as his gatekeeper, with the title of chief of staff and an office next door to Spitzer. David Nocenti, Spitzer's counsel in the AG's office, was named as the governor's counsel, his in-house legal advisor. The new state budget chief was Paul Francis, a multimillionaire from his days as CFO of Priceline.com, who had led the issues team during the campaign. Peter Pope, a career prosecutor who had run the AG's criminal section, would serve as the governor's policy director. Other Spitzer loyalists filled key positions in state government. The most notable top departure was first deputy AG Michele Hirshman, who went into private law practice. The new team was long on lawyers, old ties to Spitzer, and Ivy League degrees, but conspicuously short on Albany experience. The governor-elect didn't view that as a problem. He preferred smart outsiders, the sort of people who would bring a critical eye to the capital's corrupt ecosystem.

Lloyd Constantine wanted a job in the governor's office, too. Constantine had been behind Spitzer from the start. As he saw it, no one except Silda had believed in him so unconditionally. While Constantine had chaired Spitzer's transition team back in 1998, he'd remained in private law practice during the AG years. In 2003, he'd hit the jackpot, as lead plaintiffs' counsel in a giant antitrust case against Visa and MasterCard that generated a fee of $220 million. He'd built his own weekend compound on seven acres in upstate Chatham, thirty minutes from the Spitzers' retreat, complete with a pool and a tennis court. He dubbed it "Constantinium."

During the AG years, Constantine had found himself in growing demand as a prominent intimate of Spitzer, still his weekly tennis partner. He was wary of becoming known as a fixer, but had agreed to defend one major AG target, the big insurance broker Aon, generating bad blood with Spitzer's staff. By Constantine's own description, he was an egomaniac with no feel for politics; at a 2004 roast in his honor, a friend joked that Constantine had "never met a bridge he didn't burn." During the campaign, he had told a reporter he'd been offered $1 million just to set up a single meeting with the attorney general. After the comment appeared in print, the AG's top deputies were beside themselves—it sounded like Lloyd was talking about people trying to bribe him! Spitzer handed Baum the task of telling his old friend that such remarks were "unhelpful." But when Baum phoned, Constantine exploded. "He screamed at me," Baum recalls. *Do you know what I've done for Eliot? How important I've been to his career? Who are you to tell me what to do?* Says Baum: "Most people, I'd go tell them, 'Bite my ass!' But I couldn't do that with Lloyd." "Lloyd's relationship with Eliot was unique," says Marlene Turner. "He always had Eliot's best interests at heart, but thought that only he knew what Eliot's best interests were."

Now Constantine, at fifty-nine, wanted a spot on the governor's staff. With the stakes getting serious, he was ready to play a bigger role in the "long-term game plan." Says Constantine: "This was supposed to be a national government in training. . . . I was working alongside this guy all these years, to get him to be governor, president, master of the universe—and I was going to be there with him."

Constantine says he had thought all was in readiness for his appointment to a top job in the executive chamber. He'd even made arrangements with his law partners. But after Election Day, he endured a string of slights: Eliot's official biography made no mention of his years at Constantine's firm; Constantine was excluded from a group picture of the incoming administration; and the announcement of his appointment had been repeatedly delayed. Earlier, Eliot had even tried to persuade him to accept a commission appointment instead of a job on the governor's staff—perhaps something in another building. Certain that Baum and Dopp, jealous of his relationship with Spitzer, didn't want him around, Constantine prepared a blunt letter to his old friend, withdrawing from consideration for the job he hadn't received and offering "the hope that our friendship can be salvaged."

"You have handled this badly," Constantine wrote. "You should have viewed my offer as a valuable asset instead of a painful predicament. . . . I know you well but really can't figure out what this flaw in your makeup is. . . . I realize now that I have been overly concerned with your success and welfare." Constantine said his withdrawal freed him "to once again candidly advise you." With that, he blasted Spitzer's gubernatorial transition, in which Constantine had served as one of six co-chairs, calling it "badly conceived and badly executed"—in stark contrast to the one he had run after Spitzer's election as AG, "which produced now world-famous results." Several pages later, Constantine concluded: "I have to stop worrying about your future and focus on mine. . . . As my mother said to me a few times, 'I love you but I don't like you very much.' That's the truth right now."

Constantine never actually delivered his angry letter, but says he had an appointment to tell Spitzer he was pulling out on the very day his job finally came through. In the end, he got exactly what he wanted: he would receive the title of senior advisor, report directly to the governor, and work on unspecified major projects. (Constantine later described his role as "monster man.") Spitzer certainly knew Constantine could be impolitic and difficult. But, as always, he placed a huge premium on brains and loyalty. "Lloyd at the end of the day was only going to report emotionally to one person—and that was me," Spitzer later explained. "You ask yourself, 'Is it worth the tension to get the upside of an incredibly smart person who cares a lot?' He felt that I was his kid who'd done good. He earned the right to report directly to me."

Constantine was puzzled by the entire episode. In large part, he blamed Baum and Dopp. But it also wasn't at all like Eliot, he thought, to be so vacillating and indecisive. "The nature of our conversations changed in 2006," says Constantine. "I kept on feeling: *what is wrong with this guy? Who is he?*"

PART TWO
442 DAYS

If you look at the CEOs and the others who have been involved in most of the corporate scandals, they began to think that, somehow, the law didn't reach them, the moral boundaries that every one of us understands didn't apply to them. And this was captured in a brilliant T-shirt—and I don't often end by quoting T-shirts, but it was given to me by an investment banker friend of mine, the last one I had—and on the front it said: HUBRIS IS TERMINAL.

—ELIOT SPITZER, HARVARD LAW SCHOOL SPEECH, 2005

Chapter 8: The Haunted House

THE CAPITOL BUILDING OF NEW YORK IS THE PERFECT MONU-
ment to democracy in the Empire State: it was finished scandalously
late, ran massively over budget, and is the product of unholy compromise.

A five-story jumble of turrets and towers, the capitol was built on a
hill overlooking downtown Albany and the Hudson River, on a site covered with quicksand. It is both grand and grandiose. Construction began
in 1867; it took thirty-two years to complete. The original architect was
fired eight years in, with just two stories finished, after scandalous cost
overruns had exhausted a $4 million budget, prompting a string of inves-
tigations and editorial outrage. The new architects didn't like the Italian
Renaissance design, so they built the remaining three stories in Ro-
manesque style instead. Everything about the capitol is massive. It oc-
cupies five and a half acres; its granite walls are five feet thick. The
vaulted sandstone ceiling in the assembly chamber was the widest ever
constructed—until it started collapsing and had to be scrapped. When
finally completed in 1899, at a price of $25 million, it was the most ex-
pensive government structure ever built—twice the cost of the U.S. Capitol in Washington.

The building's interior is dark and Gothic, filled with long corridors,
arched windows, marble columns, tall unmarked doors, even a secret
entrance to the governor's office. It is dominated by three huge, ornate
stairways that seem to rise endlessly skyward in unknowable directions,
like something out of an Escher lithograph. The most remarkable, known

as the "Million Dollar Staircase," contains 444 steps and took fourteen years to build. It is adorned with scores of faces painstakingly carved in place out of stone. Most are famous: Christopher Columbus, Ulysses S. Grant, Walt Whitman. But the five hundred carvers also memorialized wives and children, animals and random citizens. Some of the images—a cherub and a tiny devil's head—are tucked in nooks and crannies, visible only with a flashlight. To new arrivals, like Spitzer's staff, the building seemed unknowable and vaguely mysterious, filled with secrets. Rich Baum, Spitzer's top deputy, came to call it "the Haunted House."

———

When Teddy Roosevelt was first elected to serve in the state government of New York, biographer Edmund Morris wrote, the Tammany Hall lieutenants in Albany ridiculed the wealthy, Ivy League–educated, reform-minded upstart. They even laid plans to humiliate the young assemblyman by tossing him in a blanket. After getting wind of this scheme, Roosevelt marched up to the largest of his adversaries, a towering ex-prizefighter named "Big John" McManus, and warned him to back off: "By God, if you try anything like that, I'll kick you, I'll bite you, I'll kick you in the balls, I'll do anything to you—you'd *better* leave me alone." When another Tammany figure insulted Roosevelt in a bar, TR knocked him down over and over, then bought him a glass of beer and lectured him on manners.

This was Eliot Spitzer's role model.

As he prepared to assume office, Spitzer wanted to land a swift, painful blow of his own. And with good reason: New York's state legislature was a catastrophe unlike any other—wasteful, undemocratic, and corrupt. An eye-opening study by an NYU think tank had come up with a single word to describe it: *dysfunctional*. And it had been that way for decades. The legislature operated on a winner-takes-all basis: whichever party controlled each chamber called the shots, and whoever led that majority wielded enormous personal power. The senate, where Republicans had held sway for forty years, was run by majority leader Joseph Bruno, a silver-maned seventy-seven-year-old who lived on a horse farm outside Albany. The assembly, under Democratic control for thirty-two years, was led by speaker Sheldon Silver, sixty-two, an Orthodox Jew and personal-injury lawyer from the Lower East Side of New York City.

Different as the two men were, both resolutely pursued Albany's prime imperative: political survival.

Each maintained tightfisted control over patronage and legislation in his own chamber. This included the unilateral right to dole out office space, staff, and hefty salary stipends—known in Albany as "lulus"—to favored lawmakers. Those in the majority, of course, got the lion's share of everything. The senate Democrats, for example, received just thirty treasured parking spaces near the capitol; Bruno's Republicans got eight hundred. This principle extended to New York's institutionalized form of pork barrel, known as "member items." Each year, the senate and assembly received $85 million apiece (another $30 million went to the governor). Without any public review or debate, Bruno and Silver then handed out pots of taxpayer money to individual lawmakers to spread around their districts at will. (In 2005, these awards included grants to the Museum of Comic and Cartoon Art and the Kitty Karetakers of Queens.) A majority legislator might get ten times as much as his minority counterpart—especially if his seat was in jeopardy. Brazen gerrymandering helped assure that majority incumbents rarely lost.

New York's legislature was the most expensive in the nation. And what did the taxpayers get? The state budget was habitually late. Legislative committees almost never held hearings or issued reports. Not a single bill got to the floor of the assembly or senate without the leader's blessing. And anything the leader brought to a vote was virtually guaranteed passage—always without amendment and usually without debate. Lobbyists were a pervasive influence. There were twenty-four of them for every lawmaker, more than in any other state. When the legislature was in session, the "electeds" raked in special-interest money at nightly fundraisers. Donation limits were sky-high.

Ethics oversight? It was a joke. The state's disclosure requirements didn't even require lawmakers to publicly reveal their outside income. Bruno's legal staff quietly advised Republican senators to hand-deliver their ethics filings to avoid the risk of mail-fraud charges. The lawmakers had established a separate legislative ethics panel to police themselves behind closed doors. It rarely met; nothing short of a felony conviction had prompted even a public reprimand. To limit scrutiny of their operations, the lawmakers had even exempted themselves from the state's open-records laws. All this was symbolized by the method through which every major issue was resolved in Albany: closed-door horse trading between the governor, speaker, and majority leader—a process infamously known as "three men in a room."

Beyond Albany, all right-thinking New Yorkers were fed up—and Spitzer, the avatar of reform, had won an overwhelming mandate. The question: how to make it happen? In the weeks before the inauguration, Dopp privately suggested a frontal assault: a Moreland Act commission to investigate the legislature. Under a 1907 law, the governor could appoint a special commission to probe any department. The panel could subpoena witnesses and documents and take testimony under oath. Previous governors had used Moreland commissions to investigate nursing-home scandals and wasteful school spending. A Moreland probe, Dopp argued, would expose the corrupting influence of money in Albany. By revealing individual legislators' conflicts from political contributions, lobbyist gifts, and outside income, it could generate an unstoppable outcry for wholesale reform—just like the shocking e-mails from Spitzer's lawsuits in the AG's office.

It would also constitute a declaration of nuclear war. Public shaming worked with CEOs. But New York's governor, powerful as he was, couldn't pass anything without the legislature. Even Spitzer decided it was too dramatic. Silver and Bruno loomed as his foremost obstacles. He'd vowed to end the tradition of one-man control, and he was determined to turn up the heat on the leaders. But he wasn't ready to do something that would immediately set the entire legislature against him. He was too smart to make that mistake.

———

Looking back, it's a little remarkable that Eliot Spitzer ever thought he might turn Joe Bruno into an ally. Spitzer was a frenetic Democrat firebrand, bent on changing everything. Bruno was the state's last powerful Republican; he personified the status quo.

But in New York, practical accommodations often trumped the usual party alignments. As the state grew ever more liberal, Bruno had shrewdly adapted. He'd been elected in 1976 as a conservative, and ousted the Rockefeller Republican serving as majority leader in 1994, with help from George Pataki. In the dozen years that followed, Bruno had often battled the Republican governor, taking some surprising positions: he had backed a ban on workplace smoking, a medical marijuana law, legal benefits for same-sex partners, and an extension of healthcare coverage to the uninsured. To be sure, business interests bankrolled Bruno's senate campaign committees, which existed to preserve the dwindling GOP majority. But the senate Republicans' biggest patron, improbably enough, was New York's most potent labor union, SEIU 1199, which represents healthcare workers. At campaign time, the union pulled out all the stops for the Republican senators, donating hundreds of thousands and dispatching armies of campaign workers. In return, Bruno had fiercely protected their interests.

By background and temperament, the governor and majority leader couldn't have been more different. One of eight children, Bruno had grown up in the gritty upstate town of Glens Falls. His father, an Italian immigrant, shoveled coal in a paper mill; his mother died when he was seventeen. Bruno made money driving an ice truck. After marrying his childhood sweetheart, he'd earned a business degree at Skidmore College and served as an infantry sergeant in Korea, where he was a boxing champ. Then he'd gone into business and politics, though it was sometimes hard to separate the two. His biggest early venture was a telephone-equipment company that did business with government agencies.

Wisecracking and unpretentious, Bruno oozed charm—he was a hard man not to like. Silda Spitzer once encountered him at the base of the capitol steps while she was bringing a piece of birthday cake to one of the troopers on security detail. "That looks *really* good," Bruno told her, with an impish smile. "Can I *have* it?" (He did.) Bruno prided himself on his rugged, Marlboro Man looks, which he assiduously preserved through daily workouts and use of a tanning machine he kept at home. While governor, Mario Cuomo had mocked him as "the handsomest man in Albany."

Bruno wasn't much for the details of issues, but he was a canny deal-maker, adept at swapping the senate's support to get what he wanted from the governor and the speaker. He took special pride in bringing home the bacon for his upstate district: Troy's minor league Joseph L. Bruno Stadium, known as "the Joe" ($14 million); the Albany International airport ($65 million), where a bronze bust of Bruno greeted travelers; the University of Albany's Nanotechnology Center ($33 million); the Albany Amtrak station ($10 million). A theater group in Bruno's district got new offices and more state operating money than any other in New York; a bronze plaque identified its building as THE SENATOR JOSEPH L. BRUNO CENTER.

There was always a scent of scandal about Bruno, though nothing had ever been proven. Part of it was his unapologetic old-school politics. Bruno saw nothing wrong with trading favors, dishing out patronage, holding court over boozy dinners with lobbyists, or jetting to a Florida golf outing (and steak dinner at an upscale strip club) on a friend's private plane—all behaviors that Spitzer scorned as sleazy and repellent. Bruno's brother and eldest daughter spent time on the state payroll, reportedly receiving favored treatment. His son had actually gone to work lobbying the legislature. Bruno had dipped into his campaign fund to pay for landscaping and pool equipment on his horse farm. (He explained that he used it for political meetings.) He'd even spent tens of thousands from the campaign kitty to cover the tab for his wining and dining.

The biggest revelation came in December 2006. With the story about to break in the press, Bruno confirmed that federal prosecutors were investigating his private business dealings. Among the areas being probed: Bruno's investment in for-profit companies to which he'd directed state grants; his real estate partnership with a lobbyist; his friendship with a businessman seeking the state's Thoroughbred horse-racing franchise; and a consulting business Bruno operated to "introduce" institutional investors to a Connecticut money-management firm. As it turned out, these investors included pension funds for unions with business before the legislature.

This news came at a moment when the Republicans' hold on the senate was looking shaky. Bruno had emerged from the November 2006 election with a slim majority—just 34–28. His GOP conference included one senator who was eighty and seven more in their seventies. New York's shifting demographics were making Republican senators an endangered species. Already, there were rumblings that Bruno would retire in 2008, at the end of his sixteenth two-year term. Bobbie, his wife of more than fifty years, was bedridden with Alzheimer's. Surely he didn't want to be on the scene when the Republicans lost control of the senate after four decades. One bold GOP senator, upon hearing of the federal investigation, had even dared call for his resignation.

All this, Spitzer reasoned, meant that Bruno wouldn't be spoiling for a fight. His political position was weak. He was staring at the new governor's monstrous mandate. And he was a man who recognized realities and liked to get things done. Bruno might even be looking for a graceful exit, aiming to end his career by sharing credit for some landmark legisla-

THE HAUNTED HOUSE | 137

tive achievements. Spitzer had been encouraged in this thinking by private conversations with the senator before taking office. He'd told Bruno of his concerns about working with Silver, discussed how they were both "doers," spoken to him about being "partners." Joe seemed good with all that. But Bruno had also warned Spitzer not to campaign for Democrats running for senate seats—that, under Albany tradition, governors didn't threaten the lawmakers' turf. "Let us do our thing, and we'll get along," said Bruno. Spitzer was flabbergasted—he wasn't interested in some kind of crazy nonaggression pact. "We're going to have a schizophrenic relationship," he told the senator. "Politically, I'm going to support Democrats. And we're going to work together in the legislature. We're going to get along great."

"You can't do that," Bruno declared. "It's an act of war."

––––––

Mike Balboni was bored out of his mind. He'd spent seventeen years in the legislature, the last nine in the state senate, representing a chunk of Long Island. Then forty-seven, Balboni was an articulate, handsome lawyer with regular guy charm—widely regarded as one of the state Republicans' rising stars. His senate peers, noting Balboni's ambition, had nicknamed him "Statewide." In fact, he wasn't going anywhere. Bruno wouldn't let him.

Balboni had wanted to run for attorney general in 2006, when Spitzer's departure left the job up for grabs. He'd put the word out a year earlier and had begun to raise cash for a statewide campaign. Then the money suddenly dried up, as if a tap had been turned off. Bruno summoned him for a sit-down. "You're not running for anything," Balboni recalls Bruno telling him over lunch at Jack's Oyster House, a lawmakers' haunt near the capitol. "I love you. But you can't run—I can't let you. If you run, we lose your seat."

Balboni's senate district made him one of the Republican Party's "marginals." Measured by registered voters, it had already gone Democratic. Balboni was so personally popular he'd probably keep winning reelection as long as he wanted. But if he left, the seat might well flip. So Bruno had passed the word to the big donors: no campaign money for Mike.

Balboni dutifully stayed put, coasting to reelection in November 2006. But by then, the prospect of another two years in the senate was too much. "The conferences were like [the film] *Groundhog Day*—the same people talking about the same issues with the same outcome. I couldn't take it anymore," Balboni says. He recalls thinking to himself: "Eliot's going to be governor; Cuomo's going to be attorney general. It's going to *suck* to be a Republican in this state." He began making plans to quit in mid-2007 and take a full-time job outside government.

Rich Baum called him on the day after Thanksgiving. Balboni chaired the senate's homeland security committee, and had volunteered his advice to Spitzer on the subject during the campaign. Balboni cared passionately about security issues. He had lost friends on 9/11, had drafted several state anti-terrorism laws and spent time in Washington serving on national advisory committees. He'd even been granted national security clearance. After days of conversation, Spitzer offered him a job—as the state's homeland security chief.

"Senator Balboni has all the skills we need," Spitzer declared at his press conference announcing Balboni's appointment, on the day after Christmas. "This is not a part of any other ulterior scheme." But, of course, it was. Spitzer had displayed bipartisanship by appointing an able Republican to a key job. He'd also put another senate seat in play, increasing the pressure on Bruno. A pragmatist, Balboni offered no apologies for his move. He was going nowhere in Republican politics, he liked what he'd seen of Spitzer, and he loved the job. He'd even brought his wife and four kids up from Long Island for the big announcement. "A terrorist bomb will never discriminate between Democrat and Republican," he reminded reporters.

Bruno was shocked when Balboni called to give him the news. He recovered quickly enough to be gracious. "What an opportunity!" he told Balboni. But that wouldn't last for long.

———

Albany was usually bitter cold in January. But as "Day One" loomed, Spitzer decided that he wasn't going to wear an overcoat at his swearing-in. Breaking with convention, he was holding the New Year's Day event outside, just like they did in Washington, and the JFK symbolism—young, coatless, and vigorous—was too tempting to resist.

Spitzer's "people's inaugural" tapped a string of evocative notes, many of them presidential. Like Bill Clinton, he'd rise before dawn to lead a brisk, two-mile "Day One Run" around the capital, with the press and security puffing along. He'd be heralded with a nineteen-gun salute. And afterward, he and Silda would throw open the doors to the governor's mansion to receive the citizenry, just as Andrew Jackson famously did at the White House back in 1829. Spitzer had even collaborated in a photo chronicle of the "adrenaline-fueled" journey that had brought him to Albany. Titled "The Making of a Governor," the exhibit would be displayed in Vanderbilt Hall at New York City's Grand Central Terminal, paid for partly with campaign funds.

Intent on demonstrating that everything—or at least something—really *was* changing on Day One, Spitzer signed five executive orders at 8 A.M., imposing fresh ethics restrictions on state employees. His twenty-minute inaugural address, given with steam issuing from his lips, contained three references to Teddy Roosevelt and yet another JFK touchstone: he urged "a politics that asks not what is in it for me, but always what is in it for us."

Still, the most memorable note of the day was all Spitzer. With Pataki and his wife, Libby, looking on from the front row, the new governor proclaimed that New York, "like Rip Van Winkle," had "slept through much of the past decade while the rest of the world has passed us by." Members of his staff had thought this was a little too nasty for the occasion. But Spitzer, as in the past, had refused to soften his words to avoid giving offense.

The traditional private swearing-in had already taken place, right after midnight at the governor's mansion, with Spitzer's parents, three daughters and two dogs, reporters, and several dozen friends in attendance. Federal judge Robert Sweet, who had married the Spitzers, presided at both ceremonies. Constantine brought the champagne, a $2,000 Balthazar of Veuve Clicquot, and bloodied his hand opening the giant bottle with a wrench.

Even veteran members of Spitzer's staff viewed this governor's inauguration as an occasion of great portent. On Day One, Dopp began keeping a private diary of life in the Spitzer administration, reflecting the sky-high hopes and expectations. "The photo of the gathering in West Capitol Park will last forever, but the moment itself came and went quickly," Dopp wrote on January 1. "The weather held, the people came and ES delivered his remarks well."

———

If anyone clung to the hope that the new governor would abide by Albany's unwritten rules, Spitzer quickly shattered those illusions. Balboni's appointment required a special election on February 6 to fill his Long Island senate seat, which had been Republican for more than a century. Democrat Craig Johnson, a popular county legislator, was running against Republican Maureen O'Connell, the Nassau County clerk. Ignoring Bruno's threats, Spitzer immersed himself in the race.

His top political operatives—including Toohey, who had gone to work at Global Strategy—guided Johnson's campaign. His adman, Jimmy Siegel, prepared Johnson's commercials. His fundraising would help make the thirty-two-day contest the most expensive senate race in history, with $5 million in total spending by the two sides. Most infuriating of all—to Bruno—Spitzer's distinctive mug was everywhere. He campaigned in the district; he was plastered on Johnson's campaign literature; he appeared in a TV ad declaring the race a referendum on his reform agenda. "If you support that agenda," the governor told voters, "you *must* vote for Craig Johnson." Even Silda campaigned for Johnson. The governor stopped just short of scorching the political earth, killing a piece of campaign literature noting that Bruno, the Republican candidate's patron, was under federal investigation.

Spitzer and Baum smelled blood, thinking they might even be able to win Democratic control of the senate *before* the 2008 election. If Johnson won, Bruno's majority would shrink to 33–29. And if they could somehow flip two more seats—by persuading Republican senators to take job offers or switch parties—the senate would be deadlocked, leaving Paterson, the Democratic lieutenant governor, to cast the tie-breaking vote. Baum had already begun probing for defectors.

Bruno squawked. "One-party rule doesn't serve anybody's purpose," he told the press. He called for "a fair fight" out on Long Island and suggested that outsiders shouldn't pour in money or get involved. Never mind that the biggest donors to O'Connell were Bruno's senate campaign committee and his union ally, 1199.

———

Spitzer was already starting to struggle with the huge expectations he had worked so hard to create.

During his first weeks in office, he got Bruno and Silver to accept a better budget process, including full disclosure of all member items. (To distance himself from the pork barrel, he'd decided not to spend the governor's $30 million share.) He also won their agreement on an ethics bill that barred lawmakers from accepting travel, gifts, and speaking fees; blocked legislative staff from lobbying lawmakers for two years after leaving government; and created a new state "public integrity" commission (though it didn't have jurisdiction over the legislature). The governor's press releases characterized these developments as "sweeping" and "landmark," and Spitzer had expected widespread praise, just like he'd gotten in the AG's office. Instead, good-government groups complained that it wasn't nearly enough—and that he had negotiated the deals behind closed doors. The legislature, on the other hand, was terrified that Spitzer would do too much. "I urge a more conciliatory approach," wrote Dopp in his diary. "Lawmakers are clearly nervous."

With good reason. For the January 24 press conference announcing ethics reform, Spitzer took the unusual step of inviting the minority leaders from the senate and the assembly to participate. Spitzer was eager to suggest that Bruno and Silver weren't the only lawmakers who mattered, even though it wasn't really true. The senate's top Democrat was Malcolm Smith, an African American from Queens who had succeeded Paterson. The assembly minority leader was an upstater named Jim Tedisco.

Tedisco, fifty-six, was an ex-jock who had graduated from Union College in Schenectady with virtually every varsity basketball record in the book. He had earned a master's degree in education and worked as a high school coach and guidance counselor before entering politics. During twenty-three years in Albany, he'd finally risen to assembly minority leader in 2005. But, in truth, there were few positions in government that mattered less. Silver didn't give him the time of day; he clearly viewed Tedisco, never known for measuring his words, as both irrelevant and obnoxious. As one of Tedisco's own aides told Baum: "Whenever I get him into the party, he always insists on putting the lampshade on his head and dancing."

Tedisco hadn't even been told about the ethics deal until it had been struck in the usual Albany manner—by the governor, Silver, and Bruno. The assemblyman was so peeved about this that he hadn't bothered to respond when the governor's office called to arrange his appearance for the 11 A.M. announcement. That morning, the assemblyman was driving back from his district when Spitzer called to ask, "Are you coming to the press conference today?"

"What's it *about*, governor?" Tedisco asked sarcastically.

Spitzer had no patience for this game. He was trying to cut the minority leaders in, over objections from their counterparts. "I'm your best friend," Spitzer told him. "I've got my hands full with Silver and Bruno."

Tedisco reminded Spitzer of all his nice campaign promises about inclusion and transparency. Then he started to lecture him. If Spitzer really wanted to make a point of reaching out, Tedisco said, he needed to involve him from the start, on an equal basis with Silver and Bruno. If Spitzer wasn't going to do that, why should he appear for his dog-and-pony show?

With that, the fifty-fourth governor of New York turned guttural. Tedisco would be there if he *told* him to be there. "I'm a fucking steamroller, and I'll roll over you and anyone else!" Spitzer growled. "I've done more in three weeks than any governor in the history of the state!

"Are you coming to the press conference or not?"

Tedisco said he would be there.

Dopp spoke to his boss shortly after this conversation. Spitzer insisted that he hadn't really threatened Tedisco; the "steamroller" reference came from a famous James Taylor song he liked, called "Steamroller Blues":

Well, I'm a steamroller, baby.
I'm bound to roll all over you.

Dopp noted the event in his diary: "ES tells Tedisco that he's a 'fucking steamroller.' Meant to be a semi-humorous statement."

The semi-humor of the situation had clearly escaped Tedisco. He quickly related the exchange to Bruno and his veteran press aide, John McArdle. Though Bruno and Spitzer were still on cordial terms, sizing each other up, the senator wasn't about to pass up an opportunity to embarrass the new governor. McArdle—who was Bruno's Dopp—quickly tipped off the single reporter in the statehouse who was certain to make the most of it: Fred Dicker of the *New York Post*. And he wasn't disappointed.

Six days later, the story appeared, beneath the tabloid headline ELIOT

SPITZ FIRE. Dicker reported that the "enraged" governor had "viciously berated" Tedisco, and quoted "sources familiar with the conversation" on Spitzer's precise language: "I am a f—ing steamroller." The article, which recounted previous Spitzer outbursts, was accompanied by a crude cartoon of Spitzer driving a steamroller.

Dopp went into damage-control mode, declining comment on a "private discussion" while insisting that Dicker's account of the episode was "embellished." But as the story rippled out through Albany and beyond, Spitzer appeared to bask in the "steamroller" image. Machiavelli had written that it was better for a leader to be feared than loved; New York's governor seemed to agree.

Baum wasn't so sure. He'd been in Brooklyn at the time of the eruption, packing up his apartment to move to the new home his family had just purchased in Albany. Dopp had called to tell him what happened. This wasn't any way for the governor to act, Baum told Dopp—especially with a pipsqueak like Tedisco. It made everyone in Albany want to take him down a notch. In the public's eye, it was good for Spitzer to appear tough enough to get important things done. But he didn't want to look like an out-of-control asshole.

————

Spitzer didn't begin his term just berating Republicans. He was battling the Democratic assembly, too. At issue was the selection of a new state comptroller to finish the term of Democrat Alan Hevesi, who had resigned as part of a criminal plea bargain in yet another Albany scandal: Hevesi had improperly used state employees to chauffeur his ailing wife and run personal errands. As Spitzer saw it, the decision on Hevesi's replacement was the first big test of whether Albany was ready to change its ways. Never mind that the governor had no formal authority to play any part in it.

Under the state constitution, Hevesi's successor was to be chosen by majority vote of the 212 legislators, meeting in combined session. That meant it was up to Silver, assuming his 108 Democrats voted as a bloc, as they invariably did. The assembly members were already drooling at the prospect of picking one of their own; several had begun lining up votes. Everything the comptroller did involved money. He managed the state's $145 billion pension fund, audited government agencies, and provided financial estimates used to set the budget. But the office, which was also a rich source of patronage and required statewide election, was almost always filled by a politician.

Spitzer had other ideas. When Hevesi announced his resignation, a *Times* editorial had urged selection of a "first-rate" replacement, "a watchdog from the outside" with financial expertise. "As a starting point," the paper wrote, "the new comptroller should not be an Albany insider." The governor agreed completely, and said so publicly. This put him on a collision course with Silver, whose influence depended entirely on the exercise—and protection—of legislative prerogative.

No one wielded power quite like Shelly Silver. A Spitzer deputy who watched the speaker at work in Albany came to think of him as "the artist of time." The speaker's special tool was delay. Silver held his tongue and kept his counsel. He postponed any action until the last possible moment—and beyond. He listened carefully, but never committed to anything, even when you thought he had. For the hyperkinetic governor—who grew up shouting his position across the dinner table—such tactics were maddening. Bruno could be bought or bargained; he used his power to get things. Silver was a sphinx; he used his power by refusing to act, letting bills and projects die. After dealing with the speaker for several months, Spitzer would describe him to a *Times* reporter as "an enigma, the grandmaster of the chess game of Albany maneuvers."

The son of a hardware store owner, Silver represented the eclectic district where he'd grown up in Lower Manhattan, stretching from Wall Street to Chinatown. After becoming speaker in 1994, he'd put the entire assembly on "Shelly time." That meant shutting down at sundown on Friday to observe the Sabbath, even in the midst of critical negotiations. Secretive, soft-spoken, and hardboiled, Silver didn't care about his image or the good-government urgings of Common Cause and *The New York Times*. He'd for years ignored demands to disclose his outside income and clients as a personal-injury lawyer, and seemed remarkably tolerant of the behavior that made Albany a cesspool. Silver had also played a role in one of the capitol's ugliest scandals. In 2001, the speaker had staunchly defended his chief counsel after a young legislative aide formally complained that the Silver lieutenant had sexually assaulted her. Two years later, Albany police charged Silver's counsel with raping a second aide, leading to a sexual misconduct plea. The assembly leadership paid a half-million dollars to settle a lawsuit over the speaker's inaction; Silver eventually apologized.

New York attorney general Eliot Spitzer in his Manhattan office in 2002, when his assault on research conflicts earned him his nickname the Sheriff of Wall Street.

(TED THAI, TIME&LIFE PICTURES-GETTY IMAGES)

Spitzer campaigning for governor in August 2006 at the state fair in Syracuse, where he spoke beneath the grandstand.

(MARIUS MURESANU)

By May 2006, Silda Wall Spitzer had joined her husband on the campaign trail, making a stop in Buffalo after the state convention.

(MARIUS MURESANU)

Tom Suozzi was a victim of the Spitzer juggernaut in the 2006 Democratic gubernatorial primary, despite rumors that he had dirt on the AG. He confronted Spitzer at a train stop on Long Island.

(MARIUS MURESANU)

Spitzer waiting to speak at a campaign rally in the Bronx in September 2006.

(MARIUS MURESANU)

The Spitzers walk toward the New York State Capitol in Albany on December 31, 2006, after a rehearsal for his New Year's Day inauguration as governor.

(JAMES ESTRIN, *NEW YORK TIMES*-REDUX)

Day One: Eliot Spitzer takes the oath of office from federal judge Robert Sweet, who also presided at the Spitzers' wedding.

(RON ANTONELLI, NEW YORK *DAILY NEWS*)

Spitzer's parents, Anne and Bernard, joined the celebration for their son's record-breaking victory as governor at campaign headquarters in Manhattan on election night 2006.

(MARK PETERSON, REDUX)

New York governor Eliot Spitzer proposes a toast shortly after midnight, minutes after his private swearing-in at the executive mansion in Albany. Daughters Elyssa, seventeen, Sarabeth, fourteen, and Jenna, twelve, joined their parents.

(MICHAEL APPLETON, NEW YORK *DAILY NEWS*)

Old friend Lloyd Constantine, seen at a 2006 campaign party, believed Spitzer was headed for the White House, and wanted a place at his side in Albany.

(MARIUS MURESANU)

The architect of Spitzer's political career, Rich Baum served as chief of staff in the AG's office and secretary to the governor in Albany. He struggled to manage Spitzer's outbursts.

(MARIUS MURESANU)

Communications director
Darren Dopp, Spitzer's longtime
spinmeister, became a media
target in the Troopergate
scandal.

(MIKE GROLL/AP/WIDE WORLD
PHOTOS)

Christine Anderson, in the
state capitol in March 2007,
handled a string of crises after
replacing Dopp as Spitzer's top
press adviser.

(NATHANIEL BROOKS, *NEW YORK
TIMES*-REDUX)

Senate majority leader Joe Bruno, seventy-seven, at his horse farm outside Albany in January 2007, had shrewdly clung to power for sixteen years. He quickly became Spitzer's nemesis.

(TIM ROSKE, AP)

Joe Bruno with Democratic assembly speaker Sheldon Silver and future governor David Paterson, then senate minority leader, at George Pataki's state of the state speech in January 2006.

(JAMES ESTRIN, *NEW YORK TIMES*-REDUX)

Spitzer with U.S. senator (and future presidential candidate) Hillary Clinton in November 2006.

(MARK PETERSON, REDUX)

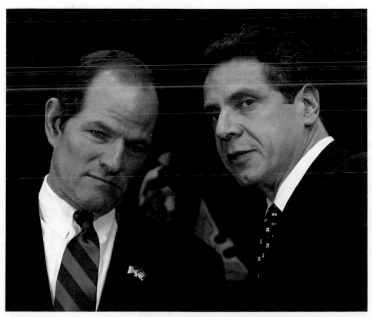

Spitzer clashed bitterly with Andrew Cuomo, who succeeded him as attorney general and had already run once for governor. They shared the podium at a November 2007 press event.

(RUBY WASHINGTON, *NEW YORK TIMES*-REDUX)

New York Post state editor Fred Dicker, Albany's most powerful journalist, hailed the new governor's election, before quickly turning on Spitzer. Dicker interviewed New York City mayor Mike Bloomberg in mid-2007 on his Albany radio show, one of the sources of his influence.

(MIKE GROLL/AP/WIDE WORLD PHOTOS)

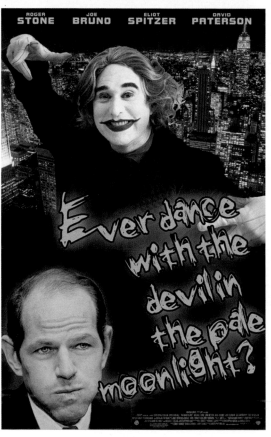

Republican dirty-trickster Roger Stone viewed himself as the Joker bedeviling Spitzer's Batman. Stone's son prepared this mock movie poster for his dad as a birthday present.

Small photo: Roger Stone.

(NYDIA B. STONE)

Former NYSE chief Dick Grasso refused to settle when Spitzer sued over his $140-million pay package. The case dragged on for years.

(LOUIS LANZANO/AP/WIDE WORLD PHOTOS)

Billionaire Ken Langone vowed revenge after Spitzer named him as a defendant in the Grasso case.

(DIANE BONDAREFF/AP/WIDE WORLD PHOTOS)

AIG chief Maurice "Hank" Greenberg, seventy-nine, joined the list of powerful Spitzer enemies after the AG's subpoena set in motion his departure from the company he had ruled for thirty-eight years.

(EMILE WAMSTEKER, BLOOMBERG NEWS/GETTY IMAGES)

Silda Spitzer joined her husband on the beach at the Ritz-Carlton in Puerto Rico during a legislative conference in November 2007. An escort from the Emperors Club left the island on the day she arrived.

(JOSE ANTONIO ROSARIO)

Mark Brener and Cecil Suwal, photographed by a friend at a Manhattan restaurant, ran Emperors Club VIP together.

(MEHAL J. ROCKEFELLER)

Cecil Suwal left the federal courthouse in Manhattan in January 2009 with her father (left) and her attorney, after being sentenced to six months in prison. Suwal says she and Brener thought having the governor as a customer would shield them from prosecution.

(BRYAN SMITH, *NEW YORK DAILY NEWS*)

Emperors Club VIP booker Temeka Lewis arranged most of the appointments for the mysterious George Fox, including his February 13 liaison in Room 871 of the Mayflower Hotel with Ashley Dupré.

(MARC A. HERMANN, NEW YORK *DAILY NEWS*)

Aspiring singer Ashley Dupré, who had worked as an escort since she was nineteen, parlayed a single encounter with the governor into a career as a celebrity. This photo was shot for an escort service in 2005.

(ZOOP-PHOTO&DESIGN)

Silda and Eliot Spitzer leave his March 10, 2008, press briefing in Manhattan without taking questions, after the governor's brief public apology for violating "any sense of right and wrong."

New York's tabloids reveled in the scandal after the *Times*'s revelation and Spitzer's cryptic admission.

Former New York governor Eliot Spitzer, in New York City, on April 10, 2009.
(CHARLES OMMANNEY, GETTY IMAGES)

The speaker viewed all the debate about government process as silly. To Silver, just two things mattered: results and retaining power. During the Pataki years, he'd kept the brakes on Republican efforts to savage liberal programs. But he'd also turned a blind eye to Albany's ethical challenges. Silver, who often likened himself to a union boss, knew that allowing his members to take a hit—even when they deserved it—would undermine his position. When Spitzer took office, there were rumblings that he was gunning to replace the speaker. That wouldn't be easy. Silver had brutally crushed a coup attempt led by the assembly majority leader back in 2000, locking him out of his office, stripping his power and perks, and ending his political career. Silver had been more attentive to the desires of his large and unwieldy conference in the years since. Nonetheless, when Spitzer publicly suggested that no assembly member was qualified to replace Hevesi, it was seen as a direct challenge.

This put Silver in a bind. He wasn't looking for a confrontation with a powerful new governor from his own party. But his assembly Democrats were uncharacteristically restive. They wanted to choose one of their own, and they deeply resented Spitzer's meddling. If Silver sided with the governor, they might revolt; the speaker might even be handing Spitzer the rope to hang him.

On January 9, the governor and Silver announced a compromise: an outside panel of three former comptrollers would screen the applicants, and present a short list of "up to five" qualified candidates to the lawmakers. To the public, this was presented as evidence that Albany was on the road to reform. The panel, Silver told reporters, "should eliminate any doubt about the process that will lead to the election of a state comptroller" and was "another solid step toward restoring the people's faith in this government." But privately, the speaker assured his members that the list would include one of them.

Mark Weprin was delighted. The forty-five-year-old Queens assemblyman was part of a New York political family. His late father had preceded Silver as speaker; Mark held his dad's seat. His brother was a New York City councilman. Weprin prided himself on being close to the new governor. Among Eliot's earliest supporters for attorney general, Weprin and his wife had been to the Spitzers' apartment for Sunday brunch; they were among the few legislative couples invited to his private swearing-in. "I was thrilled," says Weprin. "Here I was part of the inner circle." This had practical benefits. Albany insiders viewed Weprin as a conduit to Spitzer, whom few of them knew. It had already helped his fundraising. "All the lobbyists—it was palpable. People were saying, 'Mark could be my connection.'"

On the day Hevesi announced his departure, Weprin had called Spitzer to suggest the "perfect guy" to replace him—his buddy Tom DiNapoli. A twenty-year Long Island assemblyman, DiNapoli was perhaps the most popular member of the legislature—even Republicans loved him. He worked hard, knew his way around government, and wasn't a grandstander, Weprin told Spitzer. DiNapoli, itching to move up, was also close to Silver.

No dice, Spitzer told Weprin; he favored an outsider with a financial background. Weprin reported back to DiNapoli: "We're screwed." Then the special screening panel was announced. "Shelly led us to believe we had the perfect arrangement," says Weprin. "Eliot got to save face: 'We're going to have a nice open process, not operate behind closed doors.' And at least one lawmaker would make the list." DiNapoli might get the job after all, thought Weprin. Then he'd be tight with both the governor *and* the comptroller.

The choice was becoming a big media issue—before it was all resolved, fodder for four *Times* editorials. Spitzer tried to recruit a blue-chip candidate who would blow everyone away. He spoke to Sallie Krawcheck, the chief financial officer of Citigroup, and Shirley Ann Jackson, the president of Rensselaer Polytechnic Institute, but neither was interested. He was annoyed by the assembly support for the beloved DiNapoli. "What's *nice* got to do with it?" the governor asked. During their private meetings, Spitzer had taken to chatting about the stock market with Silver, who had accumulated a hefty personal portfolio and loved discussing investments. "Would you have Tom manage *your* money?" the governor asked.

Five Democratic assemblymen, including DiNapoli, were among the seventeen candidates who formally applied for the job, answering questions at a public hearing. Things were looking good. Then Weprin got a call from the governor a day before the finalists were announced.

"What makes you think DiNapoli's going to come out of the panel?" Spitzer asked.

Weprin told the governor that DiNapoli was one of the best candidates.

"He *isn't*," Spitzer responded curtly. "We shouldn't pick *anyone* from the legislature. There's more corruption in the legislature than there is in the general public."

DiNapoli was honest, Weprin protested. And supporting him would help Eliot make friends in the legislature.

Qualified? Spitzer scoffed. "DiNapoli doesn't know the difference between a swap and a debenture!" As for cozying up to the lawmakers, the thought that *that* would sway him made Spitzer even angrier. "Tell your fucking friends in the legislature I'm not interested in making any friends!"

The next day, the panel named just three finalists: the Nassau County comptroller, New York City's commissioner of finance, and an investment banker who had run for comptroller in 2002. Not a single legislator made the list. *The New York Times* pronounced itself satisfied, and so did the governor. "The committee has reported out three names of eminently qualified individuals," Spitzer commented. "We'll now wait for the legislature to pick among them—among the three—and that's as it should be."

The legislators were furious. They thought Spitzer had rigged the screening panel. "We felt like we'd been sandbagged and lied to," says Weprin. "We were trying to protect Eliot's ass by setting up this panel, and he screwed us out of having a member." At a closed-door meeting of the assembly Democrats, Silver still seemed reluctant to buck the governor. But the legislators were deeply offended that both Spitzer and the panel had judged all of them *inadequate*. "We come from all walks of life, but in our own way, we have an intelligentsia," a Queens Democrat would respond from the assembly floor. Silver polled his members: they wanted DiNapoli.

The next day, the speaker met with the governor to deliver the news. Dopp summed up the exchange in his diary: "Shelly tells Eliot that he must do a member as Comptroller. Eliot says that Shelly should abide by the agreement. Shelly says the members won't go for it. Eliot says, 'You didn't try to sell it.' Shelly says, 'I can't sell what I don't believe in.'"

So on February 7, just six weeks into his term, the governor began the day by celebrating the big victory of Democrat Craig Johnson in the special election out on Long Island. Bruno's senate majority was down to just two seats. Spitzer then endured a stinging defeat, watching the legislators elect DiNapoli—and rail about his "interference." Publicly, Silver grasped a slender reed to justify breaking his commitment to pick the comptroller from the list of finalists. The assembly had expected the screening panel to present five candidates, not three, the speaker explained. That voided the deal.

In the governor's chamber, there was debate about how sharply to respond to the rebuff by his fellow Democrats. "We talked about it: 'These are our friends we're shitting on,'" recalls Dopp; they'd need them in future battles. But Spitzer was unrelenting. To do nothing would make him look like a paper tiger. He needed to hit back—to let the lawmakers know they'd pay a price. Says Baum, "It was like a fever about how the government was corrupt." So after the vote, Spitzer publicly blasted the lawmakers for "a stunning lack of integrity," allowing "politics and cronyism" to prevail.

By the next day, the Democratic legislators were eager to move on, to patch things up with their governor. But Spitzer got even rougher. "These people in Albany, they're stuck in their ways," he declared at a breakfast meeting of his campaign donors in Manhattan. They'd learn soon enough, he ominously warned—"the knockout punch is coming." With that, Spitzer flew to Syracuse to open an upstate tour to talk about his budget proposal. But instead of discussing education funding, he attacked the local Democratic assemblyman, who had raised money for Spitzer's campaign, as a gutless puppet. "Bill Magnarelli," he declared, "is one of those unfortunate assembly members who just raises his hand when he's told to do so. . . . When Shelly Silver says 'Vote,' Magnarelli says 'How?' and doesn't ask what it's all about." For good measure, Spitzer offered his harshest attack yet on DiNapoli, calling him "thoroughly and totally unqualified for the job."

That wasn't all. Spitzer canceled a $10,000-a-seat fundraiser he was going to headline for the Democratic assembly campaign committee. He hinted that he might back challengers to Democratic incumbents who weren't truly committed to reform. He publicly called for Silver to disclose his outside income—a particularly sensitive issue for the speaker. And anonymous "sources" working for the governor floated rumors that he might even try to oust Silver. Picking up Spitzer's refrain, the *New York Post* ambushed DiNapoli on his third day in the job, while he was sipping coffee in a restaurant, and demanded he submit to a pop quiz on finance. DiNapoli foolishly agreed—and flunked: TESTY POL GETS 'F' IN FISCAL ED; ECON QUIZ BAFFLES NEW COMPTROLLER.

As always, Spitzer insisted that it wasn't personal. He was simply "presenting the facts," and he was absolutely right on the merits—why, every editorial page in the state was with him! It didn't seem to bother the voters, either—his poll numbers remained sky-high. But the legislators were aghast. No governor had ever attacked a member in his own district. This was how he treated his *friends*?

Spitzer's chief of staff, Marlene Turner, who sat thirty feet away, had certainly seen his temper at times during the AG years. But this was somehow different—more frequent and more corrosive, born of frustration. "It was hard for him to think he couldn't convince someone to see the light, to see the error of their ways—and that you didn't have to punch them," says Turner. "He would just suddenly *yell*—in pursuit of right and wrong. He's not realizing, 'Oh my God, *I just lit into the assembly minority leader!*'" When Turner asked what had happened—"You really gave it to him!"—Spitzer turned almost sheepish. "Did I really do that?" he asked. "Glad I got *that* out of my system." Says Turner: "He knew he'd exploded, but it didn't have meaning to him."

It did, of course, have meaning to others. Assemblyman Weprin, for one, was crushed by how personally Spitzer was taking their disagreement. The assemblyman's warm and valuable relationship with the governor had rapidly become neither warm nor valuable. After Weprin gave a floor speech backing DiNapoli's nomination, Spitzer had cut him off. "You'd think the honeymoon would have lasted a little longer," said Weprin. "Once Eliot started pissing on everybody, no one wanted to talk to me."

———

Mark Brener and Cecil Suwal were starting to make their mark in the world. They had recruited call girls in Los Angeles, Chicago, and Miami, and had even begun doing business in a few cities abroad. One of their top customers was England's Duke of Westminster, a billionaire. Unfortunately, Zana Brazdek, the London escort they'd hired on a quick trip to England, sold the story of her first rendezvous with the duke to a British tabloid. The article appeared in February 2007, noting that Brazdek worked for "high-class escort agency Emperors Club VIP," and even quoted e-mails from "Katie" detailing logistics for the appointment. Afterward, Suwal warned the bookers not to comment if reporters called. Strangely, the media attention didn't seem to hurt their growing business.

Brener and Suwal were becoming more creative in marketing their vision of exclusivity. In addition to ranking their call girls by diamonds (with a top rate of $3,100 an hour), they had introduced the notion of a super-elite breed of escorts, called "Icon Models," who were available only "for a handful of dates per year due to their major career commitments." These "internationally recognized faces in the fashion, media, and corporate worlds" weren't pictured, given "their unique career recognition." In fact, according to Tammy Thomas, they were the same women depicted elsewhere on the site. But when they were booked as Icon Models, they went for $5,500 an hour. Says Thomas: "That is the psychology of these guys—'Oh, she's only a thousand dollars an hour?' These people *wanted* to pay more, because paying more gives exclusivity. There's stupid money in New York—it's almost the norm there."

Day-to-day life in the business was rarely glamorous. As booker, Thomas served as a logistics hub, usually coordinating with the women by text message. Sometimes escorts were pleading for work. ("There is really nothing or you doesn't like me?") Sometimes they begged off. ("Just took [off] face & in bed," wrote Charlotta. "My period began," explained Natalie.) Tammy wrote one escort with a consumer-product inquiry. "No babe they are real," Daniella assured her. Macy, on the other hand, was planning enhancement. "I'm gonna take a break from work," she wrote Tammy at 2:11 A.M. "I'm gonna have an operation for my boops, making them little bigger!! Ha ha! So Ill be resting for 3 or 4 weeks. . . ." Rani passed on an encouraging industry indicator: "I keep hearing @ all the raises on Wallstreet . . . usually wd. B good for us . . . maybe things will pick up." But some business wasn't so desirable. "Ah, the weirdo!" texted Simone, on learning who she was about to see. "I hope he won't cry again . . . !!!" One of the agency's "doubles," unsure what role she was to play with her john, posed the existential question "Who am I?"

Even as he managed his illegal business—and avoided paying his own taxes—Brener had renewed his license to practice as a tax advisor before the IRS. He continued to insist that what they were doing was legit—that he'd found the magic loophole that would allow their enterprise to pass muster before a court of law. He even ordered business cards for Emperors Club VIP and his front company, QAT Consulting Group.

Like many entrepreneurs, Brener and Suwal harbored ambitions to diversify—to exploit their high-dollar clientele by cross-selling an array of other services. Over time, they added pages on their website pitching "exclusive" art auctions (for art that they didn't control), investment advice (which they weren't qualified to provide), and "Emperors Club VIP Concierge"—featuring weekend dates with "your favorite celebrity (retainer required)." To try to give it all an air of legitimacy, they even pasted the logos of prestigious brands like Christie's and Baccarat onto the website for their escort service. But they never made a penny on any of this, prompting one of their bookers to grumble that it was diverting eyeballs from the escorts.

The complaints had come from Temeka Lewis, a thirty-one-year-old woman who had started working at the Emperors Club in late 2005. A twin daughter of a single mother, Lewis had struggled financially since graduating from the University of Virginia as an English major in 1997. Eager to live in New York, she had worked as a waitress and a tutor and spent a couple of years in dorm-style housing operated by the Brooklyn YWCA, which twice sued her for falling behind on the rent. Responding to a classified ad in *The Village Voice*, she'd gone to work for Brener and Suwal after interviewing with them at a sushi restaurant. A bookish, strong-willed loner, Lewis was a steady presence at the Emperors Club, handling a stream of calls from an array of customers—including George Fox. When Tammy Thomas left in the spring of 2007, after perhaps a dozen conversations with him, Lewis became his exclusive handler. With her earnings from booking prostitutes, she rented her own apartment in Brooklyn. At work, she went by her middle name—Rachelle.

By 2007, the Emperors Club was prosperous enough that Brener had finally managed to repay most of his old debts. Always a penny pincher, he'd begun stockpiling cash in the New Jersey apartment. But his adult son, Greg, who had co-founded a successful IT business, still believed that Brener was a struggling tax consultant. He owned the co-op apartment where his dad lived. He'd even loaned him $4,000 to help make ends meet.

With their joint enterprise thriving, the old pimp and his girlish madam reaffirmed their mad love for each other. Brener had already proposed marriage—on Valentine's Day—but Suwal told him that she was too young to tie the knot. She was willing to memorialize her devotion, however, in her own singular way. She went to a tattoo parlor and had the words PROPERTY OF MARK BRENER inked into the flesh just above her genitals.

Chapter 9: Shark vs. Octopus

FOR A TIME, THE STEAMROLLER APPROACH ACTUALLY SEEMED to be working. New Yorkers overwhelmingly backed their governor in the comptroller fight, according to statewide polls; editorial boards pounded the lawmakers. Bruno had responded by calling Spitzer a "bully" who was "running around having a tantrum." But on Valentine's Day, with reporters in tow, Bruno walked down to the executive chamber with a playful peace offering: nine red roses. Spitzer smiled at the gift, and offered a snarky response: "One from each member of your conference!" It served as a not-so-subtle reminder: Spitzer was maneuvering to end Bruno's career as majority leader, and he remained the state's most powerful political force. In his diary, Dopp noted his boss's approval numbers and marveled: "Spitzer's political instincts are impeccable." He would soon have reason to think differently.

Spitzer quickly negotiated a pair of complex deals with the lawmakers addressing problems that had festered for years. The first overhauled the state's disastrous workers' compensation system, raising benefits for injured workers while cutting costs for business. The second provided for civil confinement of sex offenders after they had been paroled, as well as counseling before and after they were released. Both agreements had been struck in the old-fashioned Albany way—by three men in a room, without committee hearings or public debate. The legislature wasn't even in session. Formal approval by the lawmakers was, of course, a foregone conclusion.

But the big fight still loomed. In New York, the annual budget was supposed to be passed by April 1, the start of the state's fiscal year. But that had happened only twice in twenty-two years. Typically, New York went through a bizarre ritual instead. The governor proposed a budget; the senate and assembly held passage hostage, demanding hundreds of millions more for their favored interests; and everyone finally agreed, long past the deadline, after expensive, closed-door horse trading. Invariably, the process changed little about how New York's wasteful government actually did business.

Spitzer, of course, wanted to do everything differently. For starters, he wanted desperately to pass the budget on time—a late budget was the most conspicuous symbol of Albany's dysfunction. More important, he wanted to use the budget as a blunt instrument of reform, just as he'd used lawsuits while attorney general. To make that happen, Spitzer had resolved to tackle the biggest, most politically charged target of all: healthcare. It would foreshadow the ugly battle Barack Obama was to fight in Washington.

———

Healthcare spending in New York was a disaster. At $46 billion, it represented a gargantuan chunk of the $120 billion annual budget, and was growing at an unsustainable rate of 8 percent a year. New York spent more than any other state on Medicaid—measured per capita, *twice* the national average. Antiquated formulas poured money into hospitals and nursing homes with empty beds, instead of needy institutions, outpatient clinics, and home healthcare. Big, powerful teaching programs got enormous subsidies: $77,000 per medical resident, compared to $21,000 in California. And all this money produced poor results: New Yorkers died from chronic diseases more often than residents of any other state; childhood obesity was worse than the national average. Healthcare was the budget issue that towered over everything else.

The problem resulted from improbable alliances that had for years dictated decisions in Albany. In the Bizarro World of state healthcare politics, labor (in the form of SEIU Local 1199) and management (represented by the Greater New York Hospital Association) didn't fight over how to divide the pie; they teamed up to make the pie *bigger*. The point man in this potent partnership was Dennis Rivera, the union's fedora-wearing president. Most unions, of course, back Democrats, and 1199—with 210,000 members, New York's largest—usually had in the past.

But Rivera had shrewdly established another counterintuitive alliance—with Bruno, over a weekend of horseback riding on the senator's farm. In return for the union's help at campaign time, Bruno's senate did its bidding.

Over the years, this symbiotic relationship had produced truly remarkable results. Like Spitzer, Pataki had assumed office vowing to bring Medicaid spending under control. But when budget decisions actually loomed, the union got rough, spending millions on TV spots that featured frightened nursing-home patients and angry hospital workers, wondering why the heartless governor was picking on them. Many of the proposed cuts were restored. In 2002, Pataki made his own accommodation, backing a special $1.8 billion allocation to bankroll a big raise for healthcare workers; 1199 endorsed him for a third term. When the state's financial situation worsened, Pataki again proposed healthcare cuts. The union responded with the political equivalent of shock and awe, bussing in more than thirty thousand workers for an Albany rally. "Dennis Rivera is like a brother," Bruno assured the crowd. "We will make sure your needs are met." Says Spitzer: "1199 *owned* Joe."

During his own campaign, Spitzer had spoken often about the need to fix the "broken" healthcare system, even shunning the powerful union's endorsement. Now he was throwing down the gauntlet. His reforms wouldn't actually cut healthcare at all—just throttle back the projected increase to a little under 2 percent. It was a difference of about $1.3 billion. Controlling Medicaid costs was essential for Spitzer to do everything else he'd promised: fund health coverage for 400,000 uninsured children, boost state aid for needy school districts, and give a property tax cut for the middle class. That would be quite an achievement for his first year, proving that the right man really *could* tame Albany—and maybe even something bigger.

———

In government, some propositions—no matter how virtuous or necessary—are hard to sell and easy to attack. Lopping a billion dollars out of healthcare spending is one of them. Spitzer's team labored to roll out his plan with a winning spin. The governor wasn't just slashing funding—he was reforming the system, with a "patient first" approach. He wasn't targeting underpaid nurses and the desperate elderly—just waste and inefficiency. Spitzer would make this point by talking about the handful of hospital CEOs who were pulling down multimillion-dollar pay packages, casting them as the poster boys for reform. Still, the governor knew the union and the hospitals would come after him hard. When that day arrived, Spitzer vowed, he wouldn't fold, like Pataki. He'd fight back.

It didn't take long. Three weeks after Spitzer announced his budget, the union launched its first barrage. One TV ad featured Anna Rose, a ninety-four-year-old woman with a walker, who spoke slowly into the camera as the words GOVERNOR SPITZER WANTS TO CUT $450 MILLION FROM NURSING HOMES appeared onscreen. "Governor Spitzer, I want you to *look* at me," she sadly intoned. "And when you cut healthcare, I want my face to be in front of you. *Remember* me." A second ad featured another nursing-home patient wearing a hairnet. "It makes me *very* sad I voted for him," the elderly woman declared. "And if it doesn't change, I will *never* vote for him again."

Spitzer decried his opponents' "scare tactics" and "demagoguery." Then he launched a counteroffensive, buying time for his own ads. Jimmy Siegel's "Crybabies" spot scanned a maternity ward crammed with screaming newborns as a female voice explained that New York's healthcare system "rewards institutions, insurance companies, and unions, not patients." Spitzer's approach, the voice stated, "puts the money where it belongs—toward bringing patient care up and disease down, making sure that every single kid born in New York will finally have medical coverage." With that, the wailing stopped; one of the babies broke into a smile. "And the only people crying about *that*," concluded the narrator, "are the usual special interests." The union fired back with new ads. "I don't understand why Governor Spitzer is attacking me and my hospital," said a nurse dressed in her scrubs. "Let the governor walk in my shoes for a day and then call *me* a crybaby," declared another.

To fund his side of the media war, Spitzer was draining the $3 million left over from his campaign. When that ran out, he wrote a $500,000 personal check to keep the spots running. Spitzer was determined to prove his willingness to go toe to toe. But he was hopelessly outgunned. His opponents had a $65 million "education" fund—and they were spending $1 million a week to hammer him.

Spitzer tried other tactics. During a breakfast speech before a Manhattan hotel ballroom filled with civic and business leaders, he launched one of his patented broadsides. It featured a PowerPoint slide showing the logos of the union and the hospital association below the words

GUARDIANS OF THE STATUS QUO. Ken Raske, the hospital group's president, and Jennifer Cunningham, union chief Rivera's top deputy, were seated near the podium. Spitzer pointed out his "good friends" to the crowd. With charts and graphics, Spitzer then detailed how they were "flat-out wrong" about his cuts. "I have never in my professional life seen anything like that," said Raske afterward. Pursuing a divide-and-conquer strategy, Spitzer won support for his budget from a second healthcare union; courted upstaters by pointing out that the cuts would mostly hit downstate; and urged a roomful of New York City business leaders— many of them hospital trustees—to pressure the hospital association to back off. "How many people here," Spitzer asked, "really think we can keep spending like this?"

Bruno's senate, meanwhile, passed its own bloated version of the budget, restoring virtually all of Spitzer's healthcare cuts and, for good measure, adding in another $2 billion for tax rebates and education. "Profligate and pandering," declared Spitzer. Notwithstanding the comptroller ugliness, Silver and his Democratic assembly stood close to Spitzer on the budget. The speaker was laboring to assume the role of rabbinical counselor to the rookie governor. This isolated Bruno and his senate as the big-spending holdouts.

Tempers started rising as the deadline approached—midnight on Saturday, March 31. With two weeks left, Bruno met with the governor privately and railed, among other grievances, about how the Democratic leaders had lined up against him. "Every time I mention your name, he wets his pants!" Bruno said of Silver, who had often sided with him when Pataki was governor. As for the senate minority leader, Malcolm Smith, he was Spitzer's puppet, Bruno declared: *"He's got his head so far up your ass he can't see straight!"* No stranger to the use of profanity, Spitzer nonetheless responded with high umbrage: "I will not countenance that kind of vulgarity in my office!" Then he stormed out of his own office. For weeks after the shouting match was over, Baum and Dopp joked privately about a proper addendum to their boss's comment: "Unless it is uttered by me *personally!*"

A few days out, an agreement started to take shape. Then Bruno's team began stalling, correctly sensing that they could exploit Spitzer's desperation for an on-time budget to extract more concessions. Budget Director Francis sent the governor a 4:45 A.M. e-mail: "We better start lowering expectations." Silver urged Spitzer to stand firm, even if it meant a late budget, warning that Bruno was holding him hostage. Albany stood poised for a showdown that would shut down state government.

But Spitzer believed an on-time budget was one of the few issues that average voters really cared about. And there was the problem of how much more damage he'd sustain while holding out. The healthcare lobby was still pounding him with its ads, which had already taken a big toll on his approval ratings, emboldening his enemies. He needed to shut that down.

As the deadline neared, the governor spent hours with Silver and Bruno behind closed doors, wheeling and dealing. Local 1199 gave its blessing to a compromise that restored $350 million for hospitals and nursing homes, leaving about $1 billion in healthcare cuts—the kind of round number Spitzer liked. And he won a big change in the Rube Goldberg formula that distributed state school aid on a political basis, redirecting money toward needy districts. But he'd accomplished this reform—toward handing out education money on the merits—through a political deal. To win Bruno's support, he'd lavished an extra $200 million on wealthy Republican school districts out on Long Island. With that, the budget passed on Sunday morning, April 1, just hours after the deadline.

Looking back, Spitzer could fairly conclude that he had accomplished a lot. He'd reined in healthcare spending and taken the first steps toward reforming the system. He'd won medical coverage for 400,000 uninsured children. He'd closed business tax loopholes, funded stem-cell research, and cut taxes for the middle class. And he'd started to change the way New York handed out education aid.

But there was ugliness, too—especially when viewed through the prism of Spitzer's lofty campaign promises. Although he had promised to curb spending, the budget rose 7.3 percent—twice the rate of inflation. He'd bought Bruno's agreement to change the education formula with a payoff for rich suburban schools. And he'd negotiated his budget deal just as New York governors had always done it—with the senate and assembly leaders, behind closed doors. The two-thousand-page document had been presented to the rank-and-file lawmakers for their customary rubber stamp before they'd even had time to read it.

It was Day 91. Clearly, everything *hadn't* changed.

———

If Spitzer's first budget represented a promising—if flawed—landmark, it wasn't exactly seen that way in Albany. "Walking in with a 70 percent majority, it seems like an awful lot of mandate produced a mouse," grumbled one academic quoted in the *Times*. The conventional wisdom was that the wily Bruno had "rolled" Governor Steamroller, who'd failed to stand tough at crunch time. It was a spin Bruno's side had gleefully offered. Even before the budget deal was closed, the *Post's* influential Fred Dicker had taken to mocking Spitzer as "Mr. Softee."

To statehouse insiders, the good-government groups promoting reform in Albany—Common Cause, the League of Women Voters, Ralph Nader's Public Citizen—were known derisively as "goo-goos." Spitzer viewed himself as their champion. But they were up in arms, denouncing the budget process as a step *backward*. Even the *Times*, which broadly praised his budget for producing "important and fundamental changes," called the way it was negotiated "the most regrettable loss for reform." Spitzer had arrived in Albany "promising to destroy its backroom culture," the paper complained, "yet when Sunday's deadline loomed, he succumbed to horse-trading state assets behind closed doors." The paper called for future budgets to be drawn up "in the sunlight."

As Spitzer's staff saw it, their boss's reputation was suffering from public shock at his new role. "That budget was the first time anyone saw Eliot Spitzer compromise," says Baum. "He was this unyielding force of nature. It's the first time they'd seen him do the good, the bad, and the ugly to close a deal." In his diary, Dopp summed up the reaction as "mixed at best. . . . High hopes for new approach were dashed by closed process and 'high spending.' Payback from lawmakers angry about the comptroller debate was a factor. The steamroller comment hurt in the end. . . . Poll shows 16-pt drop. . . . [E]xpectations game is difficult." Francis thought Spitzer suffered from compromising too much at the end, in a way that seemed antithetical to what he stood for. "In our view, we got 80 percent of a loaf. *We won the war.* But we lost the *history* of the war."

Adds Francis: "It drove Eliot crazy."

———

Most of America's governors came to regard the blanket of round-the-clock security thrown around them as an unwelcome intrusion on their privacy. In informal chats at their national gatherings, they traded stories about the methods they sometimes used to leave their protectors in the dust. Who didn't have an occasional need for a little *space*? They even had a name for this practice: "detail ditching," they called it.

Spitzer's new job meant he was perpetually surrounded during his travels around New York by three burly plainclothes State Police troopers, and driven in a mini-caravan of two black Suburbans. As members of the elite executive services detail, these troopers took their job seriously. They'd placed surveillance cameras around the Spitzers' apartment building, which they monitered around the clock from a special room set up in the basement. One of them even followed the governor on a bicycle as he circled the Central Park Reservoir on his morning run. When Spitzer left New York, two of them went along. They were joined by even more officers from the state where they were traveling.

But Spitzer, while personally solicitous of the troopers, didn't like having an entourage. At his state office in Midtown Manhattan, he'd occasionally pop into the elevator to run down to the bank before anyone could join him. He'd also taken deliberate steps to reduce the security presence around him. Governor Pataki had armed troopers in his tail car; Spitzer's just had a driver. When Pataki spent the night at a hotel, a member of his security detail sat in a chair in the hallway as Pataki slept. But when Spitzer was out of town and said he was retiring for the evening, the State Police left for their own room. The governor didn't want anyone standing guard all night outside his door.

———

The first time that George Fox procured her services—the time when he'd seen three girls in a day—Angelina, the Emperors Club escort, really didn't much care for him. He'd been almost brutally direct with her— *wham, bam,* with no *thank-you, ma'am.* Recalls Angelina: "It was very businesslike. He was not one of those people who I would have said went out of their way to make me feel lovely and nice, like many did. It was very impersonal." So when the booker called a few months later to see if she'd be available to see him again, Angelina wasn't thrilled.

Although she was in her early thirties, several years older than the typical Emperors Club call girl, Angelina hadn't been in the business long. She'd begun escorting to supplement the uncertain income from her career in the arts, and was delighted with how much money she could make with a side job that required so little time. She'd enjoyed working for the Emperors Club. Brener and Suwal were certainly odd, but they seemed to run a tight ship, they treated her decently, and the service had a nice clientele. In their own way, they had standards. One time, Angelina walked into a room to find the customer watching porn and jerking off. She'd turned around and walked out. Suwal had been fine about it— she had even apologized.

This time, she met George Fox at the Waldorf Astoria in Midtown Manhattan. He rushed into the room with a baseball cap on, clearly trying not to be recognized, and wanting to get right to it. She insisted they *talk* first. Angelina was a four-diamond prostitute being paid $1,200 an hour. But she operated by her own rules. With George Fox, she recalls being "rather pushy," telling him: "*Listen*, we are going to sit and have a chit-chat and have a nice little date here."

Surprisingly, he seemed to like it that she pushed back. He'd brought along some Scotch, so they sat down to talk over a few drinks while listening to classical music. She asked him what he did for a living. He said he was a lawyer. What kind of law? He dodged. He asked questions about her. They joked and laughed. Says Angelina: "It ended up being kind of a fun couple of hours."

Angelina came away from the session thinking she recognized her john. She looked closely at the photos in the newspapers and watched the TV news. And soon she was certain: she knew who George Fox *really* was. When Brener and Suwal came into the city to settle up, Angelina told them excitedly in the back of the parked Honda minivan.

George Fox had seen other girls—didn't *anyone* recognize him? There'd been talk he might someday be *president*! Did they have *any* idea?

Not a clue.

Even after that, the Emperors Club proprietors couldn't really seem to appreciate why George Fox was so secretive. He still refused to give his phone number to the bookers, insisting instead on calling back. And he never used a credit card. This had greatly complicated matters when he began seeing escorts while traveling out of town. Because the service insisted on at least half payment ahead of time for trips, he'd send cash— thousands of dollars stuffed in an envelope—or money orders through the U.S. mail. George Fox also usually arranged for the agency to book the hotel room—something no other customer did. Even when traveling, he never saw a girl in his own room. "Don't you think he's being a little over the top about this security stuff?" Brener asked Suwal.

George Fox would continue to see other escorts from the Emperors Club over the months to come. But after his second visit with Angelina, he began to ask for her regularly, especially for out-of-town appointments. He rarely requested anyone else; previously, he hadn't seemed to care who he saw. He met with Angelina a half dozen times.

As they fell into something approximating a routine, she wondered how he juggled it all. George Fox clearly had more money than time. He paid for more hours than he'd use, just in case he was running late. Angelina would arrive first, and wait for him in the room. Often the appointments were late at night, when others were sleeping. Yet afterward, he'd rush off. Angelina never noticed anyone around him—no friends, no subordinates, no security. He came and went alone. "Clearly he was looking to get in and get out without being seen," she says. "It was clearly a personal thing—no one's business, affecting no one. Just *his* business."

Angelina came to like George Fox, and relish their time together. "I would insist on having a conversation before we started, because he's so smart and interesting, and I'm totally taking advantage of this," she said, laughing, in a tape-recorded interview with Alex Gibney more than a year later. "He *obliged* me. . . . I would sometimes have a little rant about what's wrong in New York City that needs to be fixed. He listened."

At times, George Fox talked about family. He spoke affectionately of his wife and daughters; they traded stories about their fathers. At one point, he asked if Angelina wore glasses or contact lenses. "No," she joked—"good eyes, good teeth!"

"Yeah," George Fox responded. "That's what my father said when I first introduced him to my wife: 'At least she has good teeth.'"

Angelina's time with George Fox honed her interest in government and politics. She read a book written about him. She pored over his newspaper coverage. She got angry at the *Post*, which really seemed to have it in for him. And as she followed his public battles, George Fox's favorite escort was privately cheering him on. "Treating people with disrespect in any circumstance is wrong," Angelina said later. "And the way he went about it was wrong. But the stuff he was trying to do is admirable. And no one else is brave enough to do it. Whether that comes from narcissism or whatever—it doesn't matter. It's like a real sense of justice."

———

Eliot Spitzer was deeply wounded by the impression left by his first budget fight: that the crafty Bruno could get the best of him; that he didn't really care about transforming Albany; and that he was, in truth, a wimp. He set out to prove each of these notions false. Spitzer embraced Dopp's advice that he needed to reclaim "the mantle of reformer." To do so, he made a single piece of legislation his top priority: campaign-finance reform. But on this issue, Bruno, with his skinny two-seat majority, would once again bedevil the governor with the record mandate.

Spitzer proposed to dramatically tighten New York's contribution limits. As things stood, they not only were the nation's highest for individual donors ($55,800 for statewide races), but contained loopholes allowing virtually unlimited contributions through business entities. Spitzer saw the influence of money in Albany as a bedrock problem, distorting the legislature's judgment on virtually every issue. But Bruno's senate Republicans, dependent on big donors, saw Spitzer's plan as a scheme to assure their extinction. They summarily rejected it.

Spitzer leapt to the attack, blasting the senate's "temporary majority" for its "addiction to the free flow of money," calling it "a narcotic to which they are beholden." Then he began touring Republican districts—starting with Bruno's—to attack the senators for blocking reform. Privately, Spitzer sent his staff to deploy a carrot-and-stick strategy, dangling the prospect of the first legislative pay raise in eight years. Baum met with the top aides to Silver and Bruno to bluntly lay out what Dopp, in his diary, described as "fork in road. Campaign finance + pay raise or no pay raise and war."

To reaffirm his belief in openness after the secret budget talks, Spitzer convened a series of public leaders' meetings in the ceremonial Red Room of the executive chamber. There, beneath a huge portrait of Teddy Roosevelt, Spitzer and Paterson sat at a table with Silver and Bruno, Tedisco and Smith, before an audience of aides, lobbyists, and reporters. They were debating the issues, much as the Spitzer family had done decades earlier at the dinner table—only the lawmakers weren't as well-behaved.

Spitzer, of course, relished the opportunity to discuss the fine points of public policy. He saw it as the best chance for individual problems to be resolved on the merits, rather than as part of a political bargain. But neither Silver nor Bruno cared for the exercise. The speaker simply didn't believe in laying his cards out on the table. And Bruno was a dealmaker, not a policy wonk. He winked and wisecracked his way through the sessions, taking potshots at the speaker and the governor while refusing to be pinned down on anything. Spitzer labored to assert his place as alpha dog, at one point scolding, "This is *my* room, and we'll play by *my* rules!"

Relations between the two men were rapidly deteriorating. With his boxer's instinct for the nasty jab, Bruno had taken to mocking Spitzer as a "spoiled brat." He gave a speech in which he reminded his audience of Spitzer's declaration that he was a "fucking steamroller," then remarked: "He got the first part right." Bruno ridiculed the very notion that money bought political influence. "If somebody wants to give us a million dollars because they believe in what we do," that's just fine, he declared. "I laugh when I read that people gain access by their contributions."

Spitzer couldn't fathom why anyone entertained such outlandish arguments. As he saw it, Bruno served as Exhibit A of how a politician could be bought by special interests. He funded his lifestyle with campaign money; he made his living by selling influence. Didn't anyone notice that he was under federal investigation for *corruption*?

Publicly, Spitzer keep insisting—absurdly—that the nastiness with Bruno was nothing personal, that they were really "good friends." But Bruno took personally everything Spitzer was doing. He knew Spitzer was trying to remove him from power. He even suspected that the governor was somehow behind the federal investigation of his business dealings. He thought Spitzer was trying to put him behind bars.

For his part, Spitzer had come to view Bruno as the single biggest obstacle to his success in Albany—the living embodiment of the evils the voters had sent him to purge. All the tides were shifting against Bruno: the age of his members, the state's demographics, the federal investigation. Time was on Spitzer's side. By the end of his first term, Bruno would surely no longer be a problem—one way or another. But that wasn't good enough. Says Dopp: "Eliot was too impatient to wait." As Spitzer saw it, he had no choice: "After the budget, he refused to deal, so I said, 'We have to take the senate.'"

Baum had met secretly with a handful of Bruno's members to try to flip the last two seats the Democrats needed. Would they accept a gubernatorial appointment? Wouldn't it be smart to switch parties before a Democrat beat them? One senator—John Bonacic, an old Baum acquaintance from Orange County who'd never liked Bruno—confided that he might accept an economic-development job. But he didn't want to go down in history as the man who turned the senate. Baum thought he'd snagged Jim Alesi, who represented the suburbs ringing Rochester. Alesi was talking about switching parties; he seemed ready to go, at the right moment. In the meantime, he'd asked Spitzer to speak to his local Lions Club. The governor would make the appearance. But Alesi wasn't quite ready to pull the trigger. Says Baum: "It was somewhere between bullshit and a breath away."

Word of this scheming further riled Bruno, even though he was no stranger to the practice of political poaching. (In a scathing 2006 memoir of his years in Albany, former Democratic senator Seymour Lachman recounted how Bruno and Pataki had courted him to switch parties with an offer of "two to three million dollars" in member items. Two other Democrats did switch sides.) In the campaign-finance fight, he'd gone after Spitzer for refusing to voluntarily abide by the limits he was proposing, even while the Republican senate blocked those limits from becoming law. After directing media attention to Spitzer fundraisers—including one where donors were invited for cocktails with the first lady—Bruno ratcheted up his rhetoric, clearly including the "missus," as he came to call her, in his assault. "I'm going to keep calling him and everyone around him a hypocrite," Bruno declared. "It's a fraud." In an e-mail to Baum, Spitzer fumed about Bruno's "fundraising bs," writing: "I want to punch back at him. He is making personal attacks and i am going [to] really go after him at some point."

———

By this time, even Spitzer's staunchest loyalists had begun worrying about how their boss was dealing with Albany. "Today was a day in which I had my own doubts about ES temperament," Dopp wrote in his diary in mid-May. "He becomes incensed that the Senate GOP, which is fighting for its life, isn't more cooperative." Dopp attempted to counsel Spitzer in the art of managing Albany, where self-interest, ego, and personal relationships regularly trumped the empirical merits of an issue. "Boss, you are *smarter* than all these sons of bitches," Dopp told him. "But you use the intelligence to engineer victories for the other guy. You engineer the outcome so they look good, and they want to work with you. If you don't—if you're slam-dunking 'em—they're going to shit all over you."

Spitzer, who considered such machinations ridiculous, responded as though Dopp were from another planet: "Why would I want to do that? Divvying up credit is a tawdry game. They should want to do it because it's the right thing." Baum brought in individual senators for the governor to court, in a bid to bypass Bruno. But Spitzer didn't put much stock in charm, either. "He hated meeting with the legislators," says Baum; he regarded them with contempt, as "a bunch of inbred assholes who never got anything done." Spitzer thought that he could exploit the senate's weak majority by bludgeoning the Republicans. If a popular governor threatened to campaign in their districts, they'd be *forced* to do the right thing. But they reacted like cornered cats. "Instead of making them scared and cooperative," says Dopp, "it made them scared and obstinate."

To a remarkable degree, Spitzer was a creature of habit—in his friends, in his choice of meals, in his speech, even in his tennis game. He seemed to know only one way to play: to *kill* every ball. After a big serve, he rushed the net, looking to put away every volley. After an opponent dropped a lob behind him, he would race to the net again on the next point. And again. And *again*. Spitzer was good—quick, strong, and breathtakingly aggressive. But he could be beaten (and driven crazy in the process) by someone throwing junk.

So it was in Albany. As AG, he could *kill*. He'd come up with the goods, bring suit, threaten to indict, and his opponents would cave. *Game, set, match.* But as governor, everything was different. The law-makers could pass a bill without him; he couldn't pass anything without them. And they didn't play by his rules. The Horace Mann motto—"Great is the truth, and it prevails"—did not apply. All this made Albany a treacherous place for Spitzer. Sheer brainpower and superior education no longer prevailed; he was facing opponents with different skills. When he smashed his serve and raced to the net, they'd hit back—and they knew how to lob and dink. His type of education hadn't prepared him for the likes of Bruno.

Amid the growing vitriol, everyone somehow managed to agree on one piece of legislation advanced by the governor: a tough new law aimed at combating human trafficking and prostitution. The law established stiff penalties for traffickers and an array of social services for their victims. Spitzer had made a special point of adding provisions making it easier to prosecute "sexual tourism," such as the Big Apple case he had brought while attorney general.

A provision of the bill also stiffened penalties for patronizing a prostitute. Johns were rarely charged in New York, but the bill elevated the offense from a Class B to a Class A misdemeanor. This raised the maximum sentence from six months to one year, to provide a stronger deterrent. "Human trafficking is modern-day slavery and among the most repugnant crimes," Spitzer said in a statement as he signed the bill into law. The common ground they had found on this issue, he added, "demonstrates what we can accomplish in Albany when we work together for the public good."

———

From the day he took office, Spitzer and his staff had wrestled with a central philosophical question, of the sort that might have been posed on a political version of *Sex and the City:* can a governor really make a difference—and keep his soul? Or was it only possible to accomplish change by plunging into the muck?

Spitzer had opted for the latter course in closing the budget, and gotten whacked for it. Now he faced that choice again. Even as Spitzer and Bruno bashed each other in the press, their staffs were laboring to assemble an Albany-style package deal. "It is a great tradition in Albany that no important bill ever emerges by itself," *Times* columnist Gail Collins wrote later that year. "It gets mixed with pork and pet projects and lobbyists' to-do lists until Bruno, Democratic Assembly Speaker Sheldon Silver, and the current governor sit down to create one huge hairball of a deal." Spitzer remained viscerally repelled by the idea of backing something he knew was wrong just to get something else he knew was right. Yet this was the grubby inevitability of politics in New York.

By mid-June, with the days winding down in the legislative session, just such a hairball had been prepared, offering something for everyone. Spitzer would get what he desperately wanted: campaign-finance reform, albeit in watered-down form. The assembly would get a legislative pay raise. And Bruno's senate would deliver the payoff for another big patron—New York City Mayor Mike Bloomberg. Bloomberg was promoting "congestion pricing," a controversial plan to cut traffic by charging drivers stiff fees to enter parts of Manhattan during peak hours. The idea had won Spitzer's support. But the legislature had been reluctant, until Bloomberg turned up the heat. It happened that the billionaire mayor—like 1199—was an investor in the senate majority; since the fall of 2006, he'd given its campaign committee $675,000. Now he'd called in his chips, improbably getting the Republicans—almost all from upstate and Long Island—to do his bidding.

To bring Bruno aboard, Spitzer had agreed to a list of pork-barrel projects and an additional property-tax cut, though not as much for either as the Republicans wanted. Dopp opposed the idea, writing in his diary that it was "an awfully expensive bowl of bouillon." But the governor and legislative leaders had all signed on.

After shaking hands with the governor, Bruno had taken the deal back to a private meeting of his conference for the customary rubber stamp. Instead, he'd faced a rebellion. Senate hardliners warned that the package would be heralded as a victory for the governor, making Spitzer even tougher to deal with. The senators also wanted more to take back to their districts, in a form they could brag about to voters: tax cuts and local projects. Spitzer wasn't giving them enough. "We're going to take home a slice of bread, and we need a loaf!" Binghamton's Tom Libous says he told his colleagues. "We're going to get the croutons! *To hell with that!*"

"This is a defining moment for us," Libous railed. "We're not going to give in to the dictatorship! We can't let him push us around!" Spitzer had suggested that the lawmakers could boast of having done the right thing, for their role in passing campaign-finance reform. To the Republicans, that didn't count for much. "In my district, taxes are too high, and there aren't enough jobs," Libous told me later. "Nobody gives a shit about campaign-finance reform except the good-government groups and *The New York Times*."

So the senators blew up the deal, voting to adjourn and leaving town.

Spitzer responded as he usually did: he called a press conference and blasted the legislators. The senate had abandoned its duties, the governor declared, after he had refused Bruno's demand to fund a list of capital projects constituting "pork that was dripping with fat." The governor then hit the road on a statewide "Where's Waldo?" tour, with a PowerPoint presentation featuring the empty senate chamber, images of the absent senators, and a list of the pressing items of public business they'd left behind.

This time, the press mostly sided with Spitzer, blaming Bruno for the gridlock. A *Daily News* columnist admiringly quoted the governor as saying he was engaged in "war" and wouldn't leave the battlefield "without a lot of scars." This prompted a pair of e-mails to Dopp from Pataki's former communications director, Mike McKeon, who had gone to work as a political consultant. "Nice comeback from tough week. Scars for everyone. . . . Truth is these guys are not used to someone who fights to the finish. We caved way too often, way too soon. So I live vicariously through you. Thanks for that."

The Spitzer administration had learned at least one lesson from its first half-year in Albany, Dopp told McKeon: "We've concluded that nothing really gets done without a crisis, a fight, or a scandal."

———

The governor's early tribulations had spawned palace intrigue by two disgruntled members of his staff: Constantine and Peter Pope. Both men, with their long-standing ties to Spitzer, felt alienated and excluded from his inner circle—and were gunning for Baum. They blamed him not only for marginalizing them, but for virtually all the administration's woes. Both thought they could do a better job.

Pope, who had forged the workers' compensation deal, was so unhappy he was already threatening to quit. Constantine vented directly to the governor in one of his long, blunt e-mails, prepared before meeting Spitzer and their wives for a birthday dinner at the Carlyle Hotel. After skewering two key gubernatorial appointees—one was "a schmoozer devoid of substance," whom Spitzer should consider firing; another was "very very smart but very bad at her job"—Constantine directed his screed at the "disorder on the second floor," where, he asserted, "nobody is in charge."

"All these bad stories go to the same source," Constantine wrote. "Rich is great at what he does but there is a lot that he simply does not do, creating havoc for the rest of us." Baum was a good behind-the-scenes strategist, Constantine argued, but in over his head as a manager. He reaffirmed his refusal to answer to Baum, declaring, "As of now I no longer report to him."

Within the administration, this view was not widely held. Baum had never run such a large operation, and the top deputies he hired hadn't either. But he was generally liked and respected. Nocenti, the governor's counsel, says Baum was "an excellent secretary," performing a "completely thankless task. You're responsible for everything that goes wrong and get credit for nothing that goes right. I think he did all of that very well."

Nonetheless, word of the conflict found its way into the *New York Post*, through leaks from unnamed "insiders" claiming that the administration was in "chaos" and "torn by rivalries." Baum was described as "invisible," Dopp as having "usurped" an outsized role by dealing with legislators himself. The two men were said to be "allied" against another "faction" led by Constantine.

Spitzer was furious about the story, which had obviously come from within the chamber. And he was certainly aware that two of his senior aides were unhappy with the state of affairs. ("Lloyd wanted to be the governor," Spitzer told me later. "And Peter wanted to be the secretary.") But he did nothing to stop the bickering. Spitzer could unleash a shocking stream of profanity at another elected official, but he couldn't bring himself to scold—much less fire—a member of his own staff. "He couldn't deliver bad news," says Turner. "He was just constitutionally incapable of it. He thought everybody was doing their best job for him."

The governor's outbursts had fed the notion that he needed a kick-ass personality to rein him in. To be sure, Baum wasn't that. He was cerebral, a bit shy, and didn't throw his weight around. Baum had a working wife and two young children; he got to his desk by 7 A.M., but went home at night to spend time with them before the kids went to bed. Baum was the sort of man who would arrange a dinner meeting at an Albany steakhouse, then wait twenty minutes for a table instead of telling the hostess that he was the top deputy to the governor. Suggests one longtime Spitzer associate: "He was not the asshole Eliot needed."

Baum thought he was doing everything humanly possible to manage his boss. For every Spitzer outburst that had erupted into headlines, there'd been a dozen more that he and Dopp had intercepted. Spitzer had become far harder to control—it had never been like this in the AG's office. "He was just at a level of volatility that was unnatural for anyone and unlike him." And the staff sniping was getting worse. Constantine and Pope, who had no day-to-day management role, were openly working to undermine him. "I hated it," says Baum. "It wasn't easy to keep people focused on important tasks when the governor's 'best friend' was telling people that I wasn't up to the job."

For a respite, Baum sometimes paused from his duties running the state government of New York to peruse the animal videos on the *National Geographic* website. Baum had a fascination with the oddities of nature. One of his favorites was a three-minute film titled "Shark vs. Octopus." It showed a surprising encounter between a menacing spiny dogfish shark and a giant Pacific octopus. The shark, a voracious predator, was prowling through the water, presumably preparing to make short work of the octopus, which was lying low near a pile of rocks. But as the shark swooped in, the wily octopus snatched it with its eight sucker-covered arms, wrapped the writhing killer into its boneless body, and held tight until the shark was dead.

Chapter 10: "Bangbang"

INCREASINGLY, THE PREFERRED VEHICLE FOR ATTACKS ON THE governor was a single Albany journalist: Fredric Uberall Dicker of the *New York Post*, sometimes known as "FUD." Within the capital press corps, the sixty-three-year-old Dicker wasn't the fairest or the most enterprising or even the most accurate reporter around. But he was surely the most influential.

Dicker was a crusty veteran of nearly thirty years in Albany, a self-described "equal-opportunity prick." His column, published every Monday, invariably relied on anonymous sources and the breathless tone of tabloid scandal. It was usually one-sided, bereft of anything resembling perspective, and frequently did someone's dirty work. A reformed social-ist who wore a beret and drove a Porsche, Dicker didn't hesitate to bully bureaucrats in his self-appointed role as advocate for the little guy. When a State Police flack didn't respond to his queries rapidly enough, Dicker warned that if he continued "to duck and dodge," his "pattern of behav-ior as a 'public information officer' will be the subject of a future article in the *New York Post*."

What made Dicker so powerful was how his voice was amplified: by his paper's screaming headlines; by his role as host of an Albany radio show (broadcast from his statehouse office) and as a local TV commenta-tor; and by his influence over the rest of the press corps, which inevitably echoed his scoops in more muted tones. What made Dicker so feared was that he was venomously fickle. He abruptly turned on his heroes, unfairly tearing them down after unfairly building them up. Romancing

Dicker was dangerous. When the love affair reached its inevitable end, he wouldn't just break your heart—he'd tear it out and eat it.

So it was with the governor. Through the inauguration, Dicker was smitten. "He gives you the sense of brilliance," he declared as Spitzer was preparing to run. Later, he'd urged the new governor to wage "an unrelenting war" on Bruno and Silver, take on the unions, spend more on education, and cut property taxes. "The good news," Dicker wrote, "is that Spitzer, who has a streak of toughness and moral righteousness that brought some of the most important leaders of Wall Street to heel, is gearing up for the battle." The governor had done many of those very things during his early months. Yet by midyear, Dicker was writing about Spitzer with an angry sense of betrayal. It was Dicker who broke the "steamroller" story; Dicker who mocked him as "Mr. Softee"; Dicker who wrote about the administration's internal "chaos." Spitzer—who had previously reveled in Dicker's praise—came to regard him as "mindlessly rabid."

Some of the governor's frustration with his treatment by the media naturally fell on his communications director. *Why didn't anyone in Albany care about the issues? How had the coverage turned critical so fast?* Dopp's skillful touch had worked wonders during the AG years—everyone had loved Spitzer except his targets. But a governor inevitably made people unhappy; he became the target. Spitzer had insisted he understood this new reality. But it clearly gnawed at him. Getting pounded in the media—when he'd done so much, fought so hard, meant so well—was almost more than he could take. "He didn't expect that he was no longer going to be revered by the press," says Peter Pope. "He became very angry that we continued to do good things, and we got no credit for it." Silda, far more thin-skinned, complained bitterly. She was incredulous when Dopp told her that Eliot would always get hammered at budget time: "You mean, we're going to have to deal with this *every year*?" She gave press secretary Christine Anderson, Dopp's deputy, a book on political messaging.

As Spitzer saw it, his conflicts with Bruno constituted a battle between right and wrong. But the Albany press corps didn't treat it that way—or even as a collision of opposing ideologies and policy prescriptions. Instead, they played it as a clash of personalities—"an asshole fight," Dopp called it—that made Bruno seem the governor's equal. The senate, meanwhile, was doing everything it could to slow Spitzer down.

This fueled a growing determination in Spitzer's camp to portray Bruno as they saw him—a sleazy man standing in the way of reform, doing the wrong thing, for the wrong reasons.

———

Bruno's fondness for state aircraft presented just such an opportunity. The story of officeholders using government planes and helicopters was a hardy perennial for statehouse reporters. Under the best of circumstances, it conveyed the image of an imperial public servant living large on the taxpayer's dime. Where the travel involved personal or political purposes—airlifting family, personal vacations, or attendance at political events—the tale readily took on the stink of scandal. "Air Cuomo" stories, about the state fleet transporting one governor's wife and children (including future attorney general Andrew Cuomo), had inevitably been followed by stories about another—"Air Pataki." Dicker had written many of them.

Spitzer had been careful to avoid such tarnish. But Bruno hadn't. Shortly after the election, the senate majority leader privately sought Spitzer's assurance that he wouldn't be "jerked around" over access to the aircraft, which fell under the governor's control. (Pataki had periodically grounded him.) Spitzer assured Bruno that he didn't consider the fleet the governor's personal toy; the senator would be welcome to use it as long as he followed the rules.

As generally understood, those rules were remarkably lax. Based on an informal ethics opinion dating back to 1995, they allowed an officeholder to use the aircraft for personal and political purposes if he conducted *any* "bona fide" state business during the trip. In theory, he could meet the legal requirement by holding a ten-minute government meeting in a hotel lobby before leaving to spend the rest of the night at a political fundraiser in the ballroom. A round-trip chopper flight between Albany and Manhattan—the senator's customary route—cost taxpayers about $4,000 a pop. Bruno also typically arranged for a plainclothes State Police investigator, paid about $70 an hour, to chauffeur him around New York in a government car.

After taking over, Spitzer's administration had sought to impose a higher standard. It drafted a new form requiring officials to legally certify that they needed the aircraft for state business. Chief of Staff Marlene Turner, who oversaw state aircraft use, had unilaterally decided she wouldn't approve a flight that didn't meet her personal smell test—a trip needed to be "more than predominantly" for government purposes. She'd make this determination based on details about the officeholder's ground schedule during the trip, which the new form also required. This process led Turner to reject several aircraft requests from the lieutenant governor, incurring Paterson's enduring wrath. But Bruno's staff had refused to provide his itineraries, insisting that it was a separation-of-powers issue. Instead, his office usually just certified that the aircraft was needed for "legislative business meetings." After conferring with Spitzer, Baum told Turner to approve Bruno's requests anyway. The governor didn't want to pick this fight.

That spring, Dicker had done some nosing around about officeholders' use of the state fleet. Eager to get ahead of the story, Dopp began gathering information about what reporters might find if they filed a public-records request. But he didn't just check on his boss—he also asked for travel records on Bruno. And he didn't seek them directly. Because the air fleet now fell under the operating control of the State Police (it had been transferred from the Department of Environmental Conservation in 1997), Dopp requested the records through assistant homeland security secretary Bill Howard, who worked in the governor's office and supervised the State Police.

Howard, forty-six, was a veteran of two decades in state government. Acting chief of staff during the last stretch of the Pataki administration, he'd suspected that he wouldn't last long on the second floor after Spitzer arrived, and had lined up a backup job in the state university system. But he wanted badly to remain in the governor's office, and his familiarity with the bureaucracy had made him valuable to Spitzer's Albany neophytes. By May 1, Baum had decided to keep him on. Howard responded with the zeal of the converted. "Thanks for today," he wrote Baum after getting the news. "Really very honored to have the opportunity to stay. Won't let you down." When the *New York Post* ran its story about the administration's "chaos," Howard e-mailed the secretary that the story was "bs," telling him to "count me as a member of 'Team Baum.'" Howard and Dopp, both Civil War buffs, had also become friendly. They'd collaborated to feed Dicker a story about how Pataki had stiffed the state on a $16,000 bill for leasing a private jet. When Dicker expressed interest, Dopp e-mailed Howard: "Think he's on the hook." After the story ran, Pataki's political action committee paid in full.

So when Dopp wanted to find out about Bruno's travels—a subject of ongoing interest within the administration—Howard eagerly took on the project. Howard had his own history with the senator on this issue. He had incurred Bruno's wrath by denying him use of the aircraft under Pataki. He'd also supported the State Police drivers' refusal to use their lights and sirens while chauffeuring Bruno, who didn't like waiting in Manhattan traffic. Now, after getting Dopp's request, Howard dealt directly with acting State Police Superintendent Preston Felton, a twenty-five-year veteran of the force. Felton, in turn, handled the matter personally, calling subordinates in the field to gather information. He then funneled what he had to Howard, who immediately passed it on to Dopp, establishing an information pipeline.

This information gathering began in earnest on May 17, when Howard picked up news that grabbed Dopp's attention: Bruno was flying that day to Manhattan for a political fundraiser—the annual Republican Party state committee dinner at the Sheraton Hotel, featuring John McCain and Rudy Giuliani. In a filing with the governor's office, Bruno had already certified that he was using the state chopper for "legislative business meetings." But Howard found out that the only meeting listed on the schedule Bruno's office had given the State Police was a midday stop at C. V. Starr—the insurance company that now served as the base for Spitzer's old enemy, Hank Greenberg. Greenberg was also a major donor to the Republican Party.

Dopp quickly drafted a proposed statement for immediate release to the press:

STATEMENT BY DARREN DOPP, COMMUNICATIONS DIRECTOR FOR THE GOVERNOR, REGARDING SENATOR BRUNO'S USE OF STATE AIRCRAFT

Our office has received inquiries regarding Senate Majority Leader Joe Bruno's use of state aircraft.

Our policy regarding use of the aircraft is clear: The state plane and helicopter may be used only for official state business.

The Senator makes periodic requests for use of a state helicopter and did so recently for use today. At the time he made the

request, the Senator attested that he and his staff required transportation to New York City for "legislative meetings."

Based upon this claim, use of the state helicopter was granted
for the Senator and three staff members to depart late this morning
and return early tomorrow morning.

Today, our office learned that Senator Bruno's "legislative
meetings" were to be held at C.V. Starr & Co. at 12:30 pm and the
Sheraton Hotel at 3:30 pm. We have asked the Senator to verify
that these meetings involve official state business.

Subsequent to receiving his reply, we will determine what action is necessary and appropriate.

At 1:45 P.M., Dopp fired off the draft to Baum. The secretary was a
bit taken aback—this was playing hardball. "Wow. I'll be back in a bit,"
he e-mailed Dopp. "My only concern is it invites scrutiny of es, but I think
we're pretty airtight."

They spoke to the governor later that afternoon. The discussion came
as Spitzer remained angry about Bruno's attacks on the "missus," and one
day after he'd vented to Baum about the senator's "fundraising bs" and
his desire to "punch back at him." Nonetheless, Spitzer and Baum instructed Dopp to hold his fire. The rules on aircraft use were so lax that
it would be almost impossible to prove Bruno violated the law, even if the
press coverage would make him look bad. Spitzer hadn't given up on getting things done during the legislative session; it wasn't worth riling
Bruno. Frustrated, Dopp e-mailed his spiked statement to press secretary
Anderson, with the notation "Argh."

But he wasn't about to let the matter drop. Information continued to
flow through his pipeline from the State Police, bringing news about the
majority leader's travels. Dopp not only received aircraft records and
ground schedules that Bruno's office had provided to the State Police, but
bulletins on changes in the senator's plans originating from the investigator driving him around. When Bruno-provided itineraries couldn't be
located for two of the trips, Felton directed the officers to write down
where they had picked up and dropped off their passenger during the day.
These brief reports—reconstructions of the missing schedules—were also
sent on to the governor's office. Howard came to refer to Bruno as "the
flying senator."

Dopp would later explain he was merely monitoring the situation, gathering information to respond to impending open-records requests from reporters, though none would actually arrive in writing for weeks. He also continued to agitate within the administration for referring the matter for formal investigation, arguing that if Bruno really was misusing state aircraft, Spitzer could be criticized for letting him get away with it. He'd discussed the matter with two chamber lawyers, David Nocenti and Peter Pope.

On June 3, Albany *Times Union* reporter Jim Odato reported that the federal criminal investigation of Bruno had broadened to include some suspiciously lucrative deals the senator had made trading Thoroughbred horses. "I guess we know why Bruno's folks have been so jumpy of late," Dopp e-mailed Baum. "Think a travel story would fit nicely in the mix."

Howard chimed in, too: "Bruno got hammered pretty good. . . . In my gut I expected charges to be filed in the spring. The story suggests that we may not be too far off. He can't survive the filing of a criminal complaint."

"I agree," Baum replied. "Doubt he would resign seat but he couldn't stay as leader."

"The impending travel stuff implies more problems. . . ." Howard wrote. "I think timing right for that move."

Odato was also a natural to expose Bruno's use of the state aircraft. Everyone in government read his paper, he had a good track record with investigative stories, he'd been tough on the majority leader, and he'd written about travel abuses in the past. Dopp had also known Odato for more than twenty years. In fact, he'd reported to Odato on his first newspaper job, as a cub reporter at the Binghamton *Evening Press*.

On June 25, Dopp began preparing a one-page, single-spaced memo, with the words "FOR BACKGROUND ONLY" at the top. The memo summed up his belief that Bruno had abused the state air fleet. During eleven trips to New York City, Dopp noted, the senator had attended political events "on at least four occasions." Bruno's itineraries showed that "the primary if not the sole purpose of these trips at state taxpayer expense was to attend political events. . . . A close examination of the facts in this situation may reveal that there was little or no legislative business and that the Majority Leader may be guilty of both misrepresenting himself and misusing state assets." Spitzer's travel records, on the other hand, showed that he used the aircraft for events "clearly connected to his official duties," Dopp wrote. He attached a raft of documents supporting his conclusions, including flight manifests for Bruno and Spitzer, the travel schedules obtained by Howard, invitations to the political fundraisers Bruno had attended, even a listing of Greenberg-related donations to the Republican Party.

Dopp would later insist that he had prepared this material to brief Nocenti, the governor's counsel. But Nocenti, a friend of Dopp's since they worked together in the Cuomo administration, later denied he had ever seen it. It was, of course, precisely the sort of "background" memo a press aide would use in dealing with a reporter to try to shape a story.

Dopp then advised Spitzer and Baum that the long-anticipated open-records request was finally about to arrive. With the end of the legislative session, Dopp explained, Odato was once again after the documents, which were already gathered. In fact, Dopp was ready to give the reporter records he wouldn't even request. (Says *Times Union* investigations editor Bob Port: "It was expressed to Jim that if he made a FOIL request, it could be promptly dealt with.")

By this point, Spitzer was no longer worried about disrupting legislative relations. Bruno's senate had just welshed on the big end-of-session deal and bolted from Albany. The governor was back in war mode.

As Spitzer later recalled events, when Dopp came in to see him on June 27, he asked his communications director to confirm that all the documents Odato would get were public records, subject to the state's Freedom of Information Law. Dopp assured him they were. In that case, Spitzer says he replied, they had no choice but to turn them over. He says he told Dopp something approximating, "Screw it, go ahead."

But Dopp has a more vivid recollection. He says that he met privately with Spitzer in his office after Baum advised him the governor was ready to release the records; he wanted to confirm that Spitzer was prepared for the ugliness that would surely follow. Dopp recalls their exchange this way:

"Boss, you're okay with the release of the plane records?"

Spitzer: "Yeah, do it."

"Are you sure? Joe will probably be pissed."

"*Fuck him!*" Dopp says the governor replied, red-faced and spitting out his coffee. "He's a piece of *shit*! *Shove it up his ass with a red-hot poker!*"

Dopp says he watched Spitzer with amazement, then quietly asked, "*Sideways*, boss?"

In politics, even a run-of-the-mill scandal can take on a life of its own, careening wildly in dangerous directions. So it was with the story of "the flying senator."

At the start, it played out precisely as the governor and his team intended. On Sunday, July 1, Odato's article led the front page of the *Times Union*, beneath a headline that was sure to provoke public outrage—STATE FLIES BRUNO TO FUNDRAISERS—with the subhead "Taxpayers finance trips of Senate majority leader to New York City political events." Citing records "obtained through a request under the Freedom of Information Law," the article closely tracked the analysis in Dopp's "background" memo. Bruno had used "taxpayer-funded state aircraft to fly to political fundraisers in Manhattan while certifying he was on state business"; his limited "business schedule" included a session with Hank Greenberg, "a generous contributor to state Republican campaigns"; Bruno's conduct could be compared to the Hevesi scandal; and Spitzer's use of the state air fleet raised far fewer questions. Bruno's staff stonewalled when asked his itinerary while traveling. But a spokesman insisted that the senator required police escort because he faced regular death threats "based on what people read in the *Times Union* and other negative reports."

Ron Ochrym, an Albany lobbyist and old friend, e-mailed Dopp that morning: "It is like the game Battleship—E-4-DIRECT HIT!!!"

The story appeared just four days after Dopp handed Odato the records. In the interim, Spitzer had been checking in expectantly on its progress, calling his communications chief at home every morning, right at ten minutes after seven. On Sunday, after scanning the *Times Union*, Dopp e-mailed Spitzer and Baum at 6:19 A.M., expressing his pleased reaction.

Spitzer, at his farmhouse in Pine Plains, needed to drive into town to get the papers. "How does it look?" he asked, writing, as usual, from his private BlackBerry.

"Gotta see to believe," Dopp e-mailed back. "Think we need to move quickly to refer it to proper authorities."

"The line about death threats and the [*Times Union*] will be taught in classes for years to come," wrote Baum.

"Will other media pick up on Bruno story?" the governor asked.

"Working it now," Dopp replied.

"Bruno story is very bad for him I think," Baum e-mailed the governor. "Really puts him in a bad spot. Can't believe it won't have some legs."

Spitzer's team sprung into action to make sure that it did.

First, they encouraged a media feeding frenzy. Dopp sent his two top press staffers a memo on what they could say—on and off the record—when reporters called. For the record, the governor's office would express its shock—*shock!*—at the paper's "findings," calling the revelations "very troubling" and adding, "We are reviewing the situation carefully to determine the appropriate course of action." Off the record? This was "a very serious situation involving possible violations of law," and they were likely to move "very quickly"—perhaps the next day—to refer the matter to the "appropriate authorities." The press secretaries could also whisper that the State Police, while still checking, knew of *no* death threats against Bruno—and that his claims suggested he was trying to justify an "improper arrangement."

"Be sure to read today's *TU*," Dopp e-mailed Liz Benjamin of the *Daily News* that morning when she checked in. "Bruno thing is serious."

"Re flights?" she e-mailed back. "Doesn't gov have to sign off on use of state plane?"

"Yes, we give sign off," Dopp replied. "But only after getting it in writing that its for official biz. Joe made written claim that it was for 'legislative meetings.' That may be false statement. Violation of law . . . Need to watch carefully."

Meanwhile, Spitzer's deputies weighed how to get someone to investigate Bruno's aircraft use—without looking like they were behind it. They could refer it to Cuomo for a civil inquiry by the AG's office, or—if they wanted to play hardball—they could send it to the DA in either Albany or Manhattan, seeking a criminal probe. In an e-mail, Baum suggested a little prosecutor-shopping: "Couldn't we call around to da/ag today or in morn so we're in position to say x has asked us for materials and we're cooperating? That way we're not instigating or deciding if criminal?"

By midday Monday, Nocenti had made the rounds and e-mailed an update to Baum and Dopp. The top deputy in the Manhattan DA's office, he reported, "says 'requesting' documents is unusual; people usual[ly] refer things to them. He needs to talk to Morgenthau. Cuomo is willing to do 'whatever we want,' but would MUCH prefer not to be the only person requesting—i.e. if Morgenthau doesn't 'request,' Cuomo won't want to either." By afternoon, it was official: both Cuomo and the Albany DA, David Soares, would look into the matter. When the AP reported that the governor's office had initiated the inquiries, Spitzer's press secretary denied it: "The DA and AG asked us for the documents. We did not refer or make the request."

All was going well. In the executive chamber, staffers were already referring to the story as "Brunogate." Then the story started to turn, transforming the governor's carefully targeted burn into an out-of-control inferno. Fred Dicker had shifted the wind.

———

Though the *Post* columnist had clearly soured on Spitzer, Dopp—who had been dealing with Dicker for more than twenty years—labored to maintain good relations. During June, the two men traded friendly e-mails about their outdoor exploits, mixing personal chat with Dicker's "return" for scoops. Dopp, who loved to unwind at his remote upstate cabin by chopping wood and writing poetry, recounted a "fine day in the country. Highlight was halting the car to let a little Amish girl walk her flock of turkeys across the road!!"

Dicker—under the heading "bangbang"—excitedly described his visit "with my cousin and his friend, who has a 200-yard shooting range in front of his house. In addition, he's an ex-Marine rifle instructor who LOVES M1s. Let me just say I had fun today." The newspaperman even offered to bring by "a real cool FBI 'terrorist' target" to give to Dopp's son. Dopp gently labored to adjust Dicker's scorn for the governor ("you're killing me with the boss"), offering flattery for his radio program ("great show") while trying to peel him away from Bruno: "Wouldn't put much stock in Joe's comments of late. Imprecise is the nicest way to characterize it."

Dicker's first reaction to Odato's article was dismissive. He'd never liked getting beat, especially on a subject he regarded as his own. "Sounds like a wild story," he e-mailed Dopp. "Legislative leaders including governors have used state aircraft to go to nycity for decades for official business, with occasionally political events thrown in. Where's the story here unless it can be shown bruno flew ONLY for political purposes?" Dicker, of course, had cranked out countless "exclusives" decrying how governors cooked up "official business" to justify flights to political events—even though it didn't violate New York's lax rules.

"Think you're right about the history," Dopp wrote back. "Issue is whether Joe crossed the line."

"What evidence is there that he may have?"

"Think TU has inside source," Dopp confided mysteriously. "Odato implied there's a lot more to come."

———

"Bruno went nuts on Dicker."

When the senate majority leader launched his counterattack Monday morning, during an appearance on his favorite Albany radio show, Dopp sounded the alarms in an e-mail.

Bruno left no doubt about whom he blamed for the exposé on his travels. "What Eliot Spitzer is trying to do is destroy me," he declared. Bruno cast the battle in class terms—pitting "an overgrown rich spoiled brat" against a kid who grew up "in the toughest part of Glens Falls, next to the boxcars," where bullies would "just punch you right in the mouth because you were Italian." He regaled reporters about a hitherto undisclosed confrontation, in which Spitzer had supposedly gotten "eight inches" from his face and told him: "I am going to hit you so hard you are going to go down and you'll *never* get up."

Dopp, who insisted the administration had done nothing more than respond to an open-records request, pointed out holes in the senator's story. Why wouldn't Bruno discuss his schedule, and explain what government business required a state helicopter and car? Why the sudden recollection of a fresh Spitzer outburst? Why, if he *really* faced security threats, had he never asked for police escort while in Albany? This was all part of a classic attack-when-under-attack response, Dopp told reporters. Some—such as Liz Benjamin of the *Daily News*—were sympathetic. "You're asking me to explain to you the thinking of a 78-year-old guy who is devoid of logic?" she e-mailed Dopp. "Um. No can do."

But Dicker was smelling a rat. He focused on the half-page itineraries Dopp had released documenting Bruno's ground travels, demanding to see identical paperwork the troopers had kept on Spitzer and Paterson, even though they routinely made public their daily schedules. Dopp needed to produce identical stop-by-stop logs the state troopers kept on *them*, Dicker asserted. "Otherwise looks like selective surveillance."

On July 5, the *Post* plastered Dicker's political espionage theory on its front page:

POLICE STATE: GOV SICCED COPS ON JOE

Gov. Spitzer targeted state Senate Majority Leader Joseph Bruno for an unprecedented State Police surveillance program that led to allegations Bruno improperly used a state helicopter for political purposes, an investigation by the Post has found.

No other state official, including Spitzer and Lt. Gov. David Paterson, was singled out for the type of detailed record-keeping the State Police maintained on Bruno, the state's most powerful Republican, official records show.

Bruno publicly demanded an immediate criminal investigation. "This is like something you'd expect in a Third World country, where some dictator has his enemies followed to see how they could either do something to them or disgrace them," the senator declared. "This is dangerous in a free country."

The governor's office denounced Dicker's story as "grossly inaccurate." The spying notion was, of course, ridiculous; Bruno was screaming about the disclosure of how he had used public resources. No one would be talking about spying if the aircraft were still being managed by the civilian bureaucrats in the Department of Environmental Conservation instead of the State Police. But Dicker had changed the dynamic. This was no longer simply a stink about Bruno's misuse of the helicopter. Now there was a competing narrative about the governor's political dirty tricks, quickly popularized as "Troopergate."

———

Bruno had become Spitzer's white whale. After the senator walked away from their big end-of-session legislative deal, the governor had resolved to bypass him whenever possible, reasoning (as he put it in e-mails to Baum) that "it will further undermine Bruno if we go around him." He was desperate to get away from "wasting time on the legislature"—to show how he could govern independently through state agencies, as New York's chief executive.

Within the Spitzer camp, there was a growing sense that Bruno had gone off the deep end. Odato's story had exposed him as a hypocrite—attacking Spitzer's fundraising and blocking campaign-finance reform, then flying off to fat-cat Republican events at taxpayer expense. When Bruno responded by unloading on Spitzer, the governor e-mailed Baum, vacationing in Florida with his family: "Have u been made aware of bruno's inane behavior today?" Baum counseled Spitzer to begin calling individual senators, "just to make them feel there's a way out of the madness and you're the reasonable one. . . . I'd just commiserate about how crazy bruno is." When Dicker's 'spying' story appeared, the governor wrote Marlene Turner that Bruno had "gone nuts. Only dicker will still carry his pablum." But the problem couldn't be dismissed—the ugly stories kept coming. Cuomo had already expanded his investigation to include the incendiary charge that administration "thugs"—as Bruno put it—had misused the State Police for political purposes. The state inspector general was conducting her own investigation. (She would ultimately defer to Cuomo's findings.)

In his diary, Dopp noted his "grudging admiration" for the way Bruno's PR team had fought back. The Republican's lieutenants had even begun probing for turncoats inside the governor's staff. One called Howard, the former Pataki staffer who had obtained the Bruno travel documents. Howard quickly reported the contact to Baum and Dopp: "Very interesting. Trying to split me away from the Administration." Balboni was approached, too, after being dispatched unsuccessfully as an emissary to the Bruno camp. "Um . . . Don't think they are in the mood to talk," he e-mailed Baum. "It was suggested to me that I 'demonstrate my independence and call for an investigation of who ordered the Superintendent to conduct the surveillance.' (Since State Police falls under my directorate.) Yeah. Right."

Spitzer's top aides grew concerned. "Bruno out of control. . . . At what point does Dicker stop?" wondered Turner. Budget Director Paul Francis wrote Baum in Florida: "I do hope this forest fire burns itself out (or Bruno gets indicted) soon." Baum had spent part of his vacation talking strategy with Spitzer from the beach. "Think it stays hot for a while because bruno needs that to obscure the story and the potential prosecution," Baum e-mailed Francis. "Need eliot to stay calm but not sure doable. I'm completely sick of the legislature. Glad I got away and wish I'd been around."

"I hope we can keep ES calm," Francis replied. "I realize this is not your responsibility alone, and that ES is who he is, and to some extent can't be changed. But there is a real risk that the cumulative weight of Bruno's charges—and ES's going toe to toe in the mudfight—will define ES in a way that he doesn't want to be defined. . . . Bruno may be committing suicide through indictment or otherwise—in which case we should get out of the way. But if Bruno survives, we've created an impression that he is the key to ES's success. . . . I know it's easier saying these things to you than it is to ES. Is he open to discussion on this, or just too mad to see straight about it?"

Publicly, Spitzer insisted that Bruno was the only angry one. But it sure didn't look that way. One day after his spying story, Dicker was hot on the trail of a new "exclusive" about Spitzer's private conversation with John Flanagan, a Republican senator from Long Island—one of the lawmakers the governor had called in his effort to prove that he was "the reasonable one." according to the senator, during their talk, the governor had called Bruno "a senile piece of shit who is under federal investigation." This juicy tidbit immediately made its way to Bruno—and then to Dicker. Dicker informed Dopp that according to Bruno's spokesman, the majority leader was "very upset" at Spitzer's remark. Did the administration have any comment?

Dopp denied it. Spitzer's calls to senators "were affirmative," he replied. "In fact, he specifically told them that he had not and would not make personal attacks on Senator Bruno, no matter what the Senator was saying about him." Indeed, Spitzer, in his calls to senators, had *boasted* of his public restraint. As he later described it to Dopp and Baum, what he'd actually told Flanagan was this: "Joe's been running around saying all kinds of things about me to the press. I *could* have responded by calling Joe *a senile piece of shit who's under federal investigation*. But I *didn't*."

Dicker's story, minus this too-cute gubernatorial nuance, ran on July 7—GOV's 'OLD' LINE A JOE BLOW. "In the latest round of the Statehouse Smackdown, the potty-mouthed governor" had "stunned" a "well-known state senator"—Flanagan went unnamed—with his "harsh and inflammatory language," Dicker wrote. Bruno's spokesman was quoted expressing the majority leader's "shock" at "how desperate the governor has gotten." All this made the *Daily News* "desperate" to land an interview with the governor, Liz Benjamin advised Baum in an e-mail. "I think the rationale is: if post will be mouthpiece of bruno we are willing to retaliate." The *News* got its one-on-one.

But Dicker just kept firing, writing that Dopp had lied and changed his story. Robert Bellafiore, a former Pataki press secretary, e-mailed Spitzer's spokesman to offer his support.

"I guess everyone who sits here hits a rocky period at times. No?" Dopp asked.

"Very true," wrote Bellafiore. "Would it help if I told you this seems rockier than most?"

———

Just seven months into a four-year term, the heady hopes for the Spitzer administration already seemed an ancient memory. In a peculiar interview with the *Times*' two Albany reporters, Danny Hakim and Nicholas Confessore, the governor talked about the toll the job had taken—on his wife. The fight with Bruno had gotten so ugly that Silda wondered whether it was all worth it, he told the *Times*. "You know what she's been telling me? She looks at me and says: 'Do you really want this stuff? And do you want this for your kids and do you want them to see this stuff?' That's the hard part. She says, you know: 'What was wrong with going into the family business? That wouldn't have been so bad.'" Spitzer insisted the conflict hadn't caused *him* any doubts—"but that's Silda's view."

Virtually everyone around Spitzer regarded this plaintive interview as a disaster—a self-pitying bid for sympathy that made him look weak and indecisive. Spitzer seemed to be playing Hamlet on the public stage— *Do I really want to be governor? Do I not want to be governor?*—while blaming his wife for his ambivalence.

Silda was furious. "Never express hesitation or doubt," she scolded her husband. "Our life and soul are invested in this." The truth was that Silda had found her position as first lady enormously gratifying, after more than a decade of shelving her own ambitions. She had taken on three challenging projects—promoting "green" buildings, encouraging community service, and trying to stem the population exodus from upstate. Eliot's comments not only made him look silly, but made her seem unsupportive. She insisted the words her husband quoted had never come out of her mouth. "You know me," she told Chrissy Stevens, her twenty-two-year-old deputy chief of staff. "I would *never* say that." Three weeks later, Stevens was in Pine Plains with the Spitzer family, in the kitchen with Elyssa, helping squeeze oranges for juice, when Silda saw the remarks in question repeated in a *Times* op-ed column. A door-slamming confrontation with the governor ensued. Says Stevens: "Her frustration was very clear."

To those close to the couple, it was apparent that their new roles had put a serious strain on the Spitzer marriage. Eliot was short with Silda, sometimes in public. Silda had felt the growing distance, and responded by throwing herself deeper into her duties. Always a perfectionist, she worked long hours, often late into the night. Says Stevens: "She was hopeful that if she could help him this way, that things would be better between them and he would be proud of her. . . . She was really trying to pretend things were the way they were before."

Spitzer had always seemed a happy warrior during his days as attorney general, exulting to his staff after slam-dunking a CEO, *"This job is really fun!"* But being governor *wasn't* fun. After half a year, he seemed different—brooding and joyless. "He was an incredibly optimistic, positive person," says Baum. "He just became darker." Spitzer had always been able to succeed by being smarter and working harder than anyone else. But in Albany, that didn't seem to matter. He kept charging into walls, sleeping less than ever, rarely pausing for a break. And Silda was right there with him, urging her husband on.

———

"Gov tells reporters of toll on family," Darren Dopp wrote in his diary on July 10. "Silda complains to Christine about lack of message. Acquaintances call to inquire about my well-being. I'm reminded of what [Edmund] Burke said, 'Do not despair, but if you do, work on in despair."

Stunned at finding himself a media target, Dopp was struggling to do just that. Everyone seemed to care far more about how he'd handled public records than about how Bruno had wasted public money. And Cuomo's two-pronged investigation—one part Bruno, one part Spitzer—was moving remarkably fast. The AG had made clear from the start that he wasn't eager to step into this quagmire; now he seemed determined to race to judgment.

When public officials become the target of an investigation, they inevitably face a tension: should they respond more like white-collar defendants—or politicians? The first strategy, anticipating legal perils around every corner, is typically adversarial: it dictates locking down, saying and releasing as little as possible. But that poses political danger, risking the media and public outrage that results from anything smacking of cover-up. In this highly charged case, unfolding in the political hothouse of Albany, Spitzer placed his chips on the white-collar strategy. As point men for handling Troopergate, he designated as "special counsel" three administration lawyers: Peter Pope, Lloyd Constantine, and First Deputy Secretary Sean Patrick Maloney, who was new to the Spitzer camp.

Baum had protested the involvement of Pope and Constantine, who were clearly disgruntled. "They'll use it," he told Spitzer on hearing the news. "People you care about will get hurt, and I don't think we'll all be here when it's over."

"Well, it's done," the governor replied.

As they reviewed internal e-mails to turn over to Cuomo's prosecutorial SWAT team, Pope and Maloney asked Dopp for evidence that he'd really begun gathering records in response to media inquiries, rather than in an effort to tarnish Bruno. There was no such proof—he explained that he had acted in anticipation of formal requests. They soon ordered Dopp to cease all contact with anyone—including Baum and Spitzer—about the events under investigation. Dopp kept coming into work, but the communications director was suddenly under a cone of silence on the issue. He couldn't defend himself or the administration to the press. He couldn't plot strategy with his bosses, whom he'd been speaking to dozens of times a day for the past eight years. During the final days of Cuomo's investigation, Eliot would stop talking to him altogether.

"The pressure of being at the center of controversy has weighed heavily on me," Dopp wrote in his diary. "Trouble sleeping, anxiety, and a sense that resolution won't come for a long time. Today, Sean Maloney and Peter Pope inform me of worst-case scenario—that an aggressive prosecutor might think I'd committed official misconduct. I am incredulous and protest that charges of 'political spying' are outrageous. Their view however is that I might have improperly accessed info about Bruno."

An AP reporter e-mailed Dopp with Dicker's latest fulminations: "Did you hear FUD today? Raised the idea that you may be in witness protection program after Bruno-gate."

Chapter 11: "Animals"

LOOKING BACK, IT'S A LITTLE HARD TO UNDERSTAND WHAT all the stink was about. One politician had hoped to hurt another by handing damaging information—in this case, *public* information—to a reporter. To be sure, it was sneaky. If Spitzer really wanted to halt the travel abuse, rather than expose Bruno, he could have simply changed the aircraft policy. And the involvement of the State Police—in re-creating missing records and providing field dispatches on Bruno's whereabouts—was foolish; it inevitably raised the ugly specter of using law enforcement for political ends. But it certainly wasn't the first time a politician had planted a damaging story about his adversary—Bruno did it all the time. If Watergate was a third-rate burglary, Troopergate was a two-bit leak. For Spitzer, the real problems were that he'd gotten caught playing hardball—and how disastrously he'd handle the aftermath. Yet in the funhouse of New York politics, it became the scandal without end.

Cuomo's investigation set the stage, though he would complete it in just twenty-one days and took even less time to reach his two central conclusions: there was no evidence that the State Police had spied on Bruno, and the senator's use of state aircraft fit within the slack boundaries of New York's rules. In short, nothing illegal had taken place. But that wasn't the end of the matter. Cuomo's investigators advised Spitzer's staff that they had uncovered "troubling" behavior, and planned to release a report on their findings. All of the "troubling" behavior, as it turned out, was on the administration side of the inquiry.

Bruno got a pass. Cuomo's investigators had interviewed witnesses who affirmed that the senator had conducted at least some government meetings on each of ten helicopter trips to New York City during the first six months of 2007. On at least one occasion, the public business had totaled less than an hour. Yet they'd made no further effort to determine whether this "business" was simply a pretext for traveling to political fundraisers. Only one Bruno-related witness was asked to testify under oath; the AG hadn't reviewed any of their e-mails. Cuomo had also dismissed the issue of whether Bruno's use of the choppers provided any personal "imputed income" benefit, requiring a special tax payment to the IRS. Having rapidly concluded that there was no way to prosecute Bruno, the AG simply recommended tightening the porous rules that permitted "mixed-use" travel.

The governor's side of the investigation was similarly rushed but less forgiving. Cuomo's investigators had interviewed only one chamber employee—Howard—and had reached their findings before key documents were unearthed. They made no effort to trace whether the governor had played any role. Instead, they focused primarily on alleged abuses of the open-records process, pillorying Dopp for bypassing the staffers who usually handled such matters (and thus providing documents *too* readily) and Felton for departing from usual State Police records procedures. They also chastised Dopp and Howard for dragging the State Police into a political fight and Felton for being too compliant—even though he was responding to inquiries from his boss about the use of public assets. Cuomo would vigorously defend this effort, saying his team had gotten it right and he'd given the affair all the attention it merited.

There'd been sparring between the two sides along the way, giving Spitzer's staff a taste of what it was like to deal with aggressive tactics from an ambitious attorney general. Howard had been summoned for sworn interrogation in a late-night phone call to his home and was never advised that he could bring a lawyer; one of Cuomo's investigators had warned the State Police attorney that if he didn't produce witnesses on her rapid-fire schedule, "they would read about it in the *New York Post*." The governor's team, in turn, wasn't about to volunteer anything that hadn't been explicitly requested. At 12:12 A.M. on July 16, Maloney warned Pope about "private e-mails" after realizing that the personal mailboxes and nongovernment BlackBerrys some staffers used might contain messages the AG would want. "If the investigators get smart, they ask for Darren's private e-mails and then others'," Maloney wrote. "That'll be a rich source of info now that I think about it." To cover themselves in responding to the AG's document requests, Maloney suggested a little wordsmithing. "We should include in our first production letter a key adjective: 'we have searched CHAMBER records and produce herewith those CHAMBER items responsive to your request.'" None of the "private" e-mails were produced.

Yet even before getting all the evidence they had requested, the AG's team had opened negotiations to wrap up the affair. Cuomo had launched the discussions personally, speaking privately to Nocenti—who had worked for his father—about the "endgame." Like his predecessor, Cuomo was eager for validation. He wanted the governor to formally embrace his report and to punish the wrongdoers he had identified: Dopp, Howard, and Felton.

This placed Spitzer in the very position confronted by the many public companies he had sued. Should he dispute the AG's findings, prompting a public battle that could drag on for months? Or should he settle the case—admit mistakes and endure the short-term hit—to put the issue behind him? In this matter, which had so strangely boomeranged, Spitzer's team of lawyers urged the governor to embrace the option usually chosen by his targets. A settlement, they told him, not only would shut down Cuomo's investigation, but would also have the benefit of keeping Dopp and Baum from having to testify. The AG's team had made noises about questioning them, but hadn't formally asked to interview them until Friday, July 20—three days before the report was to be released. They'd made the request only after the chamber had faxed over four new e-mails, which seemed to show Baum, Dopp, and Howard plotting "that move" against Bruno.

Both Baum and Dopp actually wanted to answer questions, insisting that they had nothing to hide. But the administration lawyers hated the idea. After Howard had been questioned, Cuomo's team grumbled about "inconsistencies" in his testimony; they didn't want to put Spitzer's two closest aides at risk of perjury charges. They worried about the precedent—it could jeopardize future claims of executive privilege. Such testimony could also place the mess closer to Spitzer, who might then be asked to appear himself. Although the AG's office had no subpoena power to compel anyone to answer questions, the simple truth was that if Cuomo insisted on questioning Baum and Dopp—threatening ugly headlines about administration stonewalling—the governor would likely have relented. But Cuomo never insisted; instead, the two sides pursued their negotiated settlement plan.

Troopergate was a political scandal, playing out in the court of public opinion. But on this matter, Spitzer's two top political strategists were almost entirely walled off from decisions about how to handle the crisis. Like Dopp, Baum had been barred from the discussions—until Saturday, when he'd been summoned to a strategy session in the capitol with Pope and Nocenti; Spitzer and Constantine were participating by phone. Told about the game plan, Baum protested that there was "no way" to end the matter unless he and Dopp testified—before being banished from the meeting, at Constantine's insistence. Before leaving, he'd suggested that they blunt the PR damage by at least letting him and Dopp submit written statements to the AG's office.

Spitzer signed on to the settlement plan. (He would come to deeply regret this choice, calling the decision to embrace Cuomo's findings "the biggest mistake I made.") With that, the lawyers rushed to tie up the remaining details. Spitzer didn't want the press writing that he had refused to let his aides testify; Cuomo didn't want anyone to know he'd backed off. As window dressing on this tiny farce, the AG would later publicly insist that he had merely "received"—rather than "accepted"—the written statements. Pope's handwritten notes from the discussions show that he wanted Spitzer to get "an A for cooperation"—he asked Cuomo's team to include a comment in their report saying the governor's office had "fully" cooperated. The AG refused—it hadn't. But Cuomo's camp agreed not to criticize Spitzer as long as he didn't make any such public claims.

This left a single major issue: Darren Dopp. At the point Pope first told the AG that the governor's aide wouldn't answer questions, Dopp hadn't even known about it. Even as their interests diverged, his friends in the chamber had continued to speak for Dopp until Friday, when they finally presented him with a letter saying he needed to find his own lawyer. Late that evening, Pope e-mailed Maloney and Nocenti that they should discuss their decision with Dopp's attorney: "DD cannot just read in the [AG's] report that we declined to produce him."

In fact, Dopp wanted desperately to talk to Cuomo. He *knew* Andrew. He felt certain he could explain everything, convince his crew that he had done nothing wrong. But at a Sunday-afternoon meeting in Nocenti's office, the chamber lawyers warned Dopp, finally accompanied by his own attorney, that Andrew *wasn't* his friend in this matter. The AG was a "predator" who had it in for Eliot, they said; his people were acting like "animals." If Darren signed the statement, the investigation would end, they told him. If he testified, it could lead to disaster.

The statement at issue was a mere two paragraphs, similar in length to the one Baum had agreed to sign. It had gone through multiple drafts, after being reviewed by everyone in the room, and had been approved by Spitzer himself. In it, Dopp denied directing any surveillance. He stated that he had responded to media requests about state-aircraft use by seeking information "the public had a right to know" and had received information from Howard about Bruno's travels that had been "generated" by the State Police. "I now recognize," the statement concluded, "that any requests for State Police records relating to these travels should have been handled through other channels, and I regret any appearance of impropriety that was created by the manner in which this information was sought and obtained."

Exhausted and overwrought, Dopp still wanted to tell his story. But even his attorney didn't want him to testify. Nocenti and Pope urged him to take the hit for Eliot and the team—they'd suspend him for a short while, the situation would blow over, and he'd be back on the job before long. Dopp later said he thought this was "nuts"—that the problem wouldn't go away so easily. But he finally agreed to sign the statement anyway. Then he left the capitol and went home.

Finally, there was the question of punishment. After meeting with his advisors, Spitzer had agreed to suspend Dopp indefinitely without pay for a minimum of thirty days. Constantine had wanted him fired. Howard would be transferred out of the executive chamber. Although Cuomo faulted Felton, too, the governor would not sanction him, reasoning that the veteran lawman could be excused for following orders.

By Sunday, the two sides had put the finishing touches on the rollout of their "endgame." The AG's deputies gave the governor's lawyers a detailed rundown on their report, which Spitzer had already agreed to embrace, sight unseen. The chamber sent Cuomo's team the statements from Baum and Dopp—which they didn't even mention in their report—as well as the comments the governor planned to make the next morning. Spitzer had done a mock run at answering likely questions from the press, which hadn't gone particularly well. For better or worse, all was in readiness.

Over that weekend, it had become painfully apparent that Spitzer

was about to endure his biggest setback yet. As the governor's staff prepared itself for the fallout, Pope had e-mailed Constantine: "I predict that
the next week is really going to suck."

————

The governor's team debated how to manage the bad news. Nocenti urged
a low-key response. Cuomo wasn't even doing a press briefing. Although
the headlines were sure to be ugly, there was no need to invite questions
about the governor's role by standing him in front of the cameras. He
wasn't even *mentioned* in the AG's report. But that was not Spitzer's way.
Integrity was his personal brand—any hint of ethical misconduct on his
watch demanded an immediate, overwhelming response. So Spitzer
stepped before the assembled media in Albany shortly before noon on
Monday—about five minutes after he'd finally received a copy of the fifty-
seven-page report. He hadn't even read it.

Nonetheless, the governor accepted Cuomo's findings and offered up
an overdose of contrition. Spitzer told reporters he had already apologized that morning to Bruno—personally, in a phone call. He apologized
to the men and women of the State Police for immersing their "esteemed
institution" in a political fight. He apologized to all the citizens of New
York for "letting this matter become a distraction from the vital work at
hand." Earlier that morning, he'd tearfully apologized to his staff. A few
days later, he would apologize again, in a *mea culpa* published—where
else?—on the op-ed page of *The New York Times*.

The coverage was even worse than Spitzer expected. The *Daily News*
called Cuomo's report "blistering"—"a shocking turn in the raging feud
between the governor, who rode into Albany promising to clean up the
town, and the lawmaker he has derided as a relic of old-style politics."
Dicker boasted that the AG's "bombshell" had "confirmed" his *Post* stories detailing how Spitzer aides "used the State Police as, in effect, a spy
agency as part of a broad conspiracy aimed at destroying Bruno." In fact,
Cuomo had explicitly found *no* surveillance. Even the *Times* account
failed to mention that Cuomo had dismissed the sensational spying
claims.

Meanwhile, the scandal of Air Bruno was buried beneath the media
outcry over the administration's "dirty tricks." Cuomo's report concluded that the dissemination of Bruno's itineraries represented an improper,
politically motivated disclosure. Yet two months later, Odato would un-

earth virtually identical information about Bruno's travels kept by the State Police under a previous governor—Republican George Pataki. The records showed that the senator had for years been mixing politics with a dash of government business on his downstate hops, courtesy of New York taxpayers. Yet it was this administration's eagerness to expose these habits that had become the story.

While Bruno—given a clean bill of health—was hailed as a giant slayer, the governor came under siege. It took just a day for the press to learn that Baum and Dopp had refused to testify, and to start asking why. The blood was in the water: *what did they know and when did they know it?* Dicker went after Spitzer at a raucous press conference, shouting questions and interrupting his answers. The *Post* columnist had taken, preposterously, to calling Troopergate "the biggest political scandal in modern New York history."

On a tour of newspaper editorial boards around the state, Spitzer insisted his administration had cooperated fully with the AG. This, of course, set off Cuomo, whose staff promptly told the press that it wasn't true. The governor also declared that he knew nothing about the record-collection activities by his aides; that he hadn't approved the release of the information; and that he hadn't even participated in the decision to keep Baum and Dopp from testifying. He portrayed himself as almost entirely uninvolved in the affair.

Yet nothing Spitzer did—neither his apologies nor the staff sanctions nor his embrace of the AG's findings—made the problem go away. To the contrary, Spitzer's response had transformed Cuomo's spotty report into accepted truth, elevating an overzealous media play, aimed at deploying facts to damage a political enemy, into a full-fledged scandal. And *that* story really did have "legs." The refusal to produce Baum and Dopp fed suspicions that the governor—who had his hands on everything around him—had something to hide. This fueled demands for more investigation, by someone who could force Spitzer's closest aides—and even Spitzer himself—to answer questions under oath.

———

Minutes before the governor had stepped out to offer his first public response to Cuomo's report, his senior advisor had sent him an e-mail, beneath the heading "pride." "I have never seen you better nor have I ever been prouder of a colleague or boss," wrote Lloyd Constantine. "I am precisely where I want to be. You are my brother and friend and I will help you achieve all that you hope to and more."

Constantine had used his special position on the Troopergate legal team—and his uniquely personal relationship with Spitzer, whom he playfully addressed as "stud"—to agitate for harsh discipline of the governor's aides. He e-mailed Spitzer to "stay firm," that he felt "both strongly and clearly what should be done and done now." In a message to an old acquaintance later, Constantine recounted his role during the crisis as "three weeks of 20 hour days. When I saw you we were at the end of the internal investigation which I quietly conducted and in the process of moving our friend out of the state of denial both that it had occurred on his watch and without his knowledge. And the seriousness of the situation and the likely severity of the response."

Though Spitzer had entertained doubts that the problem was as bad as Constantine thought, he'd followed most of his advice anyway. "It is cover of both tabs and lead in nyt," the governor e-mailed Constantine at 6:13 A.M., after surveying the next-day damage in the morning papers. "I suppose it is better to have been in front of it than to have been caught flat footed."

Troopergate had done considerable damage. Despite all his early battles in Albany, the governor had remained popular with New York voters. But this mess had sunk his approval rating below 50 percent. The scandal also had unfolded just as Spitzer was working to set the stage for his future ambitions. In July, his political team was preparing to send out his first national fundraising letter, with the goal of building a powerful base he could tap for future campaigns; the bad press had put that on ice. Spitzer had also established a political action committee to back "reform-minded candidates" across the country. He'd named his PAC the "Excelsior Committee," after the New York state motto—Latin for "Ever Upward." But in Albany, things were going nowhere.

Before Cuomo's report had been released, the legislative leaders had finally returned to work, agreeing to a slimmed-down "hairball" deal that included a measure of campaign-finance reform, the first steps toward Bloomberg's congestion-pricing scheme, and a legislative pay raise. But even this progress would be abandoned, falling victim to the Republicans' eagerness to thumb their noses at the beleaguered governor. State government slipped into gridlock, Spitzer and Bruno weren't speaking, and the media was rumbling about the need for a shakeup in the governor's office.

As Constantine saw it, Troopergate was part of the administration's "obsession" with toppling Bruno, for which he blamed Baum, not Spitzer. Constantine had been trying to oust the governor's top deputy for months. Now, with Dopp already sidelined and the secretary under fire, he moved in for the kill, pushing Spitzer to make "management changes." This time, the governor was listening, even as he told the press that Baum wasn't going anywhere. On Friday, four days after the Troopergate report was released, Spitzer gave an interview in his Manhattan office to the *Times*, in which he was asked whether Baum would still be in his job a month later. "Oh, yeah. Absolutely. Yes," the governor replied. That evening, Spitzer returned to Albany, where he summoned Baum to the governor's mansion and told his secretary he was "thinking about" moving him out. This wasn't because of Troopergate, Spitzer insisted; he needed to demonstrate he was embracing a fresh, less confrontational approach.

The next morning, Baum sent the governor a lengthy e-mail making a final plea for his job. He bashed his detractors. He argued that the move was stupid politically. And he played to Spitzer's guilt. "Moving me out of the position of Secretary now will have a negative effect on you at a sensitive time," Baum wrote. "Whatever we or you say . . . everyone will assume it's either because of some still-hidden culpability on my part or because of my management failure. Either way, this only moves the scandal one step closer to you and defeats our (truthful) effort to cabin it in the communications office. I know you want to show change, but I truly think the way to do it is through addition, not subtraction." Baum recalled the meeting where he'd argued that his failure to testify would make his position "untenable"—before "Lloyd objected to my presence and I was ejected. I've lived through a week of attacks on my reputation because of that decision for the team and, ultimately, you," he told Spitzer. "I don't know what to say other than it just doesn't seem right."

Spitzer had already teed up Paul Francis, his budget director, to replace Baum as secretary, and told Constantine: "Rich is gone." But Spitzer loathed making tough decisions about his own staff. He felt loyal and indebted; they'd all sacrificed to join him in public service. That was especially true of Baum, the architect of his political career. Suspending Dopp had been painful enough. He couldn't bring himself to fire Baum.

On Sunday, the governor met with his top deputy again: he wasn't being fired after all. Lloyd and Peter would be unhappy about this, the governor advised him. Yet Spitzer didn't empower Baum to rein them in, to try to halt the infighting and impose discipline. Instead, he told his secretary he needed to do more to include the two men who had tried to get him fired.

"What happened?" Constantine demanded when he found out that Baum hadn't been sacked.

"It'll be seen as a sign of weakness," the governor told him.

Constantine wasn't ready to give up. "It's a bigger sign of weakness to have someone who is terrible at his job," he said.

———   ·

July 28: Stories have Spitzer buying into AG's report, apologizing in print and saying it's time to move forward. I guess I understand, but it's all b.s.

Darren Dopp had learned of his punishment from the media, which had bombarded him with calls for comment and dispatched paparazzi to stake out his home. He'd thought he would be out for perhaps a week. No one from the governor's office had called to tell him that his unpaid suspension would last a minimum of thirty days. In fact, none of his administration friends had called at all. He'd been left to twist in the wind, to pour his feelings into his diary.

Sandy Dopp, his wife of twenty-four years, was furious. Darren had been devoted to Spitzer, tending to his every need. Why, he'd even swiped her makeup to keep him from looking shiny during TV interviews. Darren regarded Spitzer and his crew as family—for years, he'd put them ahead of his own wife, daughter, and son. She was a housewife—how were they supposed to pay their bills without Darren's $175,000 salary? And exactly *what* had Darren done wrong? *He'd followed Spitzer's orders!* Yet he wasn't willing to go public with this, choosing instead to "take the hit" himself. Meanwhile, the governor was telling the press that a staffer—obviously Dopp—had "lied" and "misled" him. He was telling everyone he knew nothing! Why did this man deserve such loyalty? Why should they suffer? Why was her husband being such a chump?

July 30: Sandy launches most vicious attack yet. I leave house for bike ride and walk at night. Spitzer in Syracuse says that if he knew what aides were doing he would have stopped it. More bs.

There were rumblings in Albany that Dopp was deeply distraught and ready to spill his guts. Andrew Cuomo had begun calling Dopp's home, urging him to talk. Cuomo didn't speak directly to Darren—that would be crossing the line. Instead, he chatted with Sandy, whom he'd known for years; the Dopps' daughter even worked in Cuomo's Manhattan office. This back-channel contact with a potential investigation witness was so dicey that the AG's chief of staff had insisted on secretly listening in; Sandy didn't know about that. But Cuomo had a blunt message for her husband: "You don't take a bullet when it's your own team that's shooting at you."

> August 1. More accounts of Spitzer confessing to things that didn't occur. . . . Sandy refuses to listen to reason—believes the worst at all turns. She wakes me up at 1 am to denounce ES—says I must set record straight. David N[ocenti] calls—says battles continue, administration is in disarray at times, and that I'm a stand-up guy who needs to hang in. Tough it out.

Dopp was struggling with his loyalties. Tough it out? Or protect himself and his family? Sandy was in a perpetual rage—he'd never seen her like this. He was beginning to have doubts. He'd even told one of his lawyers about the "red-hot poker" meeting. There were plenty of people who would *die* to hear about that. Protect Spitzer—or his family?

There was no doubt what Sandy thought. "Darren," she told her husband, "they've cut you off like a *wart!*"

George Fox was becoming more creative with his payment arrangements with the Emperors Club. He was booking more out-of-town appointments. That required a big up-front deposit, given the four-hour minimum for travel dates, plus the hotel and other expenses. When he called far enough in advance, he would simply send cash or money orders through the U.S. mail. But last-minute appointments were a problem. George Fox seemed uncomfortable with wire transfers, which were quick but easily traceable. On at least one occasion, recalls Suwal, he stopped by the bank and deposited cash directly into the QAT account. But sometimes, he couldn't make it to the bank—and was calling too late to use the mail. During the summer of 2007, this had happened on at least two occasions: George Fox had booked a date, but he'd had to scramble to figure out a way to pay for it.

———

It was in July that North Fork Bank vice president Adam Brenner, who worked on the darkly paneled private-banking floor, got a peculiar phone call from his branch's most prominent client—New York Governor Eliot Spitzer. Brenner's North Fork office, on Madison Avenue and Forty-ninth Street in Manhattan, catered to wealthy New Yorkers, many of them involved in real estate. It prided itself on service. These customers didn't come to the bank; the bankers went to them. Spitzer was, of course, a busy man. He was flying to Washington for two days on July 11. He had a breakfast scheduled for the next morning with the New York congressional delegation. Then he had separate meetings with the state's senators, Hillary Clinton and Chuck Schumer, and House speaker Nancy Pelosi, followed by dinner with his daughter Elyssa, who was there during summer break.

But Brenner couldn't fill his request. The governor wanted to send someone several thousand dollars. He had plenty of money in his personal accounts, of course. The difficulty was *how* he wanted to send it. "Is there a way to wire money where it's not evident that it's coming from me?" he asked. Spitzer explained that he'd done this once before.

Perhaps so, but not on Brenner's watch. Brenner referred the matter to his superiors. They wouldn't make this anonymous wire transfer, even for the governor. It was against all sorts of banking regulations—although it turned out that someone else at North Fork had indeed done so before. But on this occasion, the bankers noticed that the governor's desired recipient—a company called QAT Consulting—also had its account at a North Fork branch. They could make an intrabank transfer instead—anonymously. But the whole arrangement was quite unconventional; they wouldn't let him do it again. If Spitzer wanted to send money in the future without using his name, he'd have to find another way.

After his conversation with the governor, Brenner spoke with a colleague, Cindy Darrison, who had been Spitzer's chief fundraiser before going to work at North Fork back in February. Could there be some legitimate political reason for Spitzer to want to send money anonymously? No, Darrison told him—you have to disclose everything that's being spent. She was dumbfounded: *what could Eliot be trying to hide?* Was he secretly paying an opposition researcher to dig up dirt on Bruno? Quietly hiring a consultant? Surely it was *something* involving politics.

For the bank, there was no question: the incident required reporting. Any unusual money transfers or customer requests were supposed to be disclosed to the Internal Revenue Service on Treasury Form TD F 90-22.47—a "Suspicious Activity Report," known as an SAR. This was Banking 101—everyone at North Fork took an online course about it during his first day on the job. The rules had become even more stringent since 9/11—they were looking for terrorists under every rock. Politically prominent people received extra scrutiny because of their susceptibility to extortion or corruption.

While Spitzer's previous transfer had prompted no action, this one would generate an unusually detailed and lengthy SAR, which described Spitzer's transfers to QAT and the details surrounding his request. When the SAR was completed, the bank sent it in to FinCEN—the Financial Crimes Enforcement Network, a branch of the U.S. Treasury Department with offices in Detroit. There, the SAR was entered into its database, accessible to federal, state, and local law-enforcement agencies. FinCEN typically received more than 3,400 SARs a day. The North Fork filing would remain buried among them, unnoticed for months.

Chapter 12: Crossing the Rubicon

THE ARRIVAL OF ROGER STONE DURING ALBANY'S SUMMER of Tumult was heralded not with a drumroll nor a press release nor even a leak to Fred Dicker. Reporters simply started receiving e-mails from mysterious websites, trashing Eliot Spitzer.

Stone was a political consultant—a self-described "GOP hit man" and the premier dirty trickster in American politics. He'd masterminded a raft of mischief since getting his start working for Richard Nixon and palling around with Roy Cohn—most famously, the 2000 "Brooks Brothers riot," where Republican operatives staged violent protests, kicking and trampling people as they stormed a government building to help shut down the Florida presidential recount. Profiled during his younger days in a *New Republic* cover story as "the State-of-the-Art Washington Sleazeball," Stone had actually been a fringe player since 1996. That's when he'd been booted from Bob Dole's presidential campaign after the supermarket tabloids caught him and his wife advertising for sex partners in swingers' magazines. ("Hot, athletic, fit couple seeks similar couples or exceptional, muscular well-hung single men. . . . Prefer military, bodybuilders, jocks. No smokers or fats please.") Stone denied it at first, of course, insisting he'd been set up by a "sick" individual. He was a man who didn't think twice about lying, even in the face of an indisputable truth.

Stone was a master of showmanship and misdirection. He claimed credit for sleazy things he hadn't done and denied responsibility for those he had. He proudly operated by what he called "Stone's Rules." Among them: "attack, attack, attack—never defend." And "admit nothing, deny everything, launch counterattack." All this made him too much of a wild-card for mainstream candidates. In addition to his corporate consulting, Stone did political work for the desperate and those on the margins, such as Al Sharpton and Donald Trump. Hiring Stone was a Hail Mary pass. His stock-in-trade was upending the political dynamic by any means, overt or clandestine. Another of Stone's Rules: "Hit it from every angle. Open multiple fronts on your enemy. He must be confused and feel besieged on every side."

As the New York senate Republicans saw it, Stone was the perfect antidote to Eliot Spitzer. Bruno had introduced him to his conference at a meeting in mid-July, before Cuomo's report was out. "We needed to bring in somebody that could deal with this eight-hundred-pound gorilla," explains John McArdle, Bruno's communications director. At fifty-four, Stone cut a flamboyant figure, with his bleached hair transplants, dark tan, aging bodybuilder physique, and gangster suit. He wowed the senators with his pitch to stop playing defense. "We talked about how we're not going to just survive Eliot—we're going to go fucking toe-to-toe with him," says McArdle. "Roger gave everybody confidence."

Placed on the senate Republican campaign committee's payroll, at $20,000 a month, Stone set up an underground marketing network, fronted by cronies, to bombard the press with Spitzer criticism. His first website was called NYFacts.net, which reporters traced to a longtime Stone associate named Michael Caputo, who lived on a Florida houseboat with his parrot. Caputo told them he was operating on his own, out of a personal interest in New York politics. More anti-Spitzer websites soon sprang up, sending out still more e-mails, mostly about the emerging Troopergate scandal.

But Stone's biggest impact would result from a peculiar fixation on Spitzer's father—in particular, the controversy about his campaign loans to his son dating back to 1994. By mid-2007, Bernard Spitzer was eighty-three years old and suffering from Parkinson's disease, though he still came into work every day. The issue was largely forgotten. No matter. Taking its lead from Stone, Bruno's senate suddenly decided it needed to investigate the affair. Why? To assess the governor's proposal for campaign-finance reform! "In Roger's mind, the key to bringing Eliot down was the father," says McArdle. "Roger always thought Troopergate was a distraction."

———

The call came in late on the night of Monday, August 6. No one heard it until the next morning, when the receptionist at Spitzer Engineering arrived and played the voicemail:

> This is a message for Bernard Spitzer. You *will* be subpoenaed to testify before the senate committee on investigations on your shady campaign loans. You *will* be compelled by the senate sergeant at arms. If you resist the subpoena, you *will* be arrested and brought to Albany—and there's not a *goddamn* thing your *phony, psycho, piece-of-shit son* can do about it. Bernie, your *phony* loans are about to catch up with you. You *will* be forced to tell the truth. And the fact that your son's a pathological liar will be known to all.

At Bernie Spitzer's direction, his real estate lawyer, Jeffrey Moerdler, hired private investigators from Kroll, who traced the anonymous call to Roger Stone's Central Park South apartment in Manhattan; they found samples of Stone's voice from a TV interview, which sounded just like the caller. Eleven days after the call, Kroll completed a three-page report detailing its findings.

Now the Spitzers had to decide what to do. Referring the matter for criminal investigation could establish Stone's culpability in the ugly incident. It would keep the story churning in the press for weeks, maybe months, and maximize public outrage over the episode, with its damaging link to Bruno. In short, it's what the Republicans would have done in an instant. But in the wake of Troopergate—and Bruno's attempt to criminalize his administration's political conduct—the governor decided instead to treat it as nothing more than a dirty trick. The Spitzers sent letters, including the Kroll report and a copy of the recordings, to the senate investigations committee and the state ethics commission. Neither pursued the matter.

The Spitzers also informed the press. When confronted, Stone offered reporters a succession of laughable alibis. He was attending a performance of *Frost/Nixon* on Broadway when the message was left. (The theater was actually dark that night.) His landlord, a Spitzer fundraiser, had provided access to his apartment so someone could set him up. An impressionist had left the message pretending to be Stone. It was a *Spitzer* dirty trick. But no one harbored much doubt about who'd really made the call. Even by the standards of Albany, this was a shocking event. While publicly reserving judgment, Bruno announced that he was cutting Stone off the GOP payroll. Yet he remained on the case. The e-mailed attacks on Spitzer and his father continued; Stone continued to go after the governor in the media every chance he got. He was clearly not done with Spitzer.

A few days after the threatening voicemail made headlines, Moerdler received an unsolicited call from an FBI agent, who wanted to discuss the incident with his client. They met at 10 A.M. on September 6 at the offices of Spitzer Engineering. Bernie Spitzer was accompanied by Moerdler and a criminal lawyer from his firm. After a few questions about the threatening call, the two agents—one worked in the bureau's public-corruption unit—began asking about Spitzer's campaign loans to his son and the family's finances, according to Moerdler. "They wanted to inquire into the underlying events. We said, 'That's not the purpose of this investigation. This isn't a fishing expedition.' We declined to go down that road." Spitzer's lawyers terminated the meeting. The FBI agents never sought to examine any physical evidence; there is no indication they pursued any inquiry into the voicemail.

Looking back at the episode two years later, Eliot Spitzer speculates that the FBI was already looking into another matter. "The bizarre thing is they didn't look at phones or take them. They didn't ask for a recording of the call. They didn't preserve anything. What does that tell you about what they're really interested in?" In hindsight, he regrets his decision not to seek a criminal investigation of the call. "That wasn't the way I played the game." But it would have been a way to deliver a message about who was really crossing the line, says Spitzer: "What is going on when Roger Stone is running the Republican Party in Albany?"

———

Spitzer's advisors believed the governor needed to respond to Troopergate not just with apologies, but with a public display of introspection. Spitzer didn't really *do* introspection. But desperate times called for desperate measures. So during a long-scheduled appearance at the Chautauqua Institution, in western New York, Spitzer served up his own cerebral version. It combined an attack on Bush administration foreign policy, a defense of his wild seven months as governor, and the need to balance power with humility—all tied together by the theologian Reinhold Niebuhr.

His advisors agonized over this address, as only a team assembled by this particular politician could. "The governor might appear either naïve or disingenuous when he sets forth the contrast . . . between Western liberal democracy and fanaticism," wrote Nocenti to the many aides debating the draft of the speech. "I don't think we can ignore the fact that there are many individuals who reject Western liberal democracy and who do seek an 'alternative system of government' but who do not necessarily support a terrorist means to that end." Spotting a Biblical quotation, Charles O'Byrne, Paterson's chief of staff and a former Catholic priest, wondered whether the governor had "ever quoted Scripture in the past. . . . I think it will engender questions—looking to God or religious inspiration always does especially when the going is tough (unless you're Jimmy Carter or Reagan or Bush). I'd drop Micah—he really doesn't balance Niebuhr since the latter was a religious ethicist and Micah one of the minor prophets." Drew Warsaw, a policy staffer, reassured everyone that they would "vet" the remarks with "experts on national security and Niebuhrism. We are in touch with both—a Niebuhr professor from the University of Virginia and a national security expert from the Center for American Progress. . . . We will get their feedback tomorrow morning."

In the final version, Spitzer argued that the raw exercise of power was essential to upend the status quo—"even if we believed we had reason on our side . . . reason was not enough." Yet he had learned, he declared, that "we must always balance strength with humility . . . [that] a layer of self-examination and self-criticism is necessary. As a public official, the question of how to maintain that equilibrium must be one of the questions you ask yourself every day."

———

It was dark when the SUV pulled into the sprawling parking lot at the Dakota Steak House, eight miles north of Albany. Surely, no one would see them *there*. His old friend had already arrived; he was sitting in his gray Impala, with the engine running. Mike Balboni, the secretary of homeland security for the state of New York, got out of his own car and slipped into the backseat beside him.

On this warm summer night, Balboni had left his security detail back in the capital. He was on a "secret squirrel mission," carrying a message from his boss—the governor of New York. "Let's put all this aside," Balboni told Joe Bruno. "We can put a deal together." Despite all the animosity they'd traded—the governor and Bruno weren't even speaking—Spitzer was desperate to get things back on track. He'd dispatched Balboni on this assignment personally. The governor was willing to put more money in the pot—this year and even next, Balboni told the senator—if Bruno would just resume talking and finally pass Spitzer's campaign-finance bill. They should all go back to doing business.

But Bruno didn't want to hear it. "*You* have to make a decision," he told Balboni. "This guy's going *down*! I'm going to take him down. You better decide to get out." Bruno had a proposition of his own. Balboni should quit the administration, return to the Republican fold, and run for his old seat out on Long Island. "Come back to the senate," Bruno told him, "because this guy isn't going to be around. And *you're* not going to be around if you stay with him!"

With that, the peacemaking mission was over. "I got back in the car," recalls Balboni, "and swore never to talk to Joe Bruno about Eliot Spitzer again. Gandhi and Henry Kissinger could not have mediated this conflict."

———

It hadn't taken Spitzer long to experience buyer's remorse over his deal with Cuomo. The "endgame" negotiated between his staff and the AG hadn't made the controversy go away. To the contrary, the questions it left unresolved had kept the story bubbling. On the substance, Spitzer still didn't understand what the stink was about, even though he had already apologized for it. His administration had released public records about Bruno's misuse of government resources that the governor was charged with overseeing. Bruno's claims about death threats and spying had been proven to be nonsense. And the senator had hired a sleazeball who made a threatening call to Spitzer's elderly father. Yet the media only cared about whether the governor's office had followed proper procedure on a records request. Says Spitzer: "It drove me crazy. I was living in *Alice in Wonderland*."

Spitzer, of course, had affirmed this version of reality—by accepting Cuomo's report, banishing Howard, and suspending Dopp. During press interviews, he'd insisted that he knew nothing about what was going on and that his administration had cooperated fully—claims that offered a juicy target for the press, especially Dicker. Even within his staff, the notion that Dopp had acted unilaterally was widely viewed with disbelief. The governor's aides knew how voraciously Eliot kept tabs on everything, how obsessed he was with the media, and how closely he worked with Darren. They felt certain he knew what his communications director was doing—and that Dopp was getting screwed.

Three more investigations into Troopergate were already in the works. Soares, the Albany DA, was reviewing whether anyone in the governor's office had committed crimes. The public-integrity commission, which had the power to levy fines, was digging into whether anyone had violated the state ethics code. And Bruno's senate, eager to keep the controversy going, was cranking up its own inquiry; the senate would later announce plans to spend up to $500,000 in state funds to hire a former federal prosecutor with GOP ties to assist them. Unlike Cuomo, all three of these investigators had subpoena power.

By this point, the governor's office had abandoned its efforts to muzzle Baum and Dopp. Citing executive privilege, it was refusing to cooperate with Bruno's openly partisan inquiry. But it was providing documents as well as witnesses (ultimately, even Spitzer) to both the DA and the public-integrity commission.* Dopp had already been in to see Soares's investigators on August 14. He wasn't asked directly during that interview whether Spitzer had told him to release the documents, but he certainly didn't volunteer anything about it either. Dopp was still on the team—and getting hammered in the press for it, as the mastermind of a dirty trick. He agonized in his diary: "My birthday is in a few days. All I can think of is how out of thirteen generations of Dopps in America, I'm the only one to have brought shame on the family name. And for what!?"

Word finally arrived that he'd be returned to the state payroll, after thirty-six days. But he wouldn't be allowed to return to the capitol—he was too radioactive. Dopp would take accrued vacation time instead, remaining on the sidelines while the administration figured out what to do with him. "I'm doing the right thing, and I keep getting shit upon!" he bitterly told Nocenti. On his twenty-fifth wedding anniversary, Dopp made a fresh notation in his diary: "Sandy says she wants a divorce." The next day, an Albany TV station broadcast the results of a survey asking,

---

* This cooperation had limits, however. In its final report, the public-integrity commission would complain that the governor's office had delayed its investigation for months by repeatedly withholding important documents subject to subpoena and asserting "spurious" claims of privilege.

"Was Dopp punished enough?" Fifty-eight percent said *no*. Having watched this on the evening news, Dopp's twelve-year-old son, Owen, playfully started chasing his father around the house with a stick, calling out: *"Dad hasn't been punished enough!"*

———

For a moment, the clouds seemed to be parting. The ethics commission had established new rules on the use of government aircraft, allowing it only for travel that was primarily government business, mandating reimbursement for any part of a trip that wasn't, and requiring public disclosure of all activities on such "mixed-use" trips. Bruno had begun taking Amtrak, two and a half hours each way, for his travels to Manhattan. (At other times, he rode in the "Brunomobile," the senate's new $50,000 custom-outfitted van, complete with leather captain's chairs and a conference table.) On Thursday, September 20, Soares—whose investigators had questioned Dopp, Baum, and Spitzer—issued a brief statement announcing that he had found "no illegal conduct." But he went even further, concluding that the governor, his staff, and the State Police had been properly responding to informal media inquiries, not plotting to smear Bruno. The Albany DA would be making his written report public at a press conference the following morning.

After getting this news that Thursday, Spitzer's staff scrambled to come up with a press event to hold immediately after Soares's press conference on Friday, to let the governor declare the end of Troopergate and forge a new direction. He decided to roll out a plan that had been in the works for months: giving driver's licenses to illegal immigrants. On the heels of Soares's findings, this was a move that would prove Spitzer still had his mojo. Unfortunately, it was also a move that made his political advisors fear he'd lost his mind.

On the merits, it was a good idea. Barring illegal immigrants from getting licenses forced tens of thousands in New York to drive without insurance, generating more hit-and-run accidents and boosting premiums by an estimated $120 million. Many illegals were afraid to drive at all, making it hard for them to find jobs. Spitzer's plan would assure that more of them drove safely, with insurance. Law-enforcement experts even believed that it would enhance security, by creating records on many of the one million New Yorkers who were living in the shadows. Eight other states already had this policy; it had been in place in New York until 2004, when Pataki changed it.

But in political terms, the idea was suicide—a perfect target for fear, anger, and demagoguery. Spitzer had scheduled press conferences to announce the move on two occasions earlier in the year; Baum had canceled both. "I thought we couldn't take the abuse," he later explained. But now, the secretary had been hobbled, and the governor was adamant. This, Spitzer had decided, was his silver bullet. The new policy—which he'd impose unilaterally, through the Department of Motor Vehicles—would show that he remained fearless, determined to do what was right. It would also fulfill a little-noticed campaign promise, play to his liberal base, demonstrate that he wasn't dependent on the legislature, and shift the public conversation away from Troopergate. On the last point, he was certainly right.

Balboni had warned that the 9/11 families would go crazy, and they were indeed the first to pounce. "Terrorists here illegally used licenses to kill my son and thousands of others in the World Trade Center," declared the president of one family group. "If they do it again using New York licenses issued by this governor, the blood of the victims will be on Mr. Spitzer's hands." But aside from this, for a few days, there was relative calm. Even Bruno had seemed receptive, saying he could "understand the merits" of the idea. "We have hundreds of thousands of aliens here, and I'm not sure it serves the public good to deprive them of their ability to go to school, to go to work, to do the kinds of things you have to do to lead a normal life."

Then the temperature started to climb. Bruno quickly flip-flopped, accusing Spitzer of cooking up the idea to pander to Hispanic voters. Some county clerks—led by one in Bruno's district—threatened to defy the state by refusing to give licenses to illegals. The state Conservative Party began running ads on cable TV, declaring: "Along the Mexican border, we lock up illegal immigrants. In New York, Governor Spitzer wants to give them driver's licenses." And Jim Tedisco, who had once inspired Spitzer to declare himself a steamroller, added this contribution to the debate: "Osama bin Laden is somewhere in a cave with his den of thieves and terrorists, and he's probably sabering the cork on some champagne right now, saying, 'Hey, that governor's really assisting us.'" Roger Stone's anti-Spitzer websites posted a Photoshopped image of the Al Qaeda leader at the wheel of a New York City taxicab.

Determined to reclaim the mantle of righteousness, Spitzer and his team thought they could ride it out. They trotted out public endorsements of the policy from Richard Clarke, the Bush administration's anti-terrorism czar, and former New York City police commissioner William Bratton; both dismissed the roiling notion that the plan would make life easier for terrorists. When Mike Bloomberg, Spitzer's frequent ally, gently questioned the idea—even while acknowledging that it was "the governor's call"—Spitzer clubbed the mayor, calling him "wrong at every level—dead wrong, factually wrong, legally wrong, morally wrong, ethically wrong." He gave a speech complaining that "the politics of fear and selfishness" had replaced "the politics of common sense and mutual responsibility." He vowed not to "back down or flinch."

Then Lou Dobbs kicked in. The CNN anchor, who had made a career of railing against immigration reform, had been silent on the issue for a simple reason—he'd been off the air after a tonsillectomy. But when he returned, he launched a crusade against the plan—and the governor. Spitzer's license scheme, Dobbs warned darkly, was "a vast security threat to this entire nation"; it would open the door to "massive voter fraud." He called Spitzer an "arrogant abuser of his office," a "spoiled rich-kid brat," and an "idiot." (Dobbs apologized for that one.) His favorite Spitzer-bashing guest? Tedisco. In the face of this nationally televised mugging, Spitzer took solace in the support of his beloved *Times*, which backed the governor's "good, practical" plan and decried the "histrionics" of such "new demagogues." "Today's nyt edit is really good," the governor wrote Baum on October 22. "Maybe we can pivot this against them: we are the voice of reason they are dobbsian nativists. In ny in long run we win this big time by becoming symbol of reason."

But reason would not rule the day.

As elections go, November 6 was a sleepy one in New York, with just local races on the ballot. But Spitzer's top staff, heading to a 10 A.M. retreat at the governor's Pine Plains farm, was expecting fireworks. Baum was sharing a ride down from Albany with Budget Director Paul Francis and the newest addition to Spitzer's team, a former lobbyist named Bruce Gyory.

"Have you done your background reading for this meeting?" the secretary to the governor asked.

Background reading?

"*Lord of the Flies*," Baum told them.

Gyory, fifty-three, was the sort of Albany insider the Spitzer team had been lacking. He had worked as a lobbyist for twenty-four years, and had been informally advising the administration since Spitzer's inauguration, writing secret strategy memos under the pseudonym "Louis Howe"—FDR's closest political aide. He'd received the title of senior advisor to the governor.

Spitzer had summoned about twenty of his top deputies to Pine Plains for a candid assessment of the administration's performance. They gathered around the dining room table, with a stunning view of the rolling hills. In addition to the senior chamber deputies, the gathering included Silda as well as the lieutenant governor and his chief of staff, O'Byrne.

The most pressing question, of course, was driver's licenses. After six weeks of stormy debate, the idea was wildly unpopular, and not just with Lou Dobbs. One poll showed 72 percent of New Yorkers opposed; the issue was driving down Spitzer's numbers in a way Troopergate never had. *The New York Times* had actually run a story comparing him with the only governor in the state's history to be impeached and removed from office. The proposal was even hurting Hillary Clinton, whose waffling on the issue during a TV debate had become a story in the presidential campaign.

"We're right," Spitzer told his team. "But no one gives a shit." Still, he wasn't ready to give up, and Constantine was urging him on. "You are getting a reputation for backing down," he warned Spitzer. "If you back off now, you're *dead*. You're going to have great difficulty governing." Though the retreat was aimed at promoting teamwork, Constantine didn't hesitate to call for heads to roll—in front of everyone. "I have to say," he told the group, "there are some people around this table who simply don't belong here." Constantine pressed this case to the governor in a blunt, lecturing e-mail afterward. "This is so simple that it's pitiful," he wrote. To think otherwise "is just tragically wrongheaded and frankly inexplicable to me from you who is so amazingly smart in virtually all other respects."

By Friday morning, Spitzer seemed to be laying the groundwork to pull the plug on his license proposal. He was in San Juan, Puerto Rico, for the weekend, attending an annual conference of New York's Hispanic legislators. After a breakfast session, he told reporters who had accompanied him there that he was weighing whether to press on. By evening, he had received a confidential memo from his aides proposing an "exit strategy." But by Saturday night, when he convened a staff conference call from San Juan, Spitzer was once again defiant: "All of you keep on trying to stop me from doing what I want to do," he declared. "*I have crossed the Rubicon. I want you to stop trying to change my mind. There is no going back.*"

San Juan was swarming with New Yorkers that weekend, and many were keeping a close eye on Spitzer—reporters, state legislators, assorted staff members, and political activists. The governor was also accompanied by plainclothes state troopers—his usual out-of-state security detail.

Yet George Fox had tempted fate once again that weekend, by arranging for Angelina to fly in. She'd arrived Thursday evening, checked into the Courtyard by Marriott hotel, and eaten dinner. Later that evening, she'd made the ten-minute walk over to the Ritz-Carlton and met him in a room there. Angelina flew back to New York on Friday. Eliot Spitzer's wife, Silda, arrived in Puerto Rico that day to spend the rest of the weekend on the island with her husband.

On Monday, back in New York, Spitzer and Baum met at Dock's Oyster House, downstairs from his Manhattan office, with the governor's longtime political advisors from Global Strategy: Silvan, Pollock, and Toohey. The consultants brought their own polling data, which showed Spitzer's numbers falling off a cliff. "Governor, you haven't seen the floor on this," Silvan warned him. The license plan was especially anathema to upstate Republicans and independents, who had supported him in remarkable numbers less than a year earlier. He was destroying his political future, Silvan told him. "You've gotta get out."

"*Bullshit!*" the governor replied, furious at this advice. "It's the right thing to do. I'm *not* going to back down." That night, Spitzer saw Constantine at a charitable event. "This whole issue has wrecked me!" he told his old friend. Yet he insisted he was standing firm.

One day later, he wasn't. The dismal polling numbers had been sobering. Lawmakers were going to court to stop him. And the issue was threatening to give Republicans a lethal weapon to use against Democrats in their campaigns. Spitzer finally gave up after Hillary Clinton, communicating through a back channel—Queens Democratic congressman

Joe Crowley—asked him to abandon his plan before the next Democratic presidential debate on Thursday night.

"Leadership is not solely about doing what one thinks is right," Spitzer acknowledged, in announcing his about-face at a press conference in Washington, D.C., that Wednesday. "Leadership is also about listening to the public, responding to their concerns and knowing when to put aside a single divisive issue in favor of a larger agenda. . . . It does not take a stethoscope to hear the pulse of New Yorkers on this topic."

Even as he gave up, Spitzer decried the hysteria that had dominated the debate, attacking those who "equated minimum-wage, undocumented dishwashers with Osama bin Laden" for "doing nothing to offer solutions and everything to export fear." Looking back, Spitzer says he was far too slow to recognize that the cause was lost. "This is a third-rail issue that destroys you. I held on to it with two hands for as long as I could."

––––––

After more than two months on the sidelines, Darren Dopp had tired of waiting to be welcomed back into the Spitzer camp. In October, he resigned and went to work for Patricia Lynch Associates, launching a media-relations division for one of Albany's most influential lobbying firms. As Dopp saw it, this would also give him the freedom to speak his mind and clear his name—whenever the opportunity arrived. He no longer felt any obligation to protect the man he had affectionately called "boss."

On October 11, he testified for nine hours before investigators for the state's public-integrity commission. Dopp said nothing shocking or revelatory; he spent the vast majority of the time explaining why he believed no one in the administration had done anything wrong. But early on, his chief interrogator noticed scribbled notes that Dopp had in front of him; in one, Dopp had described his brief written statement to Cuomo's office as "disingenuous." The statement, of course, was so bland and unenlightening that the AG had ignored it entirely—Dopp had merely expressed regret over "any appearance of impropriety" and said that requests for State Police records should have been handled "through other channels." Questioned about his handwritten refutation, Dopp told the public-integrity investigators that he had felt pressured to sign the document—that he "didn't sincerely believe it at that moment or now."

Within days, the public-integrity commission had referred this molehill of inconsistency to Albany DA Soares for yet another investigation—

for perjury. But in the end, what became known as "Investigation D" would not focus on Dopp at all. Instead, it would follow a trail toward a larger target.

––––––

After dealing with the matter for almost half his time in office, Spitzer was sick of Troopergate. His anger about Cuomo's report had become palpable—and the attorney general knew it. *Village Voice* investigative reporter Wayne Barrett had written a lengthy piece trashing Cuomo's findings, which the AG suspected had been aided by Spitzer's staff. The governor's "aides" had also been quoted anonymously saying that Spitzer blamed Cuomo for his problems. Testifying before the senate investigations committee, the chief counsel for the State Police had openly attacked the AG's findings, calling much of Cuomo's criticism "misleading or outright wrong." There had been a final affront at a state Democratic Party event when the governor publicly snubbed Cuomo, sitting in the front row, while walking out after delivering a speech.

According to Eliot Spitzer, it was at about this time that Cuomo called him. As Spitzer tells it, the attorney general issued a warning: if the governor didn't stop criticizing the report, Cuomo would reopen his Troopergate investigation. "Andrew, you better be careful how you phrase things," Spitzer says he told Cuomo. "In layman's terms, that would be called *extortion*." Cuomo denies ever issuing any such threat. But Spitzer remains adamant about what happened. "Andrew Cuomo," he says, "does not know light from dark."

––––––

A year as governor of New York had taken a considerable toll. Spitzer had always believed in the capacity of his own hard work to solve a problem. At the staff retreat, he had vowed to go without another day of vacation for the rest of his term "if that's what it takes to get this right." Balboni thought that was crazy—the administration wasn't floundering for lack of effort. He'd never seen a group that put in longer hours. He urged the governor to have more fun—to travel the state with his family, or ski New York's tallest mountains. "You should enjoy this job," he told the governor. "You're not."

On the day after he pulled the plug on the single most politically damaging idea of his administration, Spitzer tried to follow that advice.

Bruce Springsteen was in the capital. Eliot and Silda invited some of his oldest friends to town for the occasion. Cliff Sloan, his law-school buddy, was up from Washington. Bill Taylor, his Princeton roommate, came down with his wife from Massachusetts. Lloyd and Jan Constantine were there, too. After dinner at the governor's mansion, they joined fifteen thousand others in the Times Union Arena for the concert, with seats close to the stage. A newspaper photo showed the governor in a red sweater over a white T-shirt, giving a hearty thumbs-up while standing and swaying to the music. "He was basically a guy at a concert that night," says Sloan, who spoke to Spitzer regularly. "It struck me that I had not seen him that relaxed in a long time."

The Boss was in fine form that night, too. He played an array of songs that would resonate: "Reason to Believe" . . . "Last to Die" . . . "Darkness on the Edge of Town" . . . "The Promised Land" . . . "Dancing in the Dark." And, of course, "Born to Run." When it was all over, everyone returned to the executive mansion, where they were spending the night, and stayed up until the early hours of the morning, laughing and talking over drinks.

"It was like we were back in college," Spitzer recalled wistfully. "It was the most enjoyable evening I had as governor."

Chapter 13: "A Well-Known Politician"

IT WAS LATE OCTOBER WHEN THE FEDS FIRST SHOWED UP IN the Manhattan DA's office. Dan Stein, an assistant U.S. attorney with the public corruption team at the Southern District of New York, wanted help with a prostitution investigation. It involved a shady company called QAT. FBI agents working the case had already spoken to vice detective Myles Mahady, the NYPD's resident expert on escort services.

For DA Bob Morgenthau and the handful of his deputies who knew about this, the inquiry instantly raised eyebrows. The feds didn't *do* prostitution cases. But they were certainly hot after this one. They wanted to hear about how the DA investigated and prosecuted call-girl rings. Did they know anything about QAT? How did the customers usually pay? When Morgenthau's deputies asked what this was all about, Stein told them it was *extremely* sensitive. He couldn't reveal the name, but they were investigating "a well-known politician."

With the questions about payment methods, the local prosecutors' thoughts turned to Suspicious Activity Reports. Morgenthau's office had access to FinCEN, and a former banker on staff skilled at searching the database. They sent him on a mission to find any SARs connected with the front company, QAT.

Who was this "well-known politician"?

It took him less than twenty-four hours to find out—the story was told in a pair of SARs. One, filed just a few weeks earlier, came from a branch of HSBC bank, reporting that it couldn't figure out how QAT International, a business with an account at the bank, generated its hefty cash flow. The second dated back to July, and came from a North Fork branch in Midtown Manhattan. It detailed the peculiar activity of a North Fork customer who had sent thousands of dollars to another QAT account. His name was all over the SAR:

Eliot Spitzer.

Everyone was flabbergasted. The group in on this revelation included Morgenthau, first deputy James Kindler, and investigations chief Dan Castleman. All had known Spitzer since his days as an assistant DA there two decades earlier. One of Morgenthau's lieutenants called Lev Dassin, the deputy U.S. attorney, and told him that they had figured out who the feds were targeting. *Surely* they had something wrong. Could Eliot be a victim of identity theft? Maybe he was covering for someone else who had gotten into trouble. The SARs revealed an improbable similarity between the names of the North Fork banker (Adam Brenner) and the presumed pimp (Mark Brener). Could there be a connection? Dassin offered his assurance that his investigators had explored all these possibilities and ruled them out. "I know this is shocking," Dassin replied. "But it's *him*. We *know* it's him."

The DA's team helped the feds with the investigation. Mahady and assistant DA Gene Hurley, the prosecutor on the office's escort cases, already had some familiarity with Brener. Velina Stamova, the Bulgarian prostitute who had become their cooperating witness in the aftermath of her involvement with NY Confidential, had worked for Emperors Club VIP in 2006. On this juicy investigation, there would be none of the usual turf battles among prosecutors. The feds wanted Morgenthau's office to stand down, and Morgenthau was eager to do so. His conflict was clear; the two men had been close for years.

But Morgenthau, who was then eighty-eight and had served as DA for thirty-three years, also knew that the city's tabloids, if they ever found out, would accuse him of giving his friend a pass. To protect himself, he told U.S. attorney Michael Garcia, Dassin's boss, that he wanted a letter for his files formally asking him to stand aside. Garcia readily agreed. Morgenthau's office even wrote it. Dated December 13, the letter was titled "In re Emperor's Club."

Dear Mr. Morgenthau:

This office is conducting an investigation into the Emperor's Club, an escort service operating in Manhattan. We understand that the

New York County District Attorney's Office is conducting a similar investigation of the same escort service. Based upon our recent discussions, it appears that our investigation has progressed further than yours.

We are requesting that you discontinue your investigation, except to provide whatever information and assistance we may ask of you. This action on your part would be very helpful in ensuring a successful outcome.

We appreciate your anticipated cooperation in this matter.

Very truly yours,
Michael J. Garcia

Dassin had another question for his counterparts at the DA's office. How did they handle the johns in prostitution cases—did they charge them with a crime? The DA's men told him they usually didn't. The feds were investigating the possibility that Spitzer had used state or campaign money—not his own funds—for his assignations. If he hadn't, Dassin mused, it was possible they might never find anything that merited prosecution. Perhaps it would never come out.

Morgenthau's team assured the feds that this information would be held in the strictest confidence. Among themselves, however, they couldn't imagine that it would remain secret—the story was just too explosive. Privately, they began speculating as to how long it would take to hit the headlines. Some thought it might take a couple of months, others just a couple of weeks. But no one doubted what would happen.

———

By year-end, it seemed hard to imagine how Spitzer's political situation could get worse. The latest polls showed that only 36 percent of New Yorkers viewed him favorably; 56 percent said they would rather vote for "someone else" in 2010. No significant legislation had passed since summer. Even the *Times* placed him at a crossroads: "Mr. Spitzer can either figure out how to operate the governor's office more skillfully for the next three years, or he can fail in his vital mission to reform and restart New York State."

Spitzer's political staff had also noticed some changes in the behavior of their boss. One issue was his travel habits. From the earliest days of his campaign for governor, he'd always made a point of leaving early and coming back late to avoid spending nights away from home. But now that didn't seem so important to him. He seemed to be coming up with excuses to spend the night in a hotel.

Spitzer had also begun taking out some of his frustrations on those who worked for him, prompting private jokes about his temperament. After an out-of-state trip with Spitzer in December, fundraiser Kristie Stiles advised Rod Covington, head of the governor's State Police detail, about the boss's "great holiday spirits . . . you know that's sarcasm, right?"

Covington e-mailed back: "Hey, I wanted to warn you that Santa was delivering coal!"

"Was a lot more than coal!" Stiles wrote.

"Buckle up," Covington told her, "I have a feeling it's going to be a long and bumpy ride."

Constantine, meanwhile, was still trying to get Baum (among others) fired. He even complained to the governor about his decision to award Bruce Gyory the title of senior advisor; he e-mailed Spitzer that he wanted a new title—that of *principal* advisor—to signify "a distinct status which I both have and at this point deserve." A stern lecture at the November staff retreat had done nothing to stem the corrosive media leaks, several of which appeared in the pages of *The New York Sun*. This prompted Danny Hakim, of the *Times*, angry at getting scooped, to confront Constantine. "Could we have an off-rec conversation today about these leaks to the *Sun*?" Hakim wrote in an e-mail. "All signs point to you."

The media, which had propelled Spitzer's rise, now seemed the instrument of his undoing. Silda felt particularly frustrated with the *Times*, which she felt should know better; it was ignoring Eliot's many achievements. She began to suspect that Hakim had some undisclosed tie to Bruno after personally conducting Internet research about his background that revealed he had family in the senator's district. She'd given Hakim the cold shoulder at Watkins Glen while he was writing a gentle feature about the governor's fascination with NASCAR.

In the search for answers, some saw a "messaging" problem. Silda urged her husband's staff to tap the expertise of various outside experts—either personal acquaintances from New York or authors of books she'd read. One of these was Drew Westen, an Emory University psychologist who had written a bestseller about how Democrats need to appeal to voters' emotions. Silda encouraged everyone to read it. At the Spitzers' personal expense, Westen was flown up from Atlanta for a private meeting, and later was asked to make suggestions on drafts of a big speech. Jimmy Siegel, Spitzer's campaign adman, had his own solution. He proposed that the governor hire him and his partner as full-time communications advisors—to make sure that "positive accomplishments get maximum play—and any contentious ones be presented in ways to minimize the resultant blow-back." Wrote Siegel: "It's akin to a company, a brand, rolling out new products. You want to spend a lot of time figuring out how to launch them."

In the end, the administration did try a radical new approach: a kinder, gentler Eliot Spitzer. After Thanksgiving, Spitzer met privately with the assembly Democrats he'd lambasted during the comptroller fight and joked that his wife hadn't liked him at first either, but now they were happily married. In January, he delivered a remarkably conciliatory State of the State address. He endorsed a $1 billion economic-development fund for upstate and a politically popular cap on property-tax increases that he'd previously opposed as irresponsible. His declared agenda for 2008 was an exercise in conflict avoidance. Campaign-finance reform was barely mentioned. He shelved a controversial plan (from a commission he had appointed) to let state universities set their own tuition. Although he was seeking more healthcare cuts—the state was facing a big budget hole—he'd begun early talks with industry lobbyists to avoid another media war. He even endorsed a pay raise for lawmakers.

In early January, Bruno's wife of fifty-seven years had died of Alzheimer's disease. Spitzer called the senator to offer his condolences, then joined every prominent politician in the state—along with the archbishop of New York—at a memorial service a week later. The two men embraced in the church.

But there would be no easy way back—Spitzer's natural allies remained wary and his enemies remained sworn. His gestures at appeasement during the State of the State had drawn only polite applause from the gathered lawmakers. They reacted as a hostile crowd, skeptical that Spitzer, though badly weakened, was really different. And in truth, he wasn't. "That was a change of strategy, not a change of conviction," says Christine Anderson, who'd been promoted to communications director after Dopp's departure. Fred Dicker put it this way: "I'm sure Eliot Spitzer is loved by his dog and his family, but when it comes to politics and the world that I inhabit in this state capital, he has very few friends."

In early November, Baum had received a strange e-mail in his capitol office. It read: "Stone is coming for your man Spitzer—Eliot's going down." The message originated from an address for Drake Ventures. Though Baum didn't recognize it, this was the name of Roger Stone's consulting business—the dirty trickster hadn't gone away.

———

It's uncertain precisely what launched the federal case that would lead to criminal charges against the operators of the Emperors Club. But it's clear that, from the start, its real target was Eliot Spitzer. A government filing states that the investigation began in the fall, when IRS agents stumbled across evidence of Spitzer's suspicious bank transfers "in the course of a regularly conducted review." This evidence presumably took the form of the North Fork SAR, though it remains unclear how it would spontaneously surface, in the mountain of such filings, without someone drawing it to the feds' attention. As former federal prosecutor Marc Agnifilo, a criminal defense lawyer in the case, puts it: "The government very rarely gets lucky. They get a phone call."

From the IRS office in Hauppauge, Long Island, the information appears to have made a serendipitous leap into the U.S. attorney's office in Manhattan. Mike Garcia, eager to make his mark in the pantheon of legendary Southern District prosecutors, had set out to reinvigorate the public-corruption squad by focusing on financial crime. As part of that effort, he'd hired Bob Ryan, an expert on money laundering who had once worked for the IRS in Hauppauge; a friend there had alerted Ryan, who brought the SAR in to Boyd Johnson III, the prosecutor who ran the public-corruption team. The investigation of Spitzer—and, incidentally, the Emperors Club—was under way.

At first, suspicions focused on the possibility of political, not personal, corruption—perhaps blackmail or extortion. But it quickly became apparent that this was a simpler story: the governor was paying for sex. Absent the involvement of minors, johns fell outside the usual province of federal investigation, making it a stretch to charge him with a crime. If Spitzer arranged the transport of a prostitute across state lines, he'd be guilty of violating the 1910 Mann Act. But that law was generally applied only to operators of prostitution rings. They might also find something illegal in his financial transactions. Garcia decided to continue pursuing the matter. Prostitution was a crime, and Spitzer was the *governor*. It couldn't simply be ignored.

It wasn't hard to establish the nature of the business. In mid-October, an undercover FBI agent had called the phone number listed on the Emperors Club website, posing as a customer. Temeka Lewis answered, and the agent recorded their conversation as she booked an appointment for him with an "all-American" brunette named Raquel. By early January, the feds were ready to take the investigation to the next level: the New York prosecutors sent the draft of a wiretap application to Washington for Justice Department approval.

This was a major step. Wiretapping is expensive and intrusive, intended for use only where other methods to investigate major felonies prove inadequate. On January 8, after getting the go-ahead, Garcia's prosecutors obtained the first of five court orders to wiretap the Emperors Club phones and gain access to its e-mail. This massive electronic surveillance effort would continue for two months, intercepting roughly five thousand calls and text messages and more than six thousand e-mails. It would provide the lawmen with a window into the daily operations of a thriving business.

Throughout this period, Brener and Suwal were busy maintaining their stable of fifty prostitutes. One new prospect was "a little bit nervous" because she had never "done anything like this before"; another decided she wasn't interested because a friend who already worked at Emperors Club VIP had once had to have sex with a customer twice in an hour—without being treated to dinner first. There were quality-control issues to deal with: one hooker was strung out on drugs; a customer complained that another was "more sex than sexy." An escort named Madison had walked out on a customer after just forty minutes; the madam blamed it on childcare problems. "The girls who have children tend to have . . . a little more baggage," Suwal noted. Some employees were demanding a promotion. Temeka Lewis voiced doubts that a Miami escort had what it took to become an Emperors Club VIP "Icon Model." But Sophie, who was working in London, might. When the overseas escort complained about how much she was making, Brener got on the phone to offer her a little career counseling. Their goal was to turn everyone into an Icon Model, he told Sophie. It is "much more pleasant for us to split $5,000 than $1,200."

Sometimes things went gratifyingly well. On a Saturday night, a repeat customer called from Los Angeles, wanting to book a last-minute date at his Beverly Hills hotel. Lewis scrambled to send over Chrissy, new to the agency. "Two A-pluses in a row!" the john gushed afterward. "I don't know where you get these young ladies." The client, who had put most of the $1,600 charge on his credit card, mused that he could "get it past my accountant and auditor as a business expense, but you sometimes hear of these agencies getting busted, you know. That's my really only concern," he explained. "That's why I don't call more often." Lewis assured the gentleman that Emperors Club VIP was a company with "real offices in New York City" and a "tax ID" as QAT Consulting. Its customers had nothing to fear, she declared, as the FBI listened in.

———

Ashley had always wanted to be a star. She dreamed of becoming a famous singer. Instead, she would settle for becoming a famous prostitute.

The world would come to know her as "Kristen," the high-priced Emperors Club escort. She was just twenty-two years old when she got her twisted version of a big break, stumbling into the single sexual encounter that would make tabloid and political history. This happenstance would deliver her, overnight, into the promised land of American celebrity. But by that point in her life, Ashley had already tried on a half dozen different identities. Like the wealthy men who patronized the Emperors Club, she was pursuing a fantasy.

She grew up on the New Jersey shore, as Ashley Rae Youmans. Her father operated a struggling landscape business. After her parents divorced, her mother married a wealthy oral surgeon, Michael DiPietro, and the family moved to upscale Wall Township, where they lived in a million-dollar home and Ashley rode to school in a Jaguar. From these comfortable surroundings, both Ashley and her older brother leapt into disaster. Kyle was incarcerated for possession and intent to distribute heroin at a local high school. Ashley ran away from home after her sophomore year to live with her dad on the Outer Banks of North Carolina. At seventeen—less than a year later—she took off on an extended spring-break trip to South Florida. Brandishing the lost driver's license of a New Jersey dental assistant, she posed as twenty-one-year-old Amber Arpaio, and was taped, drunk and topless, for a *Girls Gone Wild* video. "It's all fun and games," "Amber" told a reporter writing about the boobfest for *The Palm Beach Post*. "You might as well show off what you have before you don't have it anymore."

After dropping out of school, Ashley lived with a boyfriend in North Carolina, then moved to New York, where she began taking private voice lessons and recording songs. But that didn't pay the rent. After a few months working as a strip-club waitress and bar hostess, she signed on with pimp Jason Itzler, as "Victoria," NY Confidential's "newest seductress." It was September 2004; Ashley was nineteen. But she was a natural—pretty, fun, and designer-accessorized, with an ability to turn men into fools. "Ashley is addictive," says Shelley Everett, who booked prostitution appointments for her. "Men just love that girl. She's so chameleon, it's crazy. She has that little baby voice she puts on, and makes everybody feel, 'I'm your girl-friend.' Nobody does that shit better." Hulbert Waldroup, Itzler's top booker, used Ashley's musical ambitions as a selling point with johns. "She was a New Jersey Italian girl, working on her music career. That was her selling point—she's going to do this just six months to build up her career." Waldroup delivered the pitch to callers: "Sir, can you imagine having an appointment with *Madonna* before she's famous? Think of the bragging rights you'll have! I'll have her bring one of her CDs!"

When NY Confidential was busted, she moved to a spinoff agency that her boyfriend had started in Brooklyn. When he was arrested, she moved on again. Ashley occupied the hazy terrain of a working Manhattan party girl—hanging around rich older men at hot clubs, drinking vodka, snort-ing coke, and she performing sexual favors. She had inflated her curves with breast implants, and she decorated her body with tattoos. Ashley rationalized her prostitution simply: she was going to sleep with men any-way, so she might as well get paid for it. She'd escort enough to keep herself in designer clothes—or until she found a new sugar daddy—then drop out of sight for months. As Ashley saw it, she was just biding time until she became a pop star. She later explained her Manhattan party life as "get-ting to know the music scene, networking in clubs and connecting with the industry." She formed a company, Pasche New York, to promote her sing-ing career, and copyrighted three songs. Although she'd never actually made money in the business, she clung to the lifestyle of a diva. Even her cocker spaniel, Brooklyn, wore couture—a $400 Louis Vuitton collar, recalls Everett. Adds Everett: "She's a very expensive toy."

Wesley Mann, a young photographer, became friends with Ashley after they met in the fall of 2006 on Forty-sixth Street in Midtown Manhattan, where both of them lived. Mann and his roommate sometimes hung out at her apartment, which she shared with her dog and cat. It was a small one-bedroom, but filled with expensive stuff. She'd rigged up a recording studio in her shower, like a rap artist, and told them she knew celebrities, including P. Diddy and Vin Diesel. There were photos of Ashley with rich-looking older men, one taken on a private jet. Ashley explained that she worked as a waitress and in real estate. But they wondered. One day, Ashley asked Mann if he'd photograph her. They took the shots in Mann's apartment, after she'd made dinner—pasta fagioli—for him and his roommate. "She very quickly offered to do it without her shirt," recalls Mann. "It was Janet Jackson; she got into it fast. This was what she wants to be—a performer." After finishing the shoot and giving Ashley some prints, Mann stashed the photos at the bottom of his stack, certain he'd never look at them again.

By early 2007, Ashley had found her way to the Emperors Club. As usual, Brener and Suwal drove into Manhattan to size up the new candidate. Ashley didn't want her picture posted on the agency's website, lest any of her music contacts recognize her. This limited her marketability—customers naturally wanted to see what they were getting. She clearly had a winning, girlish personality—she signed her text messages "xoxo." But she was also a little "bottom heavy," recalls Suwal; the young madam wasn't much interested in hiring her. Brener, on the other hand, found her appealing. "She looks like a corporate girl who could really go wild!" he explained later. Tammy Thomas, the booker, had her own opinion: "I thought she looked like a girl you'd see on the train in New Jersey." So they brought her on at a bottom-rung rate—$1,000 an hour. During her years as an escort, Ashley had previously used the names Victoria and Sam. At Emperors Club VIP, she would go by Sloan, before changing to Kristen.

Ashley would later explain that she was searching during these years "for that identity of who I am," and her life certainly reflected considerable confusion. It was hard to even keep her current name straight. On a My-Space posting dated August 2007, Ashley painted a melodramatically tragic portrait of her pampered childhood: she had run away from "a broken family" and "abuse." Yet just months earlier, she'd filed court papers in New Jersey to change her legal name to Ashley Rae Maika DiPietro, explaining in legal documents that this was "a thank you" to her stepfather because he had raised her from the age of six and was "the only father I have known." In her music career, she was using a stage name, Ashley Nina Veneta. In Manhattan, meanwhile—and on MySpace—she went by yet another name: Ashley Alexandra Dupré. "My path has not been easy," she wrote in that MySpace posting. "I have been alone. I have abused drugs. I have been broke and homeless. But, I survived, on my own. I am here, in NY, because of my music. . . . Now it's all about my music. It's all about expressing me. I can sit here now, and knowingly tell you that life's hard sometimes. But, I made it, I'm still here and I love who I am."

One of her Emperors Club VIP customers was Joe Brooks, the sixty-nine-year-old Oscar-winning songwriter-director who wrote the hit "You Light Up My Life." Brooks would later be charged with multiple counts of raping aspiring starlets he'd lured to his apartment under the pretext of auditioning for an acting role. According to booker Thomas, after finishing a paid appointment with Ashley, Brooks had convinced her to spend the rest of the night with him, gratis, by promising to get her a recording contract.

For much of 2007, Ashley hadn't worked at Emperors Club VIP at all. Then she experienced a new romantic disaster, which she later described to an interviewer. She had been shocked to discover that the man she was dating, who had set her up in a stylish luxury studio in Manhattan's Flatiron District, turned out to be *married*—and the father of two children. Despite this revelation, she'd continued the relationship for six months, until he'd finally left her to pay her own rent: $3,600 a month. So in January 2008, "Kristen" rejoined the roster of escorts available for hire at the Emperors Club.

———

Darren Dopp was ready to talk. Taking a political hit was one thing; facing indictment was another.

Troopergate was in its seventh month. The Spitzer administration was in court, fighting subpoenas from the senate. The public-integrity commission probe was dragging on. But the big-stakes inquiry was unfolding in the office of Albany County DA David Soares.

For a time, the thirty-eight-year-old prosecutor had taken a serious look at indicting Dopp. Soares had begun his investigation at the request of the public-integrity panel, which had asked him to consider perjury charges after hearing Dopp recant his written statement of regret to Cuomo. Still in his first term as DA, Soares had been harshly criticized earlier for clearing the administration without putting the governor and his top aides under oath. Now he was determined to show that he wasn't anyone's puppet.

But as Soares dug into the matter, he recognized the case was too shaky and inconsequential to charge Dopp with perjury, a felony offense. Soares had also weighed—and rejected—bringing a coercion case against the administration lawyers for leaning on Dopp to sign his statement. Yet the investigation lingered into January, with nothing more than perjury-related misdemeanor charges still hanging over Dopp; he was considering entering a plea to end the matter.

Dopp's new lawyer, a former assistant U.S. attorney named Michael Koenig, had a better idea. In a private meeting with the DA, Koenig dangled the bait to make Dopp's criminal problem go away. "When is someone going to ask the one thing that's never been asked of Darren: *what did Spitzer know and when did he know it?* That's the elephant in the room," Koenig said. "If you ask him about that, you're going to hear that Spitzer knew a *lot* more than he's let on. And you're going to hear that the governor used some pretty colorful language." Soares was receptive—he'd suspected Dopp was being made a scapegoat—and they quickly hammered out a deal: Dopp would tell the rest of his story, in exchange for immunity from prosecution.

On February 5, the governor's former communications director appeared for a sworn interview with Soares and his deputies, who had already questioned him twice before for the DA's first investigation. They quickly zeroed in on the fateful decision to release the Bruno travel records. Dopp described the governor's frustration with the abrupt end to the legislative session; how Baum had told him that Eliot wanted the documents released; how he went in to hear it straight from Spitzer; and how he'd warned the governor about Bruno's certain angry response.

"I said to Eliot, 'Boss, you're okay with the release of the plane records?' He said, 'Yeah, do it.' I said, 'Are you sure?' And then he gave a very, you know, pointed, angry response that left no doubt that he wanted the records released."

"And that response was?"

"He used profanity and made it clear that he wanted the records released."

"Do you remember what he said exactly?"

Dopp hesitated, motioning toward assistant DA Linda Griggs, the former Air Force prosecutor leading the questioning. They went off the record.

"There's a lady in the room," Dopp protested.

"I'm no *lady*," Dopp recalls Griggs telling him. "Tell us *exactly* what the governor said."

Dopp resumed his story. "He said: 'Fuck him! He's a piece of shit! Shove it up his ass with a red-hot poker!'" They went through the exchange over and over. "The operative line was: 'Shove it up his ass with a red-hot poker,'" repeated Dopp.

"In addition to his words, what else led you to believe that the governor was very angry?" Griggs asked.

"Just the appearance," Dopp replied. "I mean, he turned a little red and, you know, he was drinking a cup of coffee and, you know, as he was saying it, he was *spitting* a little bit. He was *spitting* mad."

"When the governor told you to release the records, did you consider this a *directive* from the governor?" Griggs asked.

Dopp rolled his eyes: "You couldn't mistake that based upon the words that were used."

With that, the DA—who had previously concluded that the administration had done nothing really wrong in Troopergate—began exploring a new line of inquiry: *had the governor lied about his role?* Over the next four weeks, Soares gathered evidence to substantiate Dopp's story. He interviewed Sandy Dopp, who recalled how her husband had described the episode to her months earlier. He examined Dopp's diary, which contained a reference to the remark. And he questioned one of Dopp's former lawyers, who recalled how Darren, venting his belief that "the governor lied three times," had told him about the "red-hot poker" exchange back in September.

It wasn't clear where this would end up. But Soares was now exploring the possibility of charging the sitting governor of New York with perjury.

———

Eliot Spitzer, was plotting his resurrection. His decline in the polls had been startling. But he certainly wasn't the only governor to experience a rocky start—and he had three more years to get things back on track. Already, there were signs of progress. Spitzer was continuing to make nice with the lawmakers; there hadn't been a public "Irwin" outburst for weeks. And Troopergate was surely petering out. The *Times* had called for the scandal to be put "where it belongs—among the footnotes in

New York State's history books." After the governor aced his late January budget speech, his staff had decamped to El Mariachi, a Mexican restaurant near the capitol. There, a giddy Peter Pope had stood, raised his beer glass, and proposed a toast: "To turning the corner!"

The Bruno problem, of course, remained. Despite Spitzer's efforts to project a new appreciation for the virtues of "partnering," he felt more certain than ever that nothing meaningful would be accomplished until Bruno—and the senate Republicans—were out of his way. There was no question that he would outlast Joe. The FBI's criminal investigation into the senator's personal finances seemed to be heating up; it could take him out at any moment. And if that didn't topple Bruno, the November elections cycle surely would.

Spitzer was already gunning to snatch another GOP senate seat, opened up for a late February special election after the incumbent had quit to become a lobbyist. It was the longest of long shots, to be sure. Although the Democrats had a strong candidate in assemblyman Darrel Aubertine, a local dairy farmer, the rural "North Country" district, hugging the Canadian border, had been Republican for more than a century. Spitzer was throwing all his muscle into the race anyway: Jimmy Siegel was doing the ads, Ryan Toohey coordinating the campaign. The governor was so unpopular that he couldn't campaign personally—it would destroy whatever chance Aubertine had. But he was deeply involved, even reviewing cuts of Siegel's ads for Aubertine on Baum's laptop before they aired. A victory would drop Bruno's majority to a single seat.

In the meantime, Spitzer's view was that he could regain his footing by going small and going large: promoting local projects, especially upstate economic development, while speaking out on the sort of national issues that were his trademark, far beyond the bitter purview of Albany. To calibrate this effort, he'd begun holding a series of secret strategy meetings with his most trusted political advisors, over breakfast at the Tudor Hotel, in Midtown Manhattan.

For all his problems in New York, Spitzer was still a player on the national stage. Albany had a way of diminishing New York governors. The farther away Spitzer got, the better he looked. "Outside of New York," says Stiles, "everyone still thought he was going to be president someday." On January 26, he'd flown to Washington to attend the annual black-tie dinner of the Alfalfa Club, whose two hundred members included national political and business luminaries. President Bush was the featured speaker. The affair was held at the Capital Hilton. The governor would spend the night at his favorite D.C. hotel—the Renaissance Mayflower. Four blocks from the White House, across the street from *The Washington Post*, the Mayflower was a Washington landmark. It's where newly elected president Franklin Delano Roosevelt wrote the inaugural speech reassuring America that it had "nothing to fear but fear itself"—and where House impeachment prosecutors interrogated Bill Clinton's mistress, Monica Lewinsky.

As the governor hobnobbed over dinner with the rich and powerful, a team of FBI agents was on his tail, believing that he had plans to meet a prostitute from New York at the Mayflower in violation of the Mann Act, *The Washington Post* would later report. No Emperors Club VIP escort showed up.

Spitzer would return to Washington again on the evening of February 6, for a series of congressional meetings the next day. Again, Spitzer spent the night at the Mayflower, and this time, Angelina would travel to Washington for a liaison with George Fox. But the encounter apparently went unnoticed. Seven days later, the governor of New York would return to Washington—and the Mayflower Hotel—for a third time. It was on this occasion that Spitzer's unlucky stars would finally fall into perfect alignment.

———

On Monday, February 11, Governor Spitzer had a 7:30 A.M. breakfast with Felipe Calderón, the president of Mexico, at the Waldorf Astoria, in Midtown Manhattan. Calderón was an admirer of Spitzer's lawsuits on behalf of low-wage grocery store workers, many of them Hispanic, as well as his failed attempt to give licenses to illegal immigrants. Spitzer was to travel to Albany by helicopter that morning, in time to arrive for an 11 A.M. press event. But first, he had an errand to run just a few blocks away at the post office near Grand Central Station. There, the governor of New York waited in line and purchased money orders. Then he mailed them in an envelope with no return address. The destination: QAT Consulting.

At 10:53 that evening, FBI agents captured Temeka Lewis's text message to Cecil Suwal, asking the Emperors Club madam to alert her if the "package" from George Fox arrived in the mail on Tuesday. Fox had called Lewis to book an appointment in Washington for Wednesday, just two days off. He would be staying at the Mayflower. But Brener and Suwal wouldn't let it happen unless the money arrived first.

Angelina wouldn't be going on this out-of-town trip. The Emperors Club would instead be dispatching the hooker known as Kristen—Ashley Dupré. Lewis coordinated the arrangements. Ashley was to take an Amtrak train from Penn Station to Washington late Wednesday afternoon. The client would be paying for everything, from train tickets to cab fare to liquor from the hotel minibar. In a departure from his usual practice, he'd book the room where they'd meet himself. Ashley was all set to go—as soon as she got word that the money had arrived. The Emperors Club managers fumed at the continuing complexity of Fox's arrangements.

On Tuesday afternoon, Eliot Spitzer flew back from Albany to New York City. There, he made a jaunty appearance on Comedy Central's satirical *Colbert Report*. During their chat about the Democrats' presidential nominating fight, host Stephen Colbert joked about his desire to become a convention "superdelegate" like Spitzer, and asked what it was like to attain such stature. "We have capes, we have leotards, we have special outfits that we wear," explained Spitzer.

"I would like to see some pictures of you in that outfit," said Colbert.

"For that," replied the governor, "you have to pay extra, Stephen."

After the taping, Spitzer met Lloyd Constantine for dinner at Quatorze Bis, a low-key Upper East Side bistro, one of Spitzer's favorite restaurants. Constantine was unhappy. Unwilling to take on a hopeless political fight in his weakened state, Spitzer had deferred several controversial recommendations of his higher-education commission, which Constantine had labored over for months. In a conference call with senior staff, he'd even angrily scolded Constantine for pressing the matter. With that, Lloyd had insisted on a private meeting to tell the governor he wanted to quit. He wanted an appointment as chancellor of the state university system—which Spitzer wasn't about to give him.

Constantine didn't know that. Even finalizing the meeting with Spitzer had been difficult, though Lloyd was braving a storm to come down from Albany. "It was like: 'Dickhead, I'm driving down to have dinner with you in the snow!'" As Constantine saw it, this was "symptomatic of the way he'd been conducting himself all year long. He was just a very different person than the guy who had always been my friend." When they finally sat down to talk, Spitzer seemed distracted, unwilling to deal with his complaints. "He was anyplace but sitting opposite me," says Constantine. Spitzer even got up from the table twice during their dinner to make private calls; the snippets of conversation Constantine heard didn't make any sense.

Indeed, it was at 8:12 P.M. that George Fox called Temeka Lewis to see if his "package" had arrived. She told him that it had not. Had he sent it to the usual address for QAT? "Yup, same as in the past, no question about it," Fox replied. Lewis decided to see if Brener would let them finalize the appointment anyway—he had a credit with the agency of $400 or $500. She told Fox to call her back in five minutes. But Brener wouldn't go for it. When they spoke at 8:23 P.M., Lewis told Fox that the "office" needed more money up front. They agreed to talk again the next day.

On Wednesday, February 13, Spitzer left New York City early on a state plane for a daylong upstate swing, before yet another trip to Washington. This trip was part of his comeback strategy. He was making regular visits to places that rarely saw a governor, meeting with local leaders to develop city-by-city economic-development projects. On this day, Spitzer spoke with a business group in downtown Rochester, stopped by a veterans hospital in Batavia, and toured a university campus in Buffalo. His final appointment was an hour-long meeting with civic leaders from Niagara Falls at Shorty's, a local sports bar. His black SUV pulled up about twenty minutes late for the 3 P.M. session, with the press waiting outside. The governor kept everyone waiting for several minutes while making a phone call from inside his parked car.

At 3:20 P.M., with FBI agents listening in, George Fox called Temeka Lewis. The money still hadn't arrived. His date with Ashley Dupré—and scandal—hung in the balance, dependent on the efficiency of the U.S. Postal Service. Fox told Lewis that he had already reserved a room at the Mayflower, and had paid for it using his name. He said there would be a key waiting for the escort. At 4:18 P.M., Suwal finally sent word to her booker: "package arrived." Lewis immediately alerted Dupré; she was clear to board the train to Washington.

George Fox was pleased to hear the news when he called Lewis again at 4:58 P.M. They set the Washington appointment that evening for about 10 o'clock; only then did he ask who he'd be seeing. Her name was Kristen, Lewis told her customer. "Great, okay, wonderful," he replied. Lewis urged him to give Kristen "extra funds," so they wouldn't have to "go through this" the next time. Fox would see what he could do.

Eliot Spitzer, while in a holding room at the Niagara Falls airport, had convened a conference call with the press to discuss the state's horse-racing franchise at about 4:30 P.M. that day. When it was over, he'd asked the staff and security detail accompanying him to clear the room for a moment so he could make a private call. At 5:13 P.M., the governor, accompanied by two aides and a trooper, took off in the state plane for Washington.

This part of the trip hadn't really been necessary. Spitzer was going to testify the next day—Valentine's Day—before the capital-markets subcommittee of the House Committee on Financial Services. The topic for the hearing—"the state of the bond insurance industry"—wasn't exactly hot gubernatorial fodder. In fact, the subcommittee hadn't wanted Spitzer's testimony at all. But when he'd learned that his state insurance chief, Eric Dinallo, had been called, Spitzer instructed his aides to extract an invitation for him as well. For Spitzer, it was a way to remind people about his early role, back in his glory days as attorney general, sounding alarms about the subprime mortgage crisis and attacking passive federal regulators. Once his testimony had been arranged, he'd even scheduled an early-morning CNBC interview and written an op-ed for *The Washington Post* attacking the Bush administration; both were set for the day of the hearing.

Congressional witnesses are generally expected to submit their testimony days in advance. But as Spitzer landed in Washington at 6:25 on the evening before his midday appearance, he had a fresh set of revisions, even though a copy of his remarks had already been turned in to the House staff. By 9:29 P.M., Lora Lefebvre, a state finance expert who was helping from her office back in Albany, had incorporated these changes and e-mailed the latest draft for a quick final read by the governor. By then, Spitzer and his entourage had long since arrived at the Mayflower. But the quick approval never came. After briefly coming back downstairs, Spitzer had gone dark. No one had seen or heard from him.

"Still here. Any sense of timing?" wrote Lefebvre at 10:51 P.M. Danny Kanner, Spitzer's body man, was out to dinner at a Mediterranean restaurant with an old friend. When nothing more was heard from the governor, Kanner finally e-mailed Lefebvre at 11:20 P.M.: "Should definitely go home."

After arriving in Washington and checking into his own room, George Fox had spoken to Lewis at 8:47 P.M. to relay his cloak-and-dagger arrangements for Kristen. When she got to the hotel, she should go straight to Room 871. The door would be slightly ajar, but not visibly open, and there'd be a key for her inside. The booker next turned to financial arrangements. She told Fox that he owed a balance for the evening of $2,721.41, and that it would be ideal if he could give Kristen an extra $2,000 on top of that. He asked Lewis to tell him what Kristen looked like. She rattled off her escort profile: American, petite, very pretty, brunette, five foot five, 105 pounds.

By 9:32 P.M., Kristen had arrived in the room, located on a quiet club floor of the Mayflower, and checked in with Lewis for an update. George Fox was already at the hotel, and would be at her door soon. He would be giving her cash, Lewis explained: it would cover the balance of that night's four-hour booking—his customary out-of-town minimum—and provide extra money for future appointments.

He arrived at about 10:15 P.M., and was gone by midnight. Ashley Dupré immediately called her booker to deliver the escort version of an after-action report. First, they discussed the money. Fox had given her $4,300, Ashley told Lewis. Then they discussed the john. Despite his mixed reputation among the escorts—reflecting his inclination to get straight down to business—Dupré said she actually liked him. Unlike some of her professional colleagues, she wasn't put off by a client who didn't bother much with small talk. "I don't think he's difficult," she blurted. "I mean, it's just kind of like . . . *whatever* . . . I'm here for a purpose. I know what my purpose is." In this life, Ashley Dupré, at twenty-two, had no pretensions. "I am not a . . . moron, you know what I mean? So maybe that's why girls maybe think [he's] difficult. . . . Let's not get it twisted—I know what I do, you know?"

"You look at it very uniquely," Lewis told her. "No one ever says it that way." Brener and Suwal had strictly forbidden their employees to engage in telephone conversations about what went on behind closed doors; it was part of the lengthy "contract" they made everyone sign. But Lewis and Dupré, kicking back at the end of a challenging workday, continued their chatter.

Temeka said that she'd been told about another concern with the evening's client—that George Fox "would ask you to do things that, like, you might not think were *safe* . . . very basic things." Both women understood the shorthand: George Fox didn't like to use a condom.

"I have a way of dealing with that," explained Ashley Dupré, who knew how to lay it on the line. "I'd be like, *Listen, dude*: you really want the sex?"

————

By February 27, Eliot Spitzer and his team felt like they truly were turning the corner. That morning, they'd woken up to headlines about their stunning upset in the special senate election upstate—Aubertine had won. With his majority shaved to a single senator, Bruno was finally on the ropes. After a stormy closed-door caucus, the Republicans made a public show of literally standing behind their leader. Bruno told the capital press corps that Spitzer was "playing every dirty trick that can be played." But now, he seemed flailing and desperate. The governor, despite his personal unpopularity, had masterminded a victory in one of New York's most Republican quarters. The message was loud and clear: if he could beat them there, he could beat them anywhere.

The next morning, Spitzer addressed the annual power breakfast of the Association for a Better New York, being held at Cipriani, down on Wall Street. A year earlier, this event had been the occasion for the governor's shocking assault on his adversaries in the healthcare fight. But now, things were different. On this day, the governor's theme was unity: the need to put aside political and regional differences to pass a budget for "One New York." Declared Spitzer: "We are one state with one future and we will rise and fall together."

The full house for this event included members of the governor's family and many of his dearest friends. Bob Morgenthau sat at Spitzer's table. He greeted Silda warmly, and chatted with Eliot's parents, Bernie and Anne, whom he'd known for years. The Manhattan DA also exchanged pleasantries with his former assistant, who had gone on to such great things. When Spitzer's speech was over, he received a standing ovation from the crowd of six hundred.

But Morgenthau sat through it all with a secret sense of dread. He knew that the feds were hot on Spitzer's trail, surely on the brink of exposing his shocking secret. *Did Eliot have any idea?* Morgenthau didn't think so. "It was pretty difficult," he said later, "for me to watch a guy committing suicide."

At the end of the day, Spitzer headed out to LaGuardia Airport for a 9:05 P.M. JetBlue flight to West Palm Beach, where he was scheduled to speak the next day at an election-year fundraiser for the Palm Beach County Democratic Party. Two aides and a state trooper were traveling with him. They didn't understand why they were overnighting in Florida on this trip—they could have flown in the next morning. Eliot also seemed unusually agitated, becoming furious when their flight was delayed.

They would not land until 1 A.M. When they finally arrived, Spitzer and his entourage made the short drive over to their hotel, the Ritz-Carlton in West Palm Beach. Angelina was already in a room there, waiting for him.

Chapter 14: Client 9

BANG! BANG! BANG!

The knock on the door of Apartment 12-L at the Briarcliff came at about 6 A.M. on Thursday, March 6.

"FBI!"

Brener and Suwal were sleeping, as they always did, curled up together. When he stumbled out to open the door, a half dozen men—*big men*—wearing bulletproof vests and carrying guns, burst inside. Suwal, who slept naked, came out of the bedroom wide-eyed, after wrapping herself in a blanket.

"We are closing down Emperors Club VIP!" the FBI announced. "Are there firearms on the premises?"

Who did they think they were—Bonnie and Clyde?

The agents separated them immediately. Suwal was allowed to get dressed and was then brought into the kitchen. Brener was led back into the bedroom. After reading them their rights, the feds started asking questions. *The cash!* Suwal thought of it instantly; she *knew* it would get them in trouble.

In short order, the agents found it: $981,483, stuffed in a plastic garbage bag, inside a safe in the closet. Suwal hadn't particularly liked the idea of keeping all that money in the apartment—she believed in banks. (When the feds seized their accounts, they'd find another $179,730 there.) But Mark had his own ideas. Shocked and panicked, Suwal began telling the agents her story. "I'm really a good person!" she protested.

Suwal had never dreamed that it would come to this. She had taken comfort in Mark's tortured reasoning that what they were doing wasn't really prostitution. Besides, *George Fox* was one of their customers. As Suwal put it later: "I'm over here thinking that he's condoning it to a certain extent . . . *the governor of New York* is using our service! How bad can what we're doing be?" But if Suwal and Brener believed their special customer provided immunity from legal peril, they were mistaken. In fact, he was the reason they'd been busted.

———

The phone bookers had been arrested early that morning, too—Temeka Lewis at her apartment in Brooklyn; Tanya Hollander, a thirty-six-year-old part-timer who'd started ten months earlier, at her upstate home in Rhinebeck. They were all brought in for processing at the Metropolitan Correctional Center in Lower Manhattan, the forbidding twelve-story jail attached to the federal courthouse.

At 10:58 A.M., the prosecutor's office e-mailed the media a press release announcing the Emperors Club takedown: MANHATTAN U.S. ATTORNEY CHARGES ORGANIZERS AND MANAGERS OF INTERNATIONAL PROSTITUTION RING. All four defendants faced prostitution charges, which included violating the Mann Act, with a maximum sentence of five years; Brener and Suwal faced twenty more for money laundering. The release described Brener as the "ultimate decision-making authority" at Emperors Club VIP, and Suwal as its "day-to-day" manager.

There was no mention in the statement of any Emperors Club VIP client. But it contained the first hint about the true nature of the investigation, by identifying the three assistant U.S. attorneys "in charge of the prosecution"—Boyd Johnson, Dan Stein, and Rita Glavin. Their names were also on the criminal complaint, which accompanied the e-mailed media release. To courthouse cognoscenti, Johnson was known to be the chief of the Southern District's public-corruption unit.

The next clue came late that afternoon, when the defendants were marched into the courtroom of federal magistrate Michael Dolinger for their bail hearing. In a conspicuous display of force, all three prosecutors were there, as were a half dozen reporters, smelling a quick, colorful story. Joe Goldstein, courthouse scribe for *The New York Sun*, sat in the second row next to Brener's son Greg, who was clearly in shock. Greg owned the New Jersey co-op where his dad and Suwal lived; he'd loaned him $4,000 just months earlier, believing his father was still struggling to make ends meet. Now it turned out his father was a *pimp*—with a pile of cash stashed in his closet? Greg shook his head as he read the charges spelled out in the complaint. "It reads like a movie script," he said. Meanwhile, Goldstein was a bit surprised to spot Boyd Johnson in the courtroom. He didn't know his exact position, but he knew that he was a big wheel in the U.S. attorney's office. *What was he doing at a routine hearing on a chickenshit case like this?*

Alan Feuer was covering the story for the *Times*. On this slow news day, Feuer's first reaction to the press release had been prompted by the name of one of the defendants—Tanya Hollander. Could she possibly be a long-lost relative of former madam Xaviera Hollander, the legendary "Happy Hooker"? Feuer had called the desk to propose a playful little feature story, exploring whether this young woman had gone into the family business. But within an hour, he'd heard back: another reporter had reason to believe that the case involved a public official. After dashing off a brief about the bust for the *Times* website, Feuer arrived at the hearing looking to quietly suss out the tip.

All four defendants initially were represented by public defenders. Lewis and Hollander were released on their own recognizance. Suwal's bail was set at $500,000; she would remain in jail for twelve days. Brener was denied bail. Stein spoke about all the cash that the FBI had found, and how Brener had denied possessing any foreign travel documents before a search turned up two Israeli passports. They'd also found what was "believed to be a controlled substance," Stein announced. It would turn out to be Chinese herbs that the sixty-two-year-old pimp was taking for his high blood pressure. But all that was plenty to convince the magistrate to treat Brener as a flight risk.

Feuer's discreet inquiries among the defense lawyers turned up nothing to advance his colleague's tantalizing tip. Like all the other reporters present, Feuer wrote a straightforward story for the next day's paper about the federal bust of the online call-girl ring, whose prostitutes went for as much as $5,500 an hour. To avoid alerting the competition, his story contained nothing to suggest there was anything more to it than that.

———

The governor of New York was in his Midtown Manhattan office that Thursday afternoon, checking out the latest news from the *Times* website, when he spotted Feuer's posting in the City Room blog:

FEDERAL CHARGES IN ONLINE PROSTITUTION RING

A sense of dread fell over him, he recalled more than a year later. "In an odd way I knew right then: this is going to be no good and will lead inevitably where it led. I remember it very well; I remember that *moment*. . . . Contrary to what people think, I have tremendous equanimity about most things. But I knew when I saw it that this was a real problem. . . . I said to myself: *this is going to go almost inevitably to me.*"

———

In theory, there was no reason why the world had to know that Eliot Spitzer had hired prostitutes. While the feds had gathered plenty of evidence to prove it by the time of the Emperors Club bust, they hadn't resolved the issue of whether to charge him with a crime. In prostitution cases, johns not only usually weren't charged; they also usually weren't *outed*. But most johns weren't governors. And in this case, it is clear that federal law-enforcement officials took steps to ensure that Spitzer would be exposed. They would force Spitzer's hand through the press, the very weapon he had used so often—and so effectively—against his own prosecution targets. It was rough justice, to be sure. But as they saw it, this accomplished a necessary end. In their view, it was dangerous for Spitzer to remain governor because he was erratic, subject to extortion, and had broken the law. He was unfit to hold office.

By Thursday, the road map to Spitzer's demise was already in the hands of a dozen reporters: a forty-seven-page sworn affidavit, e-mailed to the media as part of the initial release. This was a truly remarkable document. Signed by Kenneth Hosey, the lead FBI agent in the case, it drew on all the evidence the government had so painstakingly gathered— from wiretapped phone calls and sidewalk surveillance, bank records and undercover work, a confidential informant and intercepted messages—to vividly portray life inside the Emperors Club. In addition to the four defendants, ten different johns made appearances in this narrative, identified only as Clients 1–10. Most were mere cameos, running just a few paragraphs. But one stood out as the story's star—*Client 9*.

The passage featuring Client 9 presented a detailed account of a liaison that had culminated in Room 871 of a Washington hotel. It ran for thirteen paragraphs and filled more than four pages. It recounted the mini-drama of whether Client 9's payment would arrive on time; recapped furtive calls between the customer and his booker; described the awkward payment arrangements, making clear that this john was a repeat customer; explained the logistics of sneaking "Kristen" up to the hotel room unnoticed; and even offered juicy post-date commentary about Client 9's sexual practices. To be sure, there was a necessary legal purpose to the affidavit: it had been filed in support of the government's applications for warrants to arrest the four defendants, search their homes, and seize evidence. But by any reckoning, this affidavit was far more detailed than necessary to obtain the required judicial permissions—or serve any other legal purpose. It would also tell a story, helping expose Client 9.

"I've covered courts for a while; I've never seen a document like that," says one *Times* reporter involved in the case. "That affidavit was written, in my opinion, to be a time bomb—and the key to setting it off was: *just look at Client 9*. It was a *talking* affidavit; it spoke in a way I'd never seen before. It was never intended to be used in an actual criminal case. This was intended to be a humiliation bomb."

On Friday morning, the *Times* began chasing the story in earnest. The paper's initial suspicions had come from a forty-eight-year-old shoe-leather reporter named Willy Rashbaum. Rashbaum had covered cops and crime in New York for more than twenty years. A colleague once wrote in *Esquire* that this had "given him the persona of a man who had seen all of the strange things at least twice." No one was better sourced inside the criminal justice system. Rashbaum knew the feds had their public-corruption team on the case; he'd interviewed Johnson and Hosey for other stories. But *who* was the public official? Rashbaum and a few others at the *Times* began compiling a speculative list of possibilities. Their first thought, for historical reasons, was Bill Clinton. They considered other names as well: Rudy Giuliani; Al D'Amato; an upstate congressman named Tom Reynolds; Bernie Kerik, the indicted former New York City police commissioner; Chuck Schumer. Even Joe Bruno. The sitting governor of New York did not make the list of suspects.

Rashbaum gleaned more guidance during the day from his sources: their man was a *New York* public official—and was identified in the affidavit as Client 9. The relevant passage offered helpful details, setting off an interstate scavenger hunt. *Room 871, in Washington*—what upscale hotels had a room with that number? *The snippets of conversation*—who spoke like that? *The dates*—who was in Washington on February 13? With word that it might be a New York figure, Danny Hakim, the Albany bureau chief, had been brought into the hunt. To kick the issue around, he phoned an old contact, newly minted PR consultant Darren Dopp, who seemed to know the scuttlebutt about everyone in state politics. They puzzled over various possibilities, considering each suspect carefully, before Dopp finally told Hakim: "I can tell you one guy it *ain't*—Eliot." They both laughed at the very thought.

———

Christine Anderson was ready to chill out. A press staffer in the Clinton White House, Anderson, thirty-one, had endured a tumultuous stretch since her battlefield elevation to communications director. She'd handled the Troopergate fallout, then dealt with the driver's-license disaster. Earlier in the week, Bruno had finally accepted Spitzer's invitation to talk, and they'd chatted amicably over coffee in the governor's mansion. With a one-seat majority and a state budget deadline looming, perhaps Bruno had finally realized that he'd have to do business with the governor.

On Thursday, Anderson had been questioned in her downstate office by investigators with the Albany DA. They'd come down to Manhattan for the final two interviews in Soares's perjury investigation—Anderson and Peter Pope. But there was nothing big on the weekend agenda. On Saturday, Eliot and Silda were issuing a statement recognizing International Women's Day and Women's History Month; the governor had a dinner to attend in Washington that night. Anderson's husband was out of town, heli-skiing in Utah. "I'm looking forward to a quiet weekend to get caught up on errands and sleep," she'd e-mailed her sister. "Also I'm totally hooked on the TV show *Lost* (I'm still on season 2, which I have downloaded on our computer) . . . so it's going to be an exciting weekend."

At about 6:30 P.M. on Friday, the governor popped into Anderson's office, as he always did at the end of the day, to check on what was cooking in the press. "What else is out there?" he asked.

"Nothing you don't know about," Anderson told him. "Oh, we did get these two crazy phone calls." Reporters from two different TV stations had called to ask about a crazy rumor they'd heard from "sources."

Her staff had blown them off, of course—it was beyond ridiculous. Anderson told Spitzer about it anyway:

"You're being blackmailed for prostitution."

They both laughed.

"That is so bizarre," the governor said.

Afterward, Spitzer called press secretary Errol Cockfield, who had fielded one of the calls. He pressed him for more details about exactly what the TV station thought it knew.

———

"Sources" were steering yet another journalist in the direction of Client 9: Jim Odato, the Albany *Times Union* reporter whose story had ignited Troopergate. On Thursday afternoon, just hours after the bust, a source—entirely unsolicited—had e-mailed Odato a copy of the Emperors Club complaint and affidavit. According to *Times Union* investigations editor Bob Port, who worked closely with him, the tipster had explicitly advised Odato to focus on Client 9; said that he was "a very important person who would be of great interest to us"; that he was "very wealthy"; and that this story would "explode." As Port told me: "We had someone drop a dime."

By Friday, after making more calls, the Albany journalists had zeroed in on Spitzer. Odato, without explaining why he was asking, had even gotten Spitzer's press office to confirm that the governor had been in Washington on the evening of February 13. None of this filtered up to the governor. The paper didn't feel like it had enough yet to publish, or even to approach him—just anonymous sources and circumstantial evidence. But it was tantalizingly close. Says Port: "My hair was on fire. I was pooping in my pants." Port called the spokeswoman for the U.S. attorney's office, telling her, "We believe Client 9 is Eliot Spitzer." He got a routine "No comment." The Southern District was "a wall we could never penetrate," says Port. But the editor was later struck by how the affidavit had set the stage for everything that followed. "It's government's use of power in a backdoor way I've never seen. It was like lighting a firecracker, putting it in someone's mailbox, and walking away. They *wanted* this to be known."

At least one high-ranking federal official was treating public disclosure of Spitzer's involvement as not only inevitable, but imminent: Mark Mershon, the assistant FBI director in charge of the bureau's New York office. With the bust of the Emperors Club one day earlier, Mershon felt certain that the press would soon identify Client 9. He decided, as a professional courtesy, to give a heads-up to the top two officials of the New York State Police: acting Superintendent Felton and Deputy Superintendent James Harney. "I did that personally, and that was for the sake of the relationship between the FBI and the State Police," Mershon explained during a series of phone interviews. He described it as "a respectful gesture. . . . I did not want them to be blindsided with a press story that we felt was going to come out."

How did he know this would become public? By that point, Mershon says, "my recollection is that our press officer learned of some inquiries being made by at least one and perhaps two newspapers. The idea was that we thought it would come out over the weekend, or at the very latest Monday, based on what we were hearing." Mershon said he discussed his plan with U.S. attorney Garcia—who clearly didn't like the idea—but that "he basically acceded to my request." At that point, Mershon says, he had no concern that such disclosure would jeopardize the work his agents had done. "This investigation at that point was sufficiently mature. We had all the evidence that was necessary."

So on Friday, he drove up to Albany. There, he privately gave the State Police brass the embarrassing news: the governor they had guarded around the clock had been consorting with prostitutes under their watch. Their reaction, Mershon recalls, was "very sober."

———

On Saturday morning, Spitzer woke up in his Fifth Avenue apartment, as he so often had since becoming governor, to something that annoyed him in *The New York Times*. In an editorial titled A ONE-PARTY NEW YORK STATE, the paper warned that the prospect of a senate controlled by Democrats, so very close at last, "should stir great public concern." Sure, Bruno and the Republicans had "held fast to business as usual," blocking vital reforms. But the Democrats needed a "counterweight"—they weren't perfect either. If they wanted voters to give them so much power, they needed to "earn" it. The governor worked his BlackBerry, venting his latest frustration in an e-mail to nine senior aides: "Can someone please explain nyt edit? Don't they realize they too essentially are supporting status quo? They are afraid of the change they pretend to want so deeply?"

After reading the paper, Spitzer went out with his wife to walk their dogs, Jesse and James. When they arrived back at 985 Fifth, the Spitzers were surprised to find a woman standing watch in the lobby of their building—a reporter from the *Times*.

They were getting closer.

"Can I help you with something?" the governor asked. No, she sheepishly replied. She was helping out with a story, but couldn't say what it was. He took her card.

When he got inside, Spitzer called Christine Anderson. The governor's communications director had other things on her mind that Saturday morning: she'd just found out that she was pregnant with her first child.

Anderson phoned the *Times* reporter staking out her boss, then Hakim, to find out what was up. By then, with Rashbaum working the phones, the *Times* had come to believe that Spitzer was Client 9. The woman at Spitzer's building, the paper's weekend police reporter, was part of a growing team that the *Times* was throwing into the top-secret task of turning up the heat on the governor—and nailing the story. Rashbaum had imagined that their Fifth Avenue stakeout might spot an angry Silda leaving with the children—or frantic aides arriving at the apartment. Later that day Ian Urbina, a *Times* reporter in Washington, would begin visiting every hotel in town that had a Room 871.

"What's going on?" Anderson asked Hakim that Saturday morning, after the governor's call had shattered her plans for a relaxing weekend. The possibility that it might be connected to the strange press inquiries on Friday hadn't crossed her mind.

"I can't tell you," he replied. "But we're working on a big story that's breaking. I need to know where the governor is all day, and where he's going."

Eliot was traveling down to Washington that afternoon for the Gridiron Club dinner, she told him. Hakim said he might need to go there to be close to him.

She relayed all this to her boss, who seemed equally mystified. Anderson and Hakim spoke several times throughout the day, but the reporter still wouldn't say what was up. "Is it Troopergate-related?" she asked. Hakim wouldn't say.

———

David Soares, the Albany DA, was at his Albany home late Saturday afternoon when Michele Hirshman called. Spitzer's first deputy during his

AG years, Hirshman had moved on to a partnership at Paul, Weiss, the powerhouse Manhattan law firm. In September, Spitzer had hired her as his personal attorney in the Troopergate investigations.

"What are you getting ready to release?" she asked Soares. The governor had told Hirshman about the *Times* reporter staking out his building. But he hadn't told her everything, leaving her to conclude that it must be something involving Troopergate.

Soares was bewildered. Nothing's up, he told Hirshman. "We just interviewed your people this week—we're not about to drop anything." Though he certainly wouldn't inform the governor's lawyer, Soares was preparing to go to a grand jury on the issue of whether Spitzer had lied about Troopergate. But any possible action on that front was weeks away.

Spitzer was taking other steps to assess his exposure. For far too many months, he'd madly tossed caution to the winds while serving in two statewide elected offices. He'd paid for prostitutes with wire transfers; made an eyebrow raising request to his bankers; spoken to call-girl dispatchers on his cell phone; used a prominent friend's name as a pseudonym. As a former criminal prosecutor—a man who'd overseen undercover operations himself—Spitzer knew precisely how lawbreakers got caught. He'd even given speeches wryly warning would-be offenders to "never talk when you can nod." Spitzer was also acutely aware of the perils presented by a public official's use of any government or campaign resource for improper personal purposes; Hevesi, the disgraced comptroller, was evidence of that. So now—doing far too little, far too late—the governor called a staffer on the payroll of his reelection campaign, Spitzer 2010, to ask who paid the monthly bill for his BlackBerry. "You pay it," a puzzled Allyson Giard told him.

———

The weather turned foul in New York City on Saturday afternoon, and the governor's American Airlines shuttle to Washington had been scrubbed. It was a perfect excuse to cancel. But Spitzer wasn't about to do that. Looking back, he had his own explanation: *manners.* "It just didn't feel right," he said. "I just thought it wasn't right not to show up. It's not credible that you can't get from New York to Washington."

But there was surely some subconscious motivation. This trip was a chance to carry on business as usual; to spend one final night in the world of the power elite; to pretend that a freight train wasn't barreling toward him. This could be his last hurrah. So Spitzer scrambled, with his trooper detail, to catch Amtrak down to the capital. He changed into his just-purchased white tie and tails in the train's bathroom.

The annual Gridiron Club dinner was a hoary Washington ritual, where six hundred journalists and political figures would chuckle over grilled veal chops and a long evening of musical satire. Some of Spitzer's chief adversaries from nine years in public office were there: President Bush, whose policies he had so often decried; News Corporation chairman Rupert Murdoch, whose *Post* had savaged him in Albany; and U.S. attorney general Michael Mukasey, whose prosecutors surely had him in their sights. But this was an evening for frivolity, and Spitzer worked the ballroom like he hadn't a care in the world.

The governor was seated near the dais, across the table from Stephanie Cutter, a Washington political consultant who would later serve as chief of staff for Michelle Obama. Cutter had never met Spitzer, but she'd sized up plenty of national politicians. She'd worked for Bill Clinton, been an advisor to Ted Kennedy and Senate majority leader Harry Reid, and served as communications director for John Kerry's presidential campaign. By the time the evening was over, Spitzer had made one final convert. "I left the dinner completely impressed," says Cutter. "He was charming, entertaining, smart, and interesting. I thought this man had a future in Democratic politics."

The governor of New York spent the night in Washington, as usual, at the Mayflower Hotel. Early Sunday morning, with the storms still churning, he climbed into a car with the troopers, who drove him back to New York City, where his wife and three daughters were waiting.

On the road back through the gloomy weather, Spitzer checked in with Anderson, asking if she'd heard anything. Hakim hadn't made it down to Washington; his flight from Albany had been canceled. "Nothing new," she wrote back. In fact, there was no news until 11:34 A.M., when Hakim e-mailed her.

"I need to make a request," he wrote. "Need the governor's travel records for the week of Feb 11, 2008—specifically Feb 11 through Feb 15. All hotels he stayed at, where he traveled to, flight records. Also any available records of receipts billed to the state. I'd rather not FOIL for it, but leave it to you. Thanks, D."

They knew.

When Anderson told the governor of this request from the *Times*, Spitzer realized there was no way out.

That afternoon, he gathered his resolve and his family—and did the hardest thing he'd ever done in his life. He told first his wife, then Elyssa, Sarabeth, and Jenna: he'd been deceiving them in a way utterly beyond their worst imagining. In tears, he begged them to someday forgive him. "The pain of looking at Silda and telling her what I had to tell her makes everything I left behind politically pale in comparison," he said later.

Unlike other families dealing with the raw revelation of such a personal betrayal, the Spitzers now had to turn immediately to a public question: *what to do?*

———

Rich Baum was at home in Albany when he received the first e-mail, shortly before dinnertime. The governor wanted to speak with him. But it took a few more exchanges before Spitzer's desires were clear. He wanted his top deputy to drive down to New York City "so we can talk over some things." *Immediately.* "I assume it's important and you would like to see me tonight. Is that correct?" Baum asked.

"Correct," Spitzer wrote back.

A single, panicked thought flashed into Baum's head: he was getting fired again. As he steered his way down the New York State Thruway, Baum's political life flashed before his eyes. He began working his phone.

Baum reached Ryan Toohey, who was kicking back on the veranda at the Ritz-Carlton in San Juan after masterminding the Aubertine senate victory; he hadn't heard a thing. The previous day, Jacob Gershman, the *Sun* reporter, had called Toohey to ask if he could think of a New York pol who might be wrapped up in a prostitution ring; he'd gotten a tip, too. But Toohey didn't make a connection. Baum called Marlene Turner at her West Side apartment; Eliot hadn't told her anything. He called Anderson. She filled him in about Hakim and the *Times*. They couldn't imagine that whatever he had was big enough to drag Baum downstate on a Sunday night. But it was clear the governor was anxious. "You have an eta?" he wrote at 9:15 P.M. "Where are you?" he e-mailed at 9:53 P.M. When Baum finally arrived a little after 10, he sent Toohey a nervous message: "I'm going in."

It was not the scene he expected. Michele Hirshman was sitting in a corner of the apartment. Silda and the girls were out of sight. Eliot was funereal. He led Baum into the study, where the two men sat down.

"I've been seeing prostitutes," the governor told him. "People know about it, and it's going to come out. I've gotta resign."

Baum was so stunned that he began asking questions to understand how such a thing was possible. "There's a sex angle with plenty of people in politics," he said later. "But with Eliot, I never got a hint of that."

"How did you do this with your security detail?" Baum asked Spitzer that night.

"I just slipped out."

"Is this a long-term thing?"

"No, about eight months," Spitzer told him.

After a few minutes of this, Baum told the governor he agreed with his assessment. "You won't be able to survive this. An affair is one thing; breaking the law is another." Then Baum excused himself to go to the bathroom. He shut the door, caught his breath, and called his wife back in Albany to tell her that their world was about to turn upside down.

———

The *Times* had spent Sunday working to nail the story with on-the-ground evidence. This was not one to screw up. Ian Urbina, down in Washington, had spent two days searching the city for the right Room 871. Hakim called Dopp at home and read him two passages from the Emperors Club affidavit: *"Yup, same as in the past, no question about it. . . . Great, okay, wonderful."* A chill ran down Dopp's spine. "That sounds like the boss," he told Hakim.

At about 7:30 P.M., Kristie Stiles, Spitzer's fundraiser, had gotten a frantic call from Donald Franklin, a self-employed town-car driver in Washington. Spitzer had used Franklin's car service during the campaign for governor, and his name had shown up in publicly filed expense reports. Now a reporter was on his doorstep, asking strange questions about how much he'd gotten paid. Stiles spoke to Spitzer at home. "Eliot, *The New York Times* is at Donald's house in Washington. What's going on?" But Spitzer didn't seem particularly interested in this bizarre news. He told Stiles he'd look into it and quickly hung up.

Christine Anderson was a bit preoccupied herself. Her second pregnancy test had turned up positive, and her husband—whom she was waiting to tell in person—was unexpectedly going straight from Utah to

Australia on business. Anderson set her alarm clock for 4 A.M. so she could drive up to Albany with other staffers to get there early Monday morning. The governor was scheduled to speak to family-planning advocates in Albany at 11 A.M.—and to meet privately with the state's Catholic bishops, who wanted restrictions on abortion rights, during the afternoon. Neither Spitzer nor Hakim had told her what was brewing.

"Danny, am I going to get some heads-up from you?" she asked him Sunday night.

"Yes," the reporter replied. "It could be as early as tomorrow."

Early Monday, Marlene Turner sent word up to Albany that the governor was sick and needed to cancel his appointments. Staffers were scratching their heads; Eliot *never* called in sick. "I have a terrible, terrible feeling about this," Danny Kanner, Eliot's body man, told another young staffer at mid-morning. Turner also made calls to the lieutenant governor's chief of staff, asking if Paterson could fill in for Spitzer at the family-planning conference and at the big afternoon meeting with the bishops. O'Byrne was suspicious. What was going on? Nothing, Turner insisted.

Hakim also had heard about the governor's canceled appointments. *I'll bet he's sick*, he thought. Hakim phoned Anderson, who'd gone into the Manhattan office: "So you know now?" She finally did. Baum had told Turner late Sunday night and Anderson early Monday morning. They all expected the *Times* story to be posted that day, on the paper's website.

Those within Spitzer's innermost circle of trust were gathering at his apartment. Constantine had driven down early from Chatham, after receiving Spitzer's tearful call on Sunday night. Emily Spitzer was up from Washington. After the girls had left for school, Constantine argued passionately against Spitzer's plan to resign. "You can't do this!" he argued. "The people *love* you. You're a fighter!" Baum thought there was no way to tough it out. "If you don't resign, you'll be impeached," he told Spitzer—and in the meantime, the battle would throw state government into chaos. Hirshman arrived with the Emperors Club affidavit, which was passed around, sobering everyone. It was just so *tawdry*. Spitzer sat down at his kitchen table and wrote out a resignation statement; he would deliver it at the New York office. At 11 A.M., after getting word from Baum, Anderson convened a conference call with her press staff in New York and Albany, which was being pelted with queries about the canceled appointments. She told them what was happening, and advised them privately that the governor would soon be announcing his resignation.

Back at the apartment, Constantine pleaded with Spitzer to wait: "Anything you do today, you'll be doing under duress, without full mental capacity. It's *irresponsible* for you to do this now." But Silda's voice was the one that mattered. Eliot's revelation had been agonizing for their family, what he'd done was horrible, and the media would surely be brutal. But there was so much at stake for New York. He'd been elected to do a job; he couldn't let the press and Republicans *beat* him. Albany was a cesspool. Who were *they* to judge? Badly as he'd screwed up, the people still needed him—they wanted change. Would the public really care what he did with a prostitute? *Should* they? Clinton had survived a sex scandal—why couldn't Eliot?

Though he felt certain it was delaying the inevitable, Spitzer deferred to his beleaguered wife. There was also something to be said for taking a deep breath before rushing into the abyss. He wouldn't quit on this day. "I feel like after all I've done to her," he told Baum, "I need to respect her wishes." With that, Baum retreated to the privacy of the Spitzers' bathroom and called David Paterson, next in line to be governor, to tell him what was about to become public.

———

The *Times Union* had fallen agonizingly short. Odato had worked the phones over the weekend, but hadn't gotten the final confirmation the paper wanted. Port conferred on Sunday night with the general counsel for Hearst, the paper's parent company, but decided they didn't have enough to publish. On Monday morning, the editor was in New York, teaching a graduate class in investigative reporting at the Columbia Journalism School. During his lecture, he'd put up slides from the portion of the Emperors Club affidavit discussing Client 9, and posed a not-so-hypothetical to his students: "We've been told that Client 9 is a public official. How might we try to figure out who he is? Who do you think it could be?"

The world was about to find out. The governor's office had advised the media that Spitzer would be making a public statement at 2:15 P.M. in the Manhattan office. This news set off panic in the offices of *The New York Times*. The paper wanted desperately to publish its scoop first, but it wasn't yet ready. The story was true, the reporters felt certain—but that was quite different from having what they needed to run it. Back in Albany, Hakim scrambled to come up with a draft and a source that would satisfy the editors. He began negotiating with Anderson for unattributed confirmation and precise language he could use. At 1:34 P.M., Hakim e-mailed her a tentative lead, asking, "Can I do this?" After some refinement, she gave them the go-ahead.

The story went online at 1:58 P.M.:

SPITZER IS LINKED TO PROSTITUTION RING

This first account began cautiously, with what Anderson had explicitly confirmed: "Gov. Eliot Spitzer has informed his most senior administration officials that he had been involved in a prostitution ring, an administration official said this morning." The story noted that Spitzer "was huddled with his top aides inside his Fifth Avenue apartment" after abruptly cancelling his appointments and had scheduled a public announcement "after inquiries from the *Times*." The hypocrisy angle made the third paragraph: "Mr. Spitzer, a first-term Democrat who pledged to bring ethics reform and end the often seamy ways of Albany, is married with three children."

In a combination of haste and an overabundance of caution, the *Times* did not immediately identify Spitzer as Client 9 and open the Pandora's box of seamy details in the Emperors Club affidavit—or even explicitly say that he was a *customer* of the prostitution ring. But all that came within hours, in a series of fresh revelations throughout the day. After a tip from Hakim directed Urbina, the Washington reporter, back to the Mayflower, he'd gotten the goods from a desk clerk, who helpfully checked the hotel's computer: room 871 had been registered on February 13 under the name of "George Fox," who had given *Spitzer's* Fifth Avenue home address. The real George Fox vehemently denied knowing anything about this. Key details in the updated story—including the identification of Spitzer as Client 9—were attributed to an unidentified "law enforcement official." Urbina, who'd slept just a few hours, was parked across the street from the Mayflower as the *Times* posted its first mention of the hotel. Within forty-five minutes, TV camera trucks began skidding up.

Back in the *Times*'s newsroom, Rashbaum needed to step away from his colleagues. While he had indeed seen almost all of the strange things at least twice, he'd never been through anything quite like this. Professionally, breaking the story about the governor had been a marvelous thing to behold. It was like being part of an orchestra; everyone had played together perfectly. But after the piece was posted, the impact of it all struck home. Spitzer's political career was finished; his life would be forever changed. And it was all because of a *prostitute*. It seemed almost silly; it had all been so intense. As he stood a few steps from the news desk, catching his breath after the chase, Rashbaum started to choke up.

So many people rushed to read about the shocking sex scandal that the *Times* website crashed. This story would draw more Web traffic than any day in the paper's online history—including September 11. By 2:35 P.M., Spitzer's press office had already received its first e-mail from a talk-show booker, inviting him to bare his soul. "I wanted to relay all my information should the Governor want to do an interview," Hunter Waters, a senior producer for CNN's *Larry King Live*, wrote. "Please keep Larry in mind, as it would be a perfect forum for the governor."

———

Shortly before 3 P.M., Eliot and Silda Spitzer, accompanied by their entourage, stepped out onto Fifth Avenue, where cameras had already begun gathering, and climbed into a black SUV for the short drive to the governor's office on Third Avenue near Fortieth Street. They entered through the garage, and went up the private elevator to the governor's two-floor suite, where the media was waiting in the briefing room.

While Silda had once snickered about Hillary Clinton standing dutifully by her cheating man, she had decided to do just that. This ritual show of support had become a cliché of the American political sex scandal, and some viewed it as yet another cruel humiliation. *Why shouldn't Spitzer have to deal with this by himself? Why should she have to showcase her pain?* In truth, her choice that afternoon didn't result from much discussion or thought. Silda was shocked and furious. But mostly, she was numb, operating on habit and instinct. Both steered her to stand by Eliot—at least for now. They'd done all of this together. She believed in that vow—for better or worse. And it was important for their girls, especially in the throes of a public cataclysm.

Both tearful, they stood in the hallway for a moment, composing themselves. Finally, he led the way out to the podium, where she stood slightly behind him. Silda was dressed tastefully, as always, in black slacks and a white top, with a powder-blue jacket and a double strand of pearls. Cameras had always loved her. But now she looked like a different woman, broken and ashen. She seemed to have aged a decade overnight. Eliot wore his customary uniform: dark pinstriped suit, adorned with American and state flag pins on the lapel; white shirt; and tightly knotted red striped tie. Silda gazed downward, looking at no one as her husband started to speak.

Unprepared to make a decision, unwilling to reveal anything new, unaccustomed to public acts of personal contrition, Spitzer began a statement that was inevitably vague and unsatisfying: "Today I want to briefly address a private matter." *(This was private?)* "I have acted in a way that violates my obligations to my family, and violates my—or any—sense of right and wrong. I apologize, first and most importantly, to my family. I apologize to the public, whom I promised better."

Spitzer tried to offer a measure of context amid the fury, expressing the long-held belief that had informed his time in Albany—the personal stuff doesn't really matter. "I do not believe that politics in the long run is about individuals," he said. "It is about ideas, the public good, and doing what is best for the state of New York. But I have disappointed and failed to live up to the standard I expected of myself. I must now dedicate some time to regain the trust of my family. I will not be taking questions. I will report back to you in short order. Thank you very much."

And with that—177 words, delivered in sixty-eight seconds—he was gone, rushing out the door with Silda, as frustrated reporters shouted after them: *"Are you resigning? Are you resigning?"*

Chapter 15: Who Killed Eliot Spitzer?

IN SOME QUARTERS, THERE WAS OPEN CELEBRATION. Whoops and cheers rang out on the floor of the New York Stock Exchange. Hank Greenberg, the deposed AIG titan, got the news in his Park Avenue office, when a deputy burst into a meeting carrying a Bloomberg bulletin about the *Times* scoop. "Get the fuck out of here!" Greenberg barked. "I'm working." Then he looked closer. That night, Greenberg went home and toasted Spitzer's crisis with his wife. Celebratory calls streamed in from friends, including an exultant Ken Langone. *"Bingo!"* Langone shouted.

The seventy-two-year-old billionaire had cast himself as the most fervent Spitzer hater anywhere, and it wasn't hard to see why. Hours after the scandal broke, a CNBC crew sought his reaction outside a Tribeca restaurant when he arrived for a charity dinner organized by Dick Grasso. Langone began by calling Spitzer a hypocrite who "destroyed reputations" and who needed to resign immediately. "So how do I feel?" he mused. "I certainly feel sorry for his daughters. Very much so. I don't know his wife. But I gotta, I have to assume she has some idea of this happening. For *him*?" Langone paused. "It couldn't be enough to please me."

Was he surprised at the news?

"Not at all!" Langone replied. "I had no doubt about his lack of character and integrity. It would only be a matter of time. I didn't think he'd do it this soon, or the way he did it." Unable to stop himself, Langone went on: "But I know, for example—I know for *sure*—he went himself to a post office and bought $2,800 worth of mail orders to send to the hooker." Langone gave the reporter a knowing nod and grinned. Spitzer's personal visit to the Grand Central post office had not been disclosed anywhere. But it was a significant event in the government investigation.

"How do you know that?" the reporter asked.

"I *know* it," Langone replied mysteriously. "I know somebody who was standing in back of him in line." And just who might *that* be? She didn't ask.

The reporter moved on: "What do you think is next for Governor Spitzer?" "You know," said Langone, "we all have our own private hells. I hope his private hell is *hotter* than anybody else's."

———

This was a sex scandal for the twenty-first century—a global, cross-platform phenomenon, rippling instantly in every direction. It made headlines in the Philippines, and generated tasteless jokes on late-night talk shows. ("Do you think it's too soon to be hitting on Mrs. Eliot Spitzer?") Israeli papers lamented a setback for electing the first Jewish American president. On *The View*, Joy Behar treated it as proof that men—especially powerful men—are pigs. ("Viagra is destroying our government!") The Spitzer marriage became a topic of public debate—on cable news, on talk radio, in the blogosphere. There were even instant polls: *should Silda leave him? Was seeing prostitutes better or worse than having an affair?*

Dan Castleman, Spitzer's old friend from the Manhattan DA's office, had watched it all unfold on CNN from the bar at the King David Hotel in Jerusalem, where he was working on a case. Morgenthau's team had gotten advance word from the feds that the Emperors Club bust was coming, and knew that the dreaded exposure of Spitzer's secret was finally at hand. The *Times*'s Rashbaum had even phoned Castleman in Jerusalem over the weekend, seeking to confirm the identity of Client 9. "How the hell would I know?" he'd told Rashbaum. "I'm in *Israel*." Says Castleman: "Once I got the call from Willy, I knew it would break within twenty-four hours. I was under no illusions. It was morbid."

New York City, of course, was ground zero. HO NO! screamed Tuesday's *Post*; GOV IN ROMP WITH HOOKER "KRISTEN." The *Daily News* branded Spitzer the LUV GUV, placed his LIFE IN RUINS, and plastered his grimacing face on the front page stamped with the words CLIENT NO. 9. *The Wall Street Journal* hopefully cited the scandal as "the last act" of a man who had demonstrated similar "recklessness" against his undeserving business targets. The *Times* lambasted Spitzer for his "short, arrogant statement," and lamented that he had given comfort to those he battled: Wall Streeters "who fumed at having to make their world fairer for ordinary shareholders" and state Republicans "who have blocked some of the most important reforms in Albany." The media served up new details, many of them attributed to ubiquitous "law-enforcement officials"; the targeted leaks that had helped expose the story had turned into a flood.

Hunkered down in his apartment—where the Spitzers avoided even a glance at the papers or TV news—Eliot had taken no calls from the press, with a single exception: *The Daily Princetonian*, whose undergraduate reporter asked Spitzer whether he'd resign. "I just can't answer the question," he politely replied. Few rose to the governor's defense. His neurosurgeon brother, Daniel, spoke to *The Wall Street Journal*, but offered the sort of Darwinian rationalization that didn't play well in mixed company: "If men never succumbed to the attractions of women, then the human species would have died out a long time ago."

For one of the Emperors Club defendants, Spitzer's period of deliberation spelled opportunity. After getting out of jail, Temeka Lewis retained Marc Agnifilo, a media-savvy criminal defense lawyer, on Monday night. When Agnifilo heard the booker's story about her dealings with George Fox, he quickly concluded that Spitzer's political career was over, that Lewis had juicy evidence—and that he could maximize her prospects for avoiding prison time by securing a cooperation agreement before the governor resigned. Agnifilo e-mailed Boyd Johnson, the lead prosecutor, the next morning at 7:05, and rushed into the U.S. attorney's office with Lewis hours later to cut a deal.

———

The governor skipped his customary early-morning run around Central Park that Tuesday. The media had begun a full-scale deathwatch, placing 985 Fifth Avenue under siege. Seventy reporters and cameramen camped out in front of the building, behind police barricades. Media helicopters hovered overhead, positioned to track any unexpected movement, as though the governor might suddenly bolt for the Canadian border. Spitzer would remain cloistered inside for more than forty hours. In America's cable-news studios, the scandal had become the latest fodder for round-the-clock speculation. *Could he remain in office if indicted? Was he cutting a plea deal with prosecutors?* In Albany, Jim Tedisco rushed to lead a growing chorus calling for Spitzer's resignation. If Spitzer didn't resign by Thursday, Tedisco told the press, he would move to impeach him.

Constantine still wasn't ready to give up. He had prepared a Hail Mary survival strategy, based on rapid-fire consultations with two rabbis and assorted counselors, including his own psychologist. It would go like this: Spitzer would call a press conference to discuss his misdeeds in detail, acknowledge that this was a public matter, and apologize profusely for his behavior. Then he'd throw himself on the mercy of all New Yorkers. He'd announce to the world that he was sick—*a sex addict*—and leave immediately to get the help he needed. Constantine had even researched where Spitzer would go: the Meadows Dakota, a rehab clinic in the Arizona desert that treats CEOs and movie stars for sexual disorders. Paterson would serve as acting governor while he was gone, and they'd all hope that Eliot wouldn't be impeached before he got back. "This is the way you can potentially stay governor," Constantine explained. He was even prepared to move into a motel near the clinic to serve as Eliot's "lifeline." Constantine later described this to me as "the full-immersion proposal—it would have symbolized his complete surrender to the reality of his sickness." Spitzer thought it was nutty. Even now, he wasn't about to bare his soul, especially in public. He wasn't prepared to surrender himself to a higher power. And he wasn't going to blame his behavior on an uncontrollable compulsion. "That wasn't the way I was going to handle this," he explained later. "Running in and out of rehab? It's just not me."

More of Spitzer's friends and family had joined the bleak debate inside his apartment. His parents were there. George and Pam Fox arrived—furious as they were about Spitzer's choice of a secret identity. Cliff Sloan had come up from Washington. "This is like sitting *shiva* without the food," Spitzer told him. To every new arrival, Spitzer professed his anguished bewilderment at his own actions: "How could I have done this? What was I *thinking*?" Hirshman went downtown to the U.S. attorney's office to find out more about the evidence against Spitzer, exploring whether the feds would drop their investigation of Spitzer if he resigned. (They wouldn't—though it was clear that would reduce the chance he'd face charges.) Meanwhile, Spitzer's entire family—including his father—still wanted him to stand and fight. In the midst of all this, Mike Balboni called to deliver the message that the U.S. Department of Homeland Security had revoked the governor's national security clearance.

While Spitzer says he remained virtually certain that he would ultimately resign, he set about determining whether survival was possible. He says it would have been "malpractice" not to do so. Shocked, devastated, and angry, his staff considered remaining in office out of the question. "There was nothing to fight," says Marlene Turner, recalling her reaction. "It was over in the blink of an eye. Eliot had made himself the paragon of virtue. That was his *brand*." When Spitzer asked, she recalls, "I gave my opinion that I'd expected him to resign immediately. He couldn't be governor—and he *shouldn't* be governor." Anderson agreed: "It was just over. There was such an immediate sense that the nails were in the coffin. This was *Eliot*—this wasn't someone else where [you] would remotely tolerate that kind of hypocrisy."

Spitzer called Shelly Silver. Any impeachment move would begin in the Democratic assembly, with a trial to take place in the senate. Only one New York governor had ever been impeached—in 1913. "What's the sentiment?" Spitzer asked. "If there's a motion regarding impeachment, do you think you can hold it off?" The speaker was not encouraging. "You know, Eliot, I don't think there's a groundswell of support for you," said Silver, with his customary understatement. "I don't think you've built up a great treasure chest of goodwill." The senate Democrats weren't any more receptive. "At that moment," says Malcolm Smith, then minority leader, "Eliot Spitzer had no friends at all. None among the Democrats. No Republicans. His *friends* weren't his friends." Bruno shrewdly limited his public comments to expressing sympathy for Spitzer's family. On the brink of being toppled from power, the senator unexpectedly found himself able to sit back and watch the governor self-destruct.

By this point, Spitzer had shed any lingering illusions. "Albany was desperate to get rid of me," he told me later. "There was no support." Ultimately, says Spitzer: "Resign or not—it was not a close call." With this resolved, Baum excused himself from the crowd inside the Spitzers' apartment and retreated once again into the bathroom, where he informed Lieutenant Governor Paterson—who had taken the job as a stepping-stone to the U.S. Senate—that he was about to become the governor of New York instead.

————

As the governor kept the world waiting, Christine Anderson and her staff spent Tuesday batting down breathless media rumors. *Spitzer was resigning at 7 P.M. in Albany. . . . Spitzer had already left for Washington to craft a plea deal. . . . The first lady's aides were cleaning out their desks and leaving.* "It's utterly depressing here," she wrote a friend. "I'm stunned, sad, and furious. This is all unreal." She e-mailed her husband, who was now heading from Australia to Hong Kong: "Still struggling to believe all this. I wake up each morning hoping it's a dream."

By early Wednesday, Anderson had begun quietly advising the press to expect a resignation. The announcement was set for 11:30 A.M. in Manhattan. Spitzer was still in his apartment, meeting with his family, three criminal lawyers, and Constantine, who made a final, futile pitch for his sex-addict strategy. Then they all headed down to the governor's office in a three-Suburban motorcade, with hovering news helicopters, broadcasting live, following every moment of their twenty-minute crawl through the Manhattan traffic.

Spitzer's one-sentence resignation letter, formally addressed to Bruno and Silver, was waiting for him on the thirty-ninth floor. Nocenti had faxed it down from Albany. Spitzer had briefly considered adding "with regret," or perhaps some words of explanation. Turner had opposed the idea: "There was no excusing what he'd done." She brought the letter into Spitzer's office, where the governor and first lady were waiting. "Eliot, you have to sign it now," she said. Mournful, he looked up at Turner, who had worked for him since his first day in public office. "It's just incredibly sad," she told him. The governor scrawled his name; the letter was whisked back to Albany.

Danny Kanner, waiting in the hallway, then led everyone into the packed briefing room, one floor below. Turner and Pope, who'd worked for Spitzer for nine years, filed in to watch the end. A number of younger staffers were lined up along the wall, several in tears. But his top press aide was absent. "Couldn't go down," Anderson wrote later. "Just too hard to look him in the eye."

Silda Spitzer once again stood by her husband as he took the podium, with her hands clasped behind her back. The governor cleared his throat and looked quickly over the crowd of reporters and photographers jostling for position. This statement lasted just two and a half minutes, delivered in a measured tone.

"In the past few days I have begun to atone for my private failings with my wife, Silda, my children, and my entire family," he began. "The remorse I feel will always be with me. Words cannot describe how grateful I am for the love and compassion they have shown me.

"From those to whom much is given, much is expected," he noted—and he had been given a great deal indeed. "I am deeply sorry that I did not live up to what was expected of me. To every New Yorker—and to all those who believed in what I tried to stand for—I sincerely apologize. I look at my time as governor with a sense of what *might* have been. But I also know that, as a public servant, I, and the remarkable people with whom I worked, have accomplished a great deal.

"I cannot allow my private failings to disrupt the people's work," he declared. "Over the course of my public life I have insisted—I believe correctly—that people, regardless of their position or power, take responsibility for their conduct. I can and will ask no less of myself. For this reason I am resigning from the office of governor." To ease the abrupt transition, at Paterson's request, he would remain in office until noon the following Monday.

Spitzer then cited an adage that had been sent to him by Ethel Kennedy: "I go forward with the belief, as others have said, that as human beings, our greatest glory consists not in never falling, but in rising every time we fall. As I leave public life, I will first do what I need to do to help and heal myself and my family. Then I will try once again, outside of politics, to serve the common good and to move toward the ideals and solutions which I believe can build a future of hope and opportunity for us and for our children." He thanked the public "for the privilege of service."

Once again, the governor and his wife left the room immediately. This time, the jarring shouted question came from a *New York Post* columnist named Andrea Peyser: *"Silda, are you leaving him?"*

———

After leaving the press behind, Spitzer returned upstairs to his office, to take it all in one last time. He spoke to junior staffers in the hallway, telling them not to be disillusioned, that they'd all go on to great things. And then Eliot and Silda left the building. Spitzer's career had always drawn true believers—those who viewed him as a noble man with a vital cause, striving to make the world a better place. He was going places, for the right reasons—maybe all the way to Washington. For them, his fall had been especially painful. Their idealism had been shattered by the sudden, shocking uncloaking of his secret life.

Kanner, his twenty-three-year-old body man, was among them. He had started working for Spitzer's campaign in 2004 as a college intern, after studying his policy positions on the Internet. He spent two summers helping him win the election, then hustled his way into a full-time job in the governor's office after graduating from the University of Maryland. Kanner had heard Spitzer promise to change everything on "Day One," and rail against the systemic corruption of Albany. He had watched him struggle through Troopergate, scheme to topple Bruno, and founder over driver's licenses. He'd waked up regularly at 4:45 A.M. to ride with Spitzer to Albany. Blissfully unaware of anything improper, he'd also been with him at the Mayflower on February 13.

"It was about big ideas," says Kanner. "It was about shaking things up. He was taking on the establishment. That's why I was there, and why I kept begging to stay on. I thought this guy was going to make *history*. It ended up being history for different reasons." After seeing the governor out the door on that fateful Wednesday, Kanner e-mailed a friend. His message reflected the new reality among the true believers in Eliot Spitzer, young and old: "We have to work on my resume tonight."

———

The next day's resignation stories were accompanied by yet another *Times* scoop: the identification of "Kristen" as Ashley Alexandra Dupré, a twenty-two-year-old aspiring musician—just four years older than Spitzer's eldest daughter, as the tabloids would quickly note. Thanks to her single fateful encounter with the governor, Dupré would become the only Emperors Club VIP escort ever publicly identified—"the star of the steamy drama," as the *Times* put it. "I don't want to be thought of as a monster," Dupré told a *Times* reporter in a series of late-night phone conversations.

The *Times* story drew heavily on Dupré's MySpace page, where she'd

posted a demo for one of her songs, a thumping, hip-hop-influenced number titled "What We Want." Within hours, hundreds of thousands of
visitors from around the world had flocked to the website, curious to
know more about Eliot Spitzer's hooker, and hear her sing:

I know what you want
You got what I want
I know what you need
Can you han-dle me?

Ooh, move your body to the beat,
Ooh, move your body to the beat,
Shake, move your body to that

Can you handle me, boy?

Ashley Dupré was a star at last.

———

"I'm thinking, *Holy cow!*" declared David Letterman to his audience,
hours after the scandal broke. "We can't get bin Laden, but by God, we
got *Spitzer*!"

To some people—then and later—it all seemed too strange. Most
obviously, there was the governor's behavior—how such a smart man
could do such a foolish thing. But there was also the improbability of how
it had all come to light. Had Spitzer jumped out a window—or been
pushed?

There was a fertile backdrop for conspiracy theories, woven from a
combination of politics and hate. Spitzer had fallen during a period when
the Bush Justice Department was immersed in its own scandal over brazenly political practices. The swath he'd cut through Wall Street had
generated powerful, bitter enemies with close ties to the Republican administration. And Spitzer's sharp-elbowed rise had antagonized a gen-
eration of federal prosecutors and regulators whom he had ridiculed and
embarrassed. Indeed, there were so many people eager to plunge a dagger
into Spitzer, it wasn't hard to imagine that one—or more—could have
played a part in his undoing.

To be sure, Spitzer patronized prostitutes and broke the law—for a longer period, and with greater frequency, than anyone knew. He had been a customer of the Emperors Club for at least two full years, and spent more than $100,000 on more than twenty appointments with perhaps ten different escorts in New York City, Washington, Dallas, Palm Beach, and San Juan. Yet many other prominent men have strayed—why did Spitzer's sexual habits become the target of federal investigative methods befitting an Al Qaeda terrorist? Did the investigation really begin with a routine IRS review that spotted a pair of Suspicious Activity Reports, buried within a database containing millions of them? Or did someone tip off the feds?

Some theories, circulated on the Internet, occupy wacko territory. One maintains that Spitzer was the victim of a Mossad takedown, and identifies Emperors Club VIP as a money-laundering Israeli front. The evidence? Brener held an Israeli passport. Others merit closer examination, focusing on the question of whether Spitzer's enemies had collaborated with federal prosecutors, perhaps even hiring private operatives to dig up dirt, which they then passed on. This is uncertain terrain, muddied by incomplete information and vehemently denied by everyone involved. But it is useful to carefully sort through precisely what is known and what isn't.

This exercise necessarily begins with Roger Stone, who clearly saw Spitzer's downfall as a business opportunity—a chance to burnish his reputation as a cunning giant slayer. In the following weeks, by my count, Stone launched three separate schemes to suggest that he had played a role in exposing the governor's involvement with hookers. In the first, just days after the scandal broke, conservative newspaper columnist Robert Novak (since deceased) reported that Stone had predicted Spitzer's fall "more than three months in advance," during a December 6 appearance on Michael Smerconish's nationally syndicated radio talk show. According to Novak's column, Stone had told radio listeners that "Eliot Spitzer will not serve out his term as governor of the state of New York"—but had refused to elaborate at the time on the basis for his pronouncement. In the aftermath of the scandal, the press cited this remark as evidence that Stone knew something. The problem: a tape of the December 6 Smerconish interview shows that Stone never made such a statement. (Stone insists he did, but offers no explanation for the discrepancy.)

Next, Stone, who has a home in Miami Beach, told *The Miami Herald* that he had tipped the FBI about Spitzer's use of prostitutes. As proof, he provided the paper with a letter that one of his lawyers supposedly sent to the FBI back in November 2007, reporting that Spitzer had "used the services of high priced call girls" in Florida. Stone, according to the letter, had learned of these activities from "a social contact in an adult-themed club." Translation (later offered by Stone himself): a hooker he'd met in a Miami swingers' club. The letter also put in play the kind of salacious detail Stone loves, reporting that Spitzer "did not remove his mid-calf length black socks during the sex act." This juicy account, not surprisingly, received widespread media coverage; even the mainstream press treated the black-socks detail as fact—an opportunity for further Spitzer ridicule. Stone added links to the coverage on his website.

Unfortunately, almost everything about this tale appears to be fiction. FBI officials say they have searched for such a letter and have found no trace of it. (Says Stone: "I'm not surprised they would deny a tip from a citizen.") Spitzer's only known Florida assignation (with Angelina, who flew down from New York) came during his trip to Palm Beach in late February—three months *after* the November 19 date on the Stone letter. As for the black socks? Both Spitzer and Angelina—in a position to know—call that claim ridiculous.

A month later, Stone planted yet another story positioning himself at the center of the Spitzer scandal. This account appeared, improbably, in an obscure one-man Fort Lauderdale blog called Politics1. Posted on April 21, 2008, amid routine dispatches about the Pennsylvania primary, the "Politics1 exclusive" began this way:

> Reliable sources informed Politics1 that DC super-lobbyist Wayne Berman—a longtime confidant of insurance executive Maurice Hank Greenberg—authorized a private Investigation that discovered the links between Spitzer and a Florida escort service ring. Operating under the alias code-name "Wallace C. Bernheim," Berman directed an 18-month effort that cost an estimated $2.2 million. The investigation was allegedly paid for by a highly-secretive shadow committee Berman directed, informally nicknamed "The Group." Sources tell Politics1 that The Group included Greenberg, Home Depot founder Ken Langone and former New York Stock Exchange Chairman Ken [sic] Grasso—all high-profile targets of Spitzer when he was Attorney General. . . . Berman also

retained veteran Republican dirty trickster Roger Stone to transmit the information to the FBI five months ago. The Group also funded an on-going effort by Stone to challenge Spitzer on the "Troopergate" and illegal immigrants driver's license issues. Berman and Stone were previously partners in the Black, Manafort, Stone & Kelly consulting firm, whose former clients included Philippine President Ferdinand Marcos, Angolan guerilla Jonas Savimbi, US Sugar, Phillip Morris Tobacco, and developer Donald Trump.

When a few mainstream media outlets picked up this report, Berman, who was co-chair of John McCain's finance committee at the time, publicly dismissed it as "total fiction." In a December 2009 interview, Stone told me that he knew nothing about "The Group"—or the origins of the Politics1 posting.

But according to the blog's author, a Florida attorney named Ron Gunzburger, Stone had spoon-fed him the entire story. Gunzburger, who has published Politics1 since 1997, is general counsel for the Broward County property appraiser's office and became friendly with Stone after meeting him at a local political event. He says they've even talked about collaborating on Stone's memoir. As Gunzburger recalls it, Stone didn't just tell him about how "The Group" brought down Spitzer—"he sent me a draft of how he thought I should write the story." Adds Gunzburger: "I wouldn't have known the players without him giving it to me. That was Roger's account of what happened." Responds Stone: "Gunzburger's not telling the truth."

None of that, of course, proves that the tale of an anti-Spitzer cabal is true. But it does seem evident that someone was bankrolling Stone's efforts to hound the governor, even after Bruno had fired him for the threatening voicemail left for Spitzer's father. Gunzburger says Stone confirmed that this was the case, telling him, "there are other sources of Republican funds in New York." Says Gunzburger, "He told me he had a client; he still was getting paid." The Florida attorney recalls Stone describing his marching orders on the New York project this way: "Bring down Spitzer; you take care of it." Adds Gunzburger: "When you become an enemy, someone he grows to despise, it's not just about Roger winning. It's about Roger winning, doing the victory dance, and dragging your dead carcass through the streets." In late 2009, Stone acknowledged retaining the services of a New Jersey private detective—a former DEA agent—in an unrelated matter. It's not hard to imagine his doing so, on behalf of a paying client, to gather dirt on Spitzer.

Was all this more Stone disinformation and bluster? It's impossible to say. When I met with Stone, over breakfast in New York, he confirmed that he has been paid by a group of Spitzer haters since his separation from Bruno. But he insisted that it was just a small amount, and that Greenberg and Langone were not among the contributors. "They were largely chickenshit," Stone declared. "They wanted to take him on, but they weren't willing to write checks." Stone says he was driven by . . . *conviction*. "Just because I go off the payroll doesn't mean I'm off the case. I'm a mercenary, but I'm also a true believer."

Which brings us to the next question in our speculation: who might have hired Stone—or even retained a detective directly? Notwithstanding Stone's denials, Greenberg and Langone remain the most obvious suspects. "If I were an FBI profiler, I'd go right to those two guys," says Eric Dezenhall, a Washington crisis-management consultant who has represented many Wall Street clients and travels in anti-Spitzer circles. "They have the motive, the means, the opportunity, and the personality." Greenberg had a long-standing reputation for deploying clandestine methods, born of his CIA contacts and his use of detectives at AIG. Langone had a palpable thirst for revenge. He'd hired a private investigator to find political ammunition to use against Spitzer during the run-up to his gubernatorial campaign. (Since October 2006, Langone and his wife had also given $130,000 to Bruno's senate campaign committees.)

In high-level Wall Street circles, there are persistent rumblings that Langone played this role. Some of these rumblings come from those with ties to him; others claim to have heard it in social settings directly from Greenberg. Langone became the chief suspect following his jaw-dropping claim to CNBC—that he was aware of Spitzer's predilections before the *Times* bombshell because he knew somebody "standing in back of him in line" at the post office when Spitzer bought "$2,800 worth of mail orders to send to the hooker." On July 17, 2009, *Fortune* writer James Bandler, interviewing Langone for a magazine profile of Greenberg, asked: did you hire a gumshoe? "I'd say 'no comment,'" Langone responded. On several other occasions, he flat out denied it—and he did so for this book, through both his lawyer and a spokesman. His PR consultant, Jim McCarthy, vehemently insists that Langone simply "misspoke" on CNBC—that he really *didn't* have any advance knowledge of Spitzer's involvement with prostitutes.

Langone would not speak to me directly. But to Bandler and Alex Gibney, he explained that he had heard about the post-office sighting late Monday afternoon, in the hours after the scandal broke. He says he was having drinks with a group of buddies at the Four Seasons, and that the story came from one of his companions sitting around the table—who had heard it from one of *his* friends. According to this accounting, this thirdhand source was the basis for Langone's claim on national television later that day: that he'd known about it all ahead of time because "I know somebody" who was standing behind Spitzer at the post office. It also doesn't explain how someone there by happenstance would have known precisely what Spitzer was doing at the post office—and where his money was going.

Langone, through his spokesman, has steadfastly refused to identify anyone in the chain of information he described. (He says that his source wants to maintain his privacy.) In his interview with Gibney, Langone said he "may" have met Stone sometime, but didn't hire him. And he insisted that he had never paid a private detective to conduct surveillance. "Everybody thought I had a spy," said Langone. "Nobody worked for me except my lawyers in connection with Spitzer—*nobody*. Nobody worked indirectly for me through those people. . . . No, I didn't have any private eyes on him. I didn't have any dirty-tricks guys on him, any of that. I had a very profound and strong belief that time wounds all heels. He certainly proved that correct." Greenberg has also denied knowing anything about the use of detectives against Spitzer, telling *Fortune*'s Bandler there was "nothing to that."

The third big player in the Spitzer haters club, Grasso, offered his own hint of some foreknowledge about the governor's extramarital activities. In the epilogue to his book about Grasso, *King of the Club*, CNBC reporter Charles Gasparino writes that Grasso made a surprising comment to him about Spitzer in early 2007: "We hear he has something going with a young girl." Gasparino adds that when he confronted Grasso about this remark more than a year later, after the prostitution scandal broke, Grasso "just laughed before hanging up the telephone."

Detectives are one possible explanation for how Spitzer's enemies might have known about his extra-marital activities. Another is that they received information from Republican friends in the Bush administration's Justice Department, sharing a few juicy details about their mutual enemy. But ultimately, on these questions, at this moment, certainty remains beyond reach. We are left with nothing more than intriguing speculation.

———

Among those close to the former New York governor, one person is more devoted to these theories than anyone: Eliot Spitzer's wife. Silda came to conclude that her husband had fallen victim to a perfect storm. His behavior had provided the opening. But he had so many enemies eager to move in—from Albany, Wall Street, and Washington. They'd viewed him as a foreign body, disrupting how things were done. They were *desperate* to get rid of him. There wasn't proof; she wanted someone to find it. But a hundred disparate threads of evidence fed her growing certainty: the bad guys had brought Eliot down.

Everyone directly involved with the investigation insisted there had been no improper influence. In a 2009 interview, Garcia put it to me this way: "It came in the right way. It went step by step the right way. It was worked the right way. We called it down the middle, as we saw the middle." The flood of media leaks at the end, however, had prompted an internal Justice Department investigation. "It was explosive," says Garcia. "And it's out there six, seven, eight months without leaking. But as the circle of those with knowledge of the case widened, it became harder and harder to control the leaks." The government's explanation of the case's "routine" inception was one of the points that quickly made it into the *Times,* offered initially by anonymous "law-enforcement sources."

But it is clear that prosecutors did not handle the issue of whether to charge the former governor in a routine matter. Their criminal investigation of Spitzer—a relatively simple case—would drag on for eight months after his resignation. And although the Justice Department's manual for U.S. attorneys generally directs that they shouldn't charge johns under the Mann Act except in cases involving minors, they seriously weighed this option. E-mails obtained through a Freedom of Information Act request show the Southern District prosecutors conducting a required consultation about this issue with the Justice Department's child exploitation and obscenity section.

"I have a wiretap case against an international prostitution and money laundering organization," lead prosecutor Boyd Johnson wrote on February 27, just eight days before the Emperors Club bust. "We are going to arrest the four managers of the business shortly, and a question has come up about prosecuting one of the customers. Basically, the customer has arranged at least eight prostitution appointments where he has conspired with one of the managers to transport prostitutes interstate to meet with him in hotels. The customer pays for the travel, the room, and all other expenses associated with the interstate transportation. None of the other customers on our wiretap are engaged in similar conduct; they just arrange for the organization's prostitutes in the cities where they are staying—in NY, LA, Miami, London, and Paris—to meet them at their hotels." Citing two sections of the Mann Act, Johnson concluded: "it seems to me that the customer who has arranged the eight appointments where he caused the interstate transportation of prostitutes [is] chargeable under both statutes." The target, Johnson wrote, "also appears to be chargeable as a co-conspirator of the four managers. . . ."

Johnson has declined to discuss this matter publicly, but he clearly understood that he was on uncertain ground. "I am wondering whether you folks are aware of any case where [federal prosecutors] charged a customer under similar facts . . . ," he wrote. "I have read a lot of Mann Act cases, and feel confident that the statutes should apply to this conduct, but have not seen any reported decisions with facts similar to ours. I'd be grateful for any thoughts you would have." The e-mailed responses—at least those that were disclosed—show that the Washington lawyers were generally supportive of this approach, but hard-pressed to identify a similar prosecution. "I'm not aware of cases charging customers," wrote attorney Wendy Waldron, a trial lawyer in the child exploitation section, "but I agree that he should be chargeable . . . under a causing or aiding and abetting theory."

On the day after the scandal broke, Agnifilo, Temeka Lewis's lawyer, brought in his client for a lengthy interview with the feds. The session included two assistant U.S. attorneys and Hosey, the FBI's lead agent. "I left that room thinking: he's getting charged," says Agnifilo. "They asked all the right questions to charge him. They established the elements of the Mann Act. They also established distinctions between Spitzer and other customers that could withstand selective-prosecution defense arguments. The people in that room wanted to charge him."

U.S. attorneys employ discretion, and it is always part of their franchise to bring high-profile cases that will deliver a message, to deter others from committing crimes. But in this case, Garcia recognized that deploying the Mann Act was a stretch—even for a former governor. Once Spitzer knew he was under investigation, the feds began a far more intensive search for signs of traditional corruption. They combed through an array of financial records, seeking evidence that he had used government or campaign funds to pay prostitutes. They found none. They scrutinized the family's charitable foundation; nothing was improper. They weighed a charge of structuring—splitting up financial transactions to avoid detection—but that was typically brought only where there was a serious underlying crime. In the end, they were left with nothing more than the Mann Act. "The key to me was public money or campaign money," says Garcia. "We didn't start out looking to do a big Mann Act case. It was possible corruption. That's what we wanted to explore. This was not the public corruption investigation I had in mind when I revitalized that unit."

For Garcia, the decision not to prosecute rested on the facts. But there were two considerations that made the choice easier. The first was Spitzer's resignation. If he hadn't left office—and his involvement with prostitutes had somehow remained secret—prosecutors would have referred the matter to state authorities on the belief that it was simply unacceptable to have a sitting governor who had broken the law. Under state law, Spitzer could have been charged with a misdemeanor, for violating the very statute that, as governor, he had toughened. The second consideration was the financial meltdown. It would have been even tougher to justify trying Spitzer, with all the resources and attention that would require, while Wall Street was blowing up. As things were, the investigation of Spitzer had raised the same issue for critics: could the effort devoted to unmasking the "Luv Guv" have exposed the likes of Bernie Madoff instead?

————

It is unclear precisely why the matter lingered until November—long after the FBI had completed its work. But to try to separate the issue from politics, Garcia announced his decision on Thursday, November 6. Two days after the Election Day that made Barack Obama president, the man once considered his political peer learned that he wouldn't face the prospect of serving time.

"We have determined that there is insufficient evidence to bring charges against Mr. Spitzer," the U.S. attorney said in a statement. "In light of the policy of the Department of Justice with respect to prostitution offenses and the long-standing practice of this office, as well as Mr. Spitzer's acceptance of responsibility for his conduct, we have concluded that the public interest would not be further advanced by filing criminal charges in this matter." Garcia noted that Spitzer had acknowledged arranging for prostitutes to travel across state lines "on multiple occasions."

Spitzer issued his own statement to the media, praising "the impartiality and thoroughness" of the investigation and acknowledging "responsibility for the conduct it disclosed. I resigned my position as governor because I recognized that my conduct was unworthy of an elected official." He apologized again for his behavior "and for the pain and disappointment those actions caused my family and the many people who supported me during my career in public life."

With the election of a Democratic president, the Spitzer decision was Garcia's last major act during his three years as U.S. attorney. He announced his resignation a few days later, and, in a valedictory interview with the *Times*, defended the origin and conduct of the investigation and the decision not to bring charges. "You try at the end of the day to do justice," Garcia said. "It's justice in that case. And I stand by it." Privately, those involved in the investigation offer no apologies for their handling of the matter. As one lawman bluntly put it: "He got treated a lot better than he would have treated others."

Epilogue: Eliot Unbound

IN THE DAYS AFTER ANNOUNCING HIS RESIGNATION, WITH the media still massed outside of his apartment, Eliot Spitzer took refuge with his family on his farm in Pine Plains. "That was his Superman Fortress of Solitude," says Constantine. "It was really calming to be up there."

But reminders of the situation were close at hand. Paparazzi camped outside the gate, which remained manned by state troopers until noon on Monday, the hour his resignation officially took effect. And the impact of what he had done was just starting to sink in. For nine years in public life, Spitzer had been the eye of a hurricane, with people and events swirling all around him. Now all that was gone—although there *were* certain things he didn't mind leaving behind. "Chutzpah," he e-mailed Christine Anderson on Sunday, after getting an interview request from Dicker. "Ugh," Anderson replied.

Constantine, who had e-mailed his own resignation to Paterson minutes after Spitzer's announcement, was concerned that his old friend might try to harm himself. "If you asked me—what chance is there that Eliot Spitzer is going to blow his brains out?—I'd say there was a 2 percent chance," Constantine told me months later. "But it was not one in a billion." Constantine arranged for Spitzer's closest male friends to check in on him regularly. "I don't think this is a time when he should be left alone," he told them.

On Monday morning, Constantine joined Spitzer in Pine Plains, certain that Day 442—his last as governor of New York—would be especially difficult. "There's an hour left," Constantine remarked at 11 A.M., seeking to lighten his friend's mood. "I want you do a bunch of things: I want you to issue a pardon to Joe Bruno!"

Spitzer grimaced. "You're not so funny, Lloyd."

Although Spitzer thought his friends were overreacting, he was glad to have their company. But that only went so far. After having so much to do for so long, he suddenly had far too much time to agonize over the question that everyone was asking: *how could he have done such a thing?*

In the period surrounding Eliot Spitzer's implosion, several prominent American politicians survived their own sex scandals. Mark Sanford, the married Republican governor of South Carolina, had disappeared south of the border to pursue his Argentinean "soul mate." Although Sanford traveled on the state tab to pursue his affair—and his wife eventually filed for divorce—he refused calls to resign and an impeachment bid went nowhere. Republican U.S. senator John Ensign, a born-again Christian from Nevada with a wife and three children, admitted a long-running infidelity with a deputy married to one of his top Capitol Hill aides. Ensign, who had voted to impeach President Clinton for the Monica Lewinsky scandal, had tried to keep the matter quiet. His wealthy parents paid his mistress $96,000, and Ensign sought to appease the woman's husband by setting him up as a Washington lobbyist. Ensign remained in the Senate without censure. In 2007, Louisiana senator David Vitter, a married father of four and a conservative Republican, admitted "a very serious sin" after his phone number was found in the records of "D.C. Madam" Deborah Jeane Palfrey. Facing at least five years in prison, Palfrey hanged herself after being found guilty in federal court of racketeering and money laundering. None of her johns faced charges. Vitter endured no government investigation, legal sanction, or Senate censure. He has announced plans to seek reelection.

Back in Albany, New York's accidental governor, David Paterson, disclosed that both he and his wife had engaged in multiple affairs during a "troubled" period in their marriage while he was serving in the state senate. Paterson confirmed the story to *Daily News* reporters on the day he was sworn in as governor. In fact, Paterson later disclosed that he had asked Spitzer to delay his resignation for five days so he could sort out how to handle the matter. In subsequent interviews, Paterson elaborated on his adultery, which turned out to include a long-running relationship with a state employee, conducted in a hotel room paid for, on at least two occasions, with campaign funds. Because using political funds for personal purposes is illegal, Paterson wrote a $253 check to repay his campaign after the revelation.

Paterson's behavior raised questions about misuse of his public office. Yet there was no giddy scramble for juicy details; this sex scandal came and went in a matter of days. A *Times* editorial dismissed it as a "tabloid moment." Even Tedisco bit his tongue, calling the revelation "a private issue." The message from Albany was clear: patronizing prostitutes was a public outrage; affairs were accepted statehouse behavior. An even more important distinction: Paterson wasn't Spitzer. Everyone basked in the ascent of a genial old Albany hand. Asked at a press conference if *he'd* ever patronized prostitutes, Paterson deadpanned: "Only the lobbyists." Declared Bruno: "It's like a new day. The sun is shining."

But for the state government of New York, things only got darker. Eager to placate Bruno, Paterson had embraced the political non-aggression pact that Spitzer had scorned. Though his party was just a single seat from claiming the senate, the new governor wouldn't lift a finger to help Democrats challenging GOP incumbents. Yet appeasement did nothing to break the Albany logjam. As a *Times* headline put it, summing up Paterson's first months in office: THEY'LL SHAKE HIS HAND, BUT THEY AREN'T PASSING HIS BILLS.

The end of Paterson's first legislative session, in June 2008, did bring one big surprise: Bruno's tearful announcement that he was leaving the senate, to be succeeded as majority leader by Dean Skelos, a hard-liner from Long Island. Bruno memorialized his thirty-two-year senate tenure by taking reporters on a bus tour of all the pork he had bestowed upon his district. Bruno's decision prompted speculation that he was getting out ahead of two landmark events: the Democratic takeover of the senate—and his own criminal indictment. Both occurred in a matter of months.

Election Day 2008 flipped the senate, as everyone had expected, after four decades of Republican control. But Paterson's hands-off approach cost the Democrats several winnable races, giving them just a 32–30 edge. It was soon clear that wasn't enough. For months, a few conservative Democrats from New York City threatened to vote with the Republicans, despite efforts to mollify them with leadership posts and hefty stipends. In June, two of the dissidents did switch sides, throwing the senate into chaos, with both sides claiming control. The Democrats locked the chamber doors; the Republicans threatened to convene in a nearby park. The balance of power in the Empire State teetered on one senator who owed $61,000 in fines for ignoring campaign-finance laws, and a second who faced assault charges for slashing his girlfriend in the face with broken glass. The stalemate finally ended after both defectors were lured back, with the scofflaw getting the title of majority leader. It all made the worst days of the Spitzer administration seem like a model of comity and achievement.

In January 2009, after more than two years under investigation, Bruno was indicted on eight counts of political corruption. When his trial began that November in federal court, three blocks from the capitol, it served as a showcase for everything that was wrong with Albany. "There is a real sense that if he is guilty of something, then the whole system is guilty of something," one lobbyist told the *Times*. Indeed. During his years presiding over the senate, Bruno had brazenly peddled his influence, accepting $3.2 million from a dozen private companies for luring business from state agencies or New York's labor unions. Among Bruno's secret deals: a private partnership with a man seeking the state horse-racing franchise, whose $440,000 in payments to the senator included $80,000 disguised as the purchase price for a worthless horse.

These relationships, prosecutors charged, helped explain why Bruno had pushed grants and contracts to specific companies—and why he so often did the unions' bidding. At trial, it became shockingly evident how Bruno mixed his public and private affairs. Hevesi, the disgraced comptroller, had pled guilty to a felony for using a state employee to run errands for his sick wife. What was revealed about Bruno's fiefdom made that seem like a trivial indiscretion. Bruno's senate secretary testified that she spent as much time on his personal business as she did handling his public duties—even balancing his checkbook and doing his Christmas shopping. Senate lawyers prepared contracts for Bruno's consulting work and provided legal advice to his clients. His state driver went to the bank to deposit his consulting fees. He used his capitol office to host meetings where his private clients—who paid him on commission—gave sales pitches to state employees and union officials.

The trial made something else apparent: Bruno's flights on the state helicopter didn't just allow him to do his political business on the taxpayer's dime; they allowed him to do his *private* business on the taxpayer's dime. After a month-long trial, the jury found him guilty in early December on two felony counts of mail fraud. Bruno, who had turned eighty, faced a $500,000 fine and a sentence of up to twenty years. Visibly crestfallen, he vowed to appeal the verdict. "In my mind and in my heart, it is not over until it's over," he told reporters outside the courthouse afterward. "And I think it's far from over. Thank you all, have a good night and Merry Christmas." With that, Bruno climbed into a waiting Mercedes-Benz and rode off.

Paterson, meanwhile, had proven a disaster. As governor, he was unfocused and vacillating, unable to convince the legislature to do anything and widely regarded as in over his head. After Hillary Clinton became secretary of state, he'd even botched his opportunity to fill her U.S. Senate seat, turning the process into a soap opera that alienated everyone. When Caroline Kennedy—the most popular choice—finally withdrew in frustration, the Paterson camp smeared her by anonymously peddling false reports that she had personal tax problems making her unsuitable. Paterson instead named upstate congresswoman Kirsten Gillibrand, a Chuck Schumer protégée. By mid-2009, polls showed some New Yorkers longing for the days of the Spitzer "steamroller"; Paterson was even less popular than his disgraced predecessor. Democrats were so worried he would torpedo their prospects that Obama privately urged him not to run in 2010.

As the national recession struck New York, Paterson tried unsuccessfully to force the lawmakers to confront the state's deepening financial crisis. Deals were cut to balance successive budgets through one-time financial gimmicks, federal stimulus money, and the draining of reserve funds. But by the end of 2009, New York was running out of money to pay its bills; Paterson was forced to withhold $750 million in aid to schools and local governments to keep the state from becoming insolvent. A massive deficit loomed in 2010.

Waiting coyly in the wings throughout all of this was a Democrat who saw the governor's mansion as his destiny: Andrew Cuomo. Cuomo had followed Spitzer's path, prosecuting a string of headline-grabbing cases, to become a wildly popular attorney general. Polls showed him trouncing Paterson—and anyone else—for governor.

For Spitzer, the notion of Cuomo's ascent was a bitter pill to swallow.

One day, he privately vented his frustrations about Paterson to Constantine, who says he promptly scolded him: "You're the *only* person in the state of New York who has no right to criticize David. He's governor for two reasons: you picked him. And you did what you did."

————

Most from Spitzer's circle didn't stick around state government for long. Rich Baum resigned immediately, sold his house in Albany, and moved his family back to Brooklyn. After two months, Baum found a job that matched his private passion—as chief operating officer of the New York Academy of Sciences, a nonprofit scientific society that once counted Charles Darwin and Albert Einstein among its members. Like everyone who worked for Spitzer, Baum received sympathetic messages from well-wishers. Among them was an e-mail from Dick Morris, Spitzer's old friend and political advisor, who had become a conservative political commentator, regularly savaging Hillary Clinton in the media. "Please pass on to Eliot my love and support," Morris wrote. "He has been a crusader for justice and is the latest illustration of the secular proverb that no good deed goes unpunished and the spiritual one that a prophet is without honor in his own house. I have and will continue to avoid public comment (ever since Eliot became governor) but please tell him that I adore him and empathize with what he is going through. As you know, I've been there . . . You have invested your entire life in Eliot, a la Louis Howe and FDR, and are entitled to better." The e-mail was signed, "Love, Dick."

Christine Anderson remained with Paterson a few weeks longer. In November 2008, she gave birth to a baby boy; four months later, she became a spokeswoman for Blackstone Group, the publicly traded private-equity fund. David Nocenti and Paul Francis stayed on until July. Nocenti became executive director of the Union Settlement Association, a social-service agency working with immigrants in East Harlem. Francis went to work for Bloomberg LP, the mayor's private media company. Marlene Turner had left immediately. She didn't return to work until January 2010, when she accepted a position as special assistant to the new Manhattan DA, Cyrus Vance Jr. Morgenthau had finally retired, at the age of ninety.

After vowing not to go back to practicing law, Lloyd Constantine returned to the law firm he had co-founded. But he also launched a new career, as an author. His first book was about his big antitrust case against the credit card companies. His second, scheduled for publication in the spring of 2010, is a memoir of his time in the Spitzer administration. While Spitzer wasn't exactly happy about this development, the two men continued to play tennis and even took a ski trip together—until an "exclusive" interview with Constantine appeared in the *New York Post*, casting Lloyd as the mastermind of Spitzer's entire political career and quoting him describing a Spitzer master plan: "Eliot was going to be governor for eight to twelve years, and then he was going to run for president." With that, Spitzer stopped speaking to him.

Darren Dopp, meanwhile, had reconciled himself to his prosperous new life as a spinmeister-for-hire at Patricia Lynch and Associates. When I visited him in Albany, he recounted how Lynch had signed him on, telling him, "Darren, we're going to be rich someday." But Dopp was still pained about his forced departure from state government, after nineteen years. "I didn't want to get rich," he recalled. He pointed out the window to the capitol, on the hill at the top of State Street. "I wanted to be up *there!*"

The Troopergate investigations dragged on, preposterously, long after both Spitzer and Bruno were gone. Three weeks after the hooker scandal broke, Soares released his final report, concluding that Spitzer had misled the public about his true role in the release of Bruno's flight records. After hearing Dopp's "red-hot poker" testimony, the DA explained, he had planned to convene a grand jury to investigate possible misconduct by the governor, but decided to drop the matter after Spitzer resigned. The public-integrity commission, however, wasn't finished. In July, after investigating for ten months and taking three thousand pages of sworn testimony, it charged Baum, Dopp, Felton, and Howard with violating New York's Public Officers Law, for engaging in conduct that would "raise suspicion" that they were doing something improper. Baum, Howard, and Felton all settled, facing no fine or further sanction. Unwilling to admit wrongdoing and negotiate his own slap on the wrist, Dopp began a long, public battle with the commission, appealing a proposed $10,000 fine.

In its report, the ethics panel complained that the four men had mishandled confidential information—and that the governor's office had delayed its probe by withholding key documents. But the commission itself then came under investigation. In May 2009, the state inspector general released his own report, concluding that the ethics panel had repeatedly leaked confidential information about its Troopergate probe to both the press and to a Spitzer administration aide—and that the full commission had ignored evidence that this was going on. New York's ethics commission now had its *own* ethics scandal. Paterson promptly demanded the resignation of all twelve commissioners. But they refused to go, deepening the public sense of chaos and moral paralysis.

———

The four Emperors Club VIP defendants all pled guilty to prostitution charges and faced more formal justice than the former governor. Tanya Hollander, the part-time phone booker, received probation; she married her fiancé and continued in her new job helping run a Buddhist conference center in the Catskills owned by the parents of actress Uma Thurman. Temeka Lewis, Spitzer's regular handler, benefited from her cooperation deal with the feds, struck just before his resignation. Her lawyer argued that her help had been decisive in winning guilty pleas from her fellow defendants and in resolving what to do about Spitzer. Though Lewis had been a major player in the Emperors Club since November 2005, she received just a year's probation. She remained in New York City, working as a waitress to pay her bills.

Suwal played the victimized girl. At sentencing, defense lawyer Al Ebanks argued that she had fallen under the spell of her older paramour while just eighteen, citing her "strategically placed" tattoo (PROPERTY OF MARK BRENER) as evidence of his sick hold on her. A psychological report noted Suwal's history of drug abuse, her "lack of insight and her extreme neediness," her need to go "to extreme lengths to obtain others' attention and approval." But now Suwal was back on track: she'd gone back to college, at Fordham in New York City, found a job, and was doing volunteer work. "It is my aim to prevent others, especially young girls, from making the kind of mistakes that I have made," Suwal, wearing a black-and-white bow in her hair, tearfully told the judge. She said she wasn't the same person who had been "deluded" into committing crimes. At twenty-four, her lawyer declared, she had "permanently severed the umbilical cord from Brener," the *real* mastermind of Emperors Club VIP. The judge was impressed. Prosecutors were pressing for a two-year prison sentence; Suwal got just six months.

Within weeks, Suwal was pitching a very different story. "Cecil

Suwal, the 'New York Madam' who procured prostitutes for former Governor Eliot Spitzer, is preparing to shop her memoir to publishers," reported a blog for *Portfolio* magazine. "In it, she will recount her years running the infamous escort service for mega-rich and influential clientele." As for severing the umbilical cord from Brener? Suwal discussed her feelings about the pimp in a filmed interview with Alex Gibney in May 2009, just days before entering prison. "We love each other," she said. "And whatever I end up doing in my future, I want him to be a part of. So I've got my chips on Mark." By the time she got out, she was having second thoughts, concluding that it was no longer possible for her to have anything to do with him.

At his own sentencing, Brener seemed a very hard man to love. His lawyer, Murray Richman, was unable to muster a single letter of support on his behalf; no one from his family was present. In pleading for leniency, Richman cited the sadness in Brener's life—the anti-Semitism, his first wife's death, his inability to "find a place for himself." Richman suggested that it was Suwal who really ran the Emperors Club—and that no one had really been hurt by his crimes. But the judge wasn't buying it. Brener got two and a half years. From prison, he repeatedly professed his own love, vowing to pursue Suwal—if she'd have him—when he got out.

At each of the four Emperors Club VIP hearings, Spitzer was the unseen presence. Defense lawyers argued that it was unfair to treat their clients harshly when others—especially the former governor—were allowed to walk away. Spitzer was the *real* target; they were just collateral damage. The judge sentencing Hollander seemed sympathetic to this point, noting that, on November 6, 2008, the government had revealed its decision "not to indict other members of the conspiracy." That, of course, was the date U.S. attorney Garcia announced that he wouldn't be charging Spitzer.

The prostitutes of the Emperors Club faced no charges. But several were brought in for interrogation by prosecutors and the FBI, where the feds asked them to identify pictures of johns and showed them surveillance photos of their furtive meetings with Brener and Suwal in the back of the battered Honda minivan. Angelina says one FBI agent pressed her for details about whether she had brought sex toys to her meetings with Spitzer. "He wanted to get some information about some kinky sex stuff . . . like the governor is into *whatever*. . . . I just said there was nothing." She was annoyed by the line of inquiry. "How on earth," she asked later, "does that relate to prosecuting either Eliot Spitzer or Emperors Club?" The agency's shutdown had sent the women back out onto the job market, and several moved into new lines of work. Angelina remained in the escort business. Now seeing clients on her own, she diversified, developing a specialty in men with a taste for fetishism, bondage, and sado-masochism. But she was actually making most of her income trading commodities— buying and selling gold, futures, and foreign currencies.

Ashley Dupré, meanwhile, became a professional celebrity. She surrounded herself with a posse of handlers to field incoming business propositions and media inquiries: a criminal lawyer, a publicist, a manager, a marketing firm. After extensive negotiations, she granted interviews to one TV show (with Diane Sawyer on *20/20*) and one print outlet (*People* magazine). She considered offers to pose nude. She labored to find a taker for *her* memoir (she also wanted to keep young girls from making the mistakes she'd made). And she found a benefactor in hip-hop mogul Russell Simmons, who hosted her occasional postings on his website.

But mostly, she became a fixture in the *New York Post*. Ashley caught cavorting at a trendy Manhattan hotel with a married New Jersey asphalt mogul. Ashley insisting she'd never exploited the Spitzer scandal and blasting her female critics for *hypocrisy*. ("I know many women who target guys with money. . . . Is what I did any more dishonest?") Ashley giving a guided tour of her nine body tattoos. Ashley posing for tacky fashion shots and touting her latest single, which the *Post*'s music critic dutifully praised. Ashley attacking Tiger Woods's mistresses for exploiting their situation. ("And I was the hooker?")

And then, incredibly, the paper announced that it was *hiring* the former escort for "Ask Ashley," a new advice column on sex, love, and relationships. The *Post* tastefully introduced this feature to its readers with the headline SPITZER'S BABE ANSWERS ALL YOUR LOVE-LIFE QUESTIONS! To promote her new career, Ashley went on Fox News's *Geraldo Live*, where she bemoaned young girls' obsession with sexuality and materialism ("Everything's, you know, fake boobs, fake hair, fake nose, fake teeth . . . it's really, it's *unfortunate*"); offered marriage advice to the Woods family ("I think that they should get divorced. . . . Tiger needs to go into therapy"); and took the microphone for a wholesome pre-Christmas rendition of "Let It Snow."

Wesley Mann, the young photographer who had done a courtesy

shoot of his shapely neighbor, thinking he'd never look at the pictures again, had suddenly found his sexy images of Ashley in high demand. For weeks, they appeared in newspapers and magazines, bringing Mann a big windfall—enough to let him quit his day job as a photo assistant and purchase the equipment that he needed to go into business on his own.

The Spitzer scandal was also advancing the careers of those who brought it to public attention. After his resignation as U.S. attorney, Mike Garcia took a partnership in the Manhattan office of Kirkland & Ellis, the blue-chip Chicago firm. Boyd Johnson, who had led the investigation, became deputy U.S. attorney; Dan Stein moved up to replace him as chief of the public-corruption unit. In April 2009, *The New York Times* was awarded the Pulitzer Prize for breaking-news reporting for its "swift and sweeping coverage" of the sex scandal. Metropolitan editor Joe Sexton and reporters Willy Rashbaum and Danny Hakim accepted the award.

In the months after breaking the story, the *Times* went to court to seek release of the government's wiretap applications, which presumably would show how the investigation had really started. U.S. District Judge Jed Rakoff ordered the records released, but the U.S. attorney's office fought the decision, and an appeals court sided with the government. An internal Justice Department investigation into the leaks surrounding the Spitzer scandal was completed; no information about it was publicly released.

Questions about the investigation's origins were also being asked by a congressional committee—the same committee, as it turned out, before which Spitzer had testified after meeting Ashley Dupré at the Mayflower. But plans for a public hearing were put on hold amid more pressing questions about how to respond to the global financial crisis.

———

Eliot Spitzer's disgrace put his wife in the national spotlight in a way his greatest achievements never had. There were nasty judgments, to be sure. *Post* columnist Andrea Peyser branded her a "doormat" and an "ass-coverer" for standing by her husband; Dr. Laura, on the other hand, blamed her for not doing enough to meet his "needs." But mostly, the situation—and Silda's stricken image—made her a subject of national pity. It was an image that launched a million water-cooler debates—and eventually a network TV show, wryly titled *The Good Wife*.

Silda resolved to get on with life, and move beyond that frozen image of a powerless, beleaguered victim. That May, she made her first post-scandal appearance in Manhattan society, arriving solo and dressed in burnt orange, for the annual Children for Children gala, held at Christie's auction house. "Shedding the shame of her husband's downfall, a radiant Silda Wall Spitzer emerged from self-imposed exile Wednesday night—looking stunning in a designer evening dress and heels," the *Daily News* gossip page reported. "She looks pretty *hot*, doesn't she?" declared ABC *Nightline* anchor Cynthia McFadden, the event's emcee, as the crowd greeted Silda with a standing ovation. "I hope that *your* spring has been less eventful," Silda puckishly told the crowd. In October, she attended *Fortune*'s "Most Powerful Women" conference in California, where she introduced herself as a "media storm survivor." Five months later, she spoke at a "Women in Power" series in Palm Beach, where she flashed before-and-after slides of herself, from the nightmarish press statement with her husband and the Christie's gala. By then, she had taken a job—earning her own paycheck again at last—as managing director at a women-run Manhattan hedge fund, Metropolitan Capital Advisors. Silda politely rejected all media requests for interviews, except for a gentle *Vogue* profile ("The Survivor") focused largely on the importance of volunteerism.

Everyone, of course, wondered if she'd divorce him. Presumptuous as it was—was there any decision more uniquely personal?—much of womankind thought she should do so. From the start, Silda had resolved to take everything a day at a time. But she wasn't bred to give up on marriage easily. There was so much at stake—twenty years of marriage, three wonderful girls. Eliot truly seemed committed to making it work. And if he really meant what he said, she was willing to give it a try, too. Soon there were public sightings of Eliot and Silda together, looking happy—at breakfast at a Manhattan deli, on their wedding anniversary; at a Yankees game in the Bronx; at a Manhattan charity dinner. Spitzer told anyone who would listen how lucky he was that she'd forgiven him.

Throughout this time, Silda privately struggled to figure out what had happened. She sought insight in books about relationships, spirituality, and the impact of high-stress jobs on adrenaline and testosterone. She thought about her husband's high-pressure upbringing, which offered so little outlet for expressions of weakness and pain. She took long walks in the city with friends, where she voiced her bewilderment: "If you figure it out, please let me know!" Silda wondered about what she might have done differently. "On some level, this is my fault," Constantine says she told him. "The wife is supposed to take care of the sex. This is *my* failing; I wasn't adequate." Constantine reassured her: "I said, 'Silda, I don't know exactly what happened here. But you're a beautiful woman. There are an awful lot of men that would die to be with you. This has absolutely nothing to do with your adequacy as a woman.'" Ultimately, she came to recognize that it wasn't a reflection of her, but of *him*—his needs, his frustrations, his psychological wiring. They went to counseling, of course—though Eliot was so uncomfortable with the notion of *therapy* he couldn't even bring himself to say the word. As one old friend put it, "He's the only Jew in New York who can't admit he's seeing a psychiatrist."

With the passage of time, Silda found solace in a larger perspective. No man is without flaws. So many others in public life had fallen prey to temptation. And although Eliot's sins had massive ramifications, they were ultimately personal failures. In Silda's eyes, he had remained true to his public promise, battling tirelessly on behalf of the citizenry against powerful forces bent on doing him in. Yes, he had succumbed to temptation. But that was the result of the impossible expectations he had created, the brutal pressures he had faced in public life—and his inbred inability to find a healthier way to deal with them.

The girls endured, too. In classic Spitzer manner, they missed not a single day of school, running the gauntlet of press each morning after the scandal broke to catch the bus for Horace Mann. Elyssa, then a senior and editor of the school paper (a position that had eluded her dad), had panicked that his disgrace would ruin her college prospects. Efforts were made, says Constantine, for her to get special early notification to allay her fears. In the end, she was admitted to Princeton *and* Harvard. After weighing the ramifications of following her dad's path, she decided—with his encouragement—to attend Harvard instead.

———

For the eight months that the government investigation dragged on after his resignation, Spitzer remained publicly—and reluctantly—silent. His criminal lawyers wanted to scrupulously avoid antagonizing the prosecutors—or to stir up public sentiment that might generate pressure to charge him. Toward this end, Spitzer retained corporate PR consultants from Sard Verbinnen, whose initial focus was keeping the Spitzers out of the press. That meant muzzling Eliot.

For a time, it wasn't a problem. Spitzer's father, suffering from Parkinson's disease, took a dire turn for the worse, requiring hospitalization. Spitzer focused on his family, and his father's care. (His dad was treated at the NYU Langone Medical Center, recently renamed after the billionaire's second $100 million gift.) As Bernie's crisis eased, Eliot started going into work every day at Spitzer Engineering, where the space that had always been waiting for him was converted from a conference room into an office. For months, he dabbled in real estate, even overseeing the addition of a Washington office building to the family holdings. But his heart wasn't in it.

During this period, every recently busted madam in Manhattan seemed to be coming out of the woodwork, telling the tabloids that Spitzer had been a customer of hers, too. The most visible of these was a buxom peroxide blonde named Kristin Davis, whose claims about his involvement and behavior—on TV, radio, and even in an e-book—became progressively more outlandish. Spitzer's PR team denounced these stories as "outrageous fabrications"—and law-enforcement officials told me there is no evidence Spitzer had ever done business with Davis. Yet much of the media treated it as fact.

Meanwhile, the global financial system had crashed. Where were the regulators? These were Spitzer's issues—the terrain on which he had built his career. The disaster proved he was *right*. Despite all his problems as governor, everyone would be clamoring for him to weigh in; he'd be an influential voice on dealing with the crisis; he'd have a platform to rebuild his public standing—*if only he hadn't seen hookers!* Then an appeals court threw out the remaining claims in the Grasso case, on the grounds that the AG no longer had jurisdiction because the NYSE had shed its nonprofit status after the suit was filed; Cuomo declined to appeal. Spitzer was left to fume over all this in private, angrily venting in my conversations with him. He often seemed more agitated by the treatment of Troopergate and his time in Albany—the missteps he'd made there—than the fallout from his sex scandal.

In November, Spitzer was finally cleared, and the cork popped out of the bottle. The textbook on post-scandal rehabilitation generally dictates that a public figure undergo an extended period of private reflection and family healing—ideally accompanied by charitable works—before attempting a comeback, three or five years later, when memories have faded and he can reasonably claim to be a changed man. Spitzer was having none of that. The cloud of prosecution was lifted on November 6, 2008. Ten days later, he published a long op-ed in *The Washington Post* on "saving capitalism from its own excesses." (It ended with a single clause acknowledging "mistakes I made in my private life [that] now prevent me from participating in these issues as I have in the past.") Three weeks later, he began writing a regular column about the financial system for *Slate*, the online magazine, titled "The Best Policy." In December, he even showed up at a *Slate* media party in Chinatown, at a massage parlor-turned-bar named Happy Ending Lounge. There, a *Financial Times* blogger asked him how he was enjoying life. "It sucks," Spitzer replied. "I used to be governor of New York." By January 2009, Spitzer had parted ways with his PR consultants.

The first TV interview—on CNN, with the decorous Fareed Zakaria—came in March. Two weeks later, it was Matt Lauer, on the *Today* show. He appeared on NPR. There was a *Newsweek* cover story — "Spitzer in Exile"— in July. In each of these interviews, Spitzer suggested he was speaking up only reluctantly—and would do so only on rare occasions—after being asked his views about issues he truly cared about. There was, of course, an obligatory discussion of the sex scandal, repeated with Lauer and in each of these early interviews. He had done something very stupid, for which "there are no excuses possible"; he had paid a heavy price for it; he owed an enormous debt to his family; he was struggling to confront the "gremlins" that had prompted his behavior. Pressed by Lauer for specifics on how frequently he had seen prostitutes, and for how long, he dodged: "Not frequently, not long, in the grand context of my life." With *that* issue addressed, the conversation shifted to the problems in America's financial system.

The regular *Slate* columns, on an array of topics related to the financial system, were Spitzer at his best—pithy, contrarian, smart, and unsparing of Democrats and Republicans alike. They raised provocative questions and offered creative answers. Within months, Spitzer was having a real impact on public debate. He was ahead of the curve on asking why Goldman Sachs didn't lose a penny in the AIG bailout; urging a breakup of the big banks; and pointing out that there wasn't a need for new regulations—just tougher regulators. By the end of 2009, he had also reemerged as a TV talking head—making frequent appearances on cable news shows. He accepted a smattering of invitations to give speeches and serve on discussion panels, and taught a political science class at City College.

All this prompted talk of a political comeback, which Spitzer naturally dismissed. But to confidants, he openly mused about his sightings of political opportunity. The unfulfilled potential of the state comptroller's office—someone deploying its untapped power as a giant institutional shareholder could transform it into a national force, much as he'd transformed the AG's office. Or the U.S. Senate seat—Gillibrand, Paterson's appointee, seemed vulnerable to attack as a woman without ideology.

Inevitably, these private discussions found their way into the press, offering a stark reminder of the circus any new Spitzer candidacy would face. SAY IT AIN'T HO! SPITZER EYES NEW RUN; SECOND COMING, screamed the first *Post* story, in September 2009. This was followed the next day by a second front-page headline, ONLY IN AMERICA, quoting Ashley Dupré's *mother* expressing her dismay at the notion of a Spitzer comeback. Mrs. Capalbo helpfully posed for the story on the beach in a skimpy bikini. When the rumbling of a 2010 run resurfaced in the *Post* for the *third* time, in December, Kristin Davis, the paroled madam, made headlines by vowing to run for office against Spitzer. The mastermind behind this stunt? Roger Stone, of course.

———

Why *had* Eliot Spitzer paid for sex?

Because in marriage, intimacy is a complex dance. It's sometimes available precisely when and how you want it. But often, it's not. For people living busy lives, a dizzying array of complications get in the way: jobs, kids, hormones, leftover squabbles, bad weather. Plenty of politicians have affairs, and women would have surely been available to Spitzer if he'd wanted them. But that would have required its own set of negotiations with another human being—and with himself.

To Spitzer, an affair—while having the distinct advantage of not being against the law—represented a far greater betrayal. He *loved* Silda. But he had needs. And in his maddeningly frenetic life, he acted to fulfill them, quickly and without complication. Money was not a problem. So women for hire—there at his call, dismissed when he was done, making no demands other than payment—provided an elegant solution. That explains his harshly impersonal behavior with the escorts. Suggests Agnifilo, Temeka Lewis's lawyer: "There's something about Spitzer that liked the efficiency of this."

Spitzer spoke openly about this for the first time in December 2009, when Alex Gibney and I met with him in his office to discuss new details we had gathered about his involvement with prostitutes. "An affair begins to connote an emotional relationship," Spitzer explained. "If I had had an affair, I'd still be governor, but I might not be married. In the grand scheme of things, I'm glad I am where I am."

During more than a year of conversations, Spitzer had repeatedly rejected the theory that his behavior was so risky he must have been sub-consciously *trying* to blow himself up—to escape from a high-pressure life he secretly hated. To the contrary, he now insisted, he had truly thought he could get away with it. "If you're looking for an outlet, you delude yourself into believing you've found an outlet that can satisfy whatever frustrations you have without doing damage to your life." Spitzer paused. "Obviously, I succeeded at none of that."

How and when had he started seeing prostitutes? When the scandal broke, he had told Bamm, among others, that it had begun about ten months earlier, in mid-2007, suggesting that it was a response to the frustrations of Albany—*Bruno had driven him to hookers!* He later ac-knowledged to me that it briefly predated his time as governor. Now, we had evidence of an Emperors Club VIP appointment in March 2006. *That's* when it began, Spitzer said. This, of course, put the kibosh on the theory that he had turned to infidelity at an especially desperate moment—as Spitzer acknowledged. "You need to understand the unbe-lievable insanity I was living through," he said, speaking of his time as governor. "None of this explains March 2006, when life is great, the world is my oyster. I was up by forty points in the polls, about to become governor, had a great wife and children, and all the money I could ever want. Yeah, life really *sucked*," he said sarcastically.

Yet even when all was going well, Spitzer says he now recognizes, he was facing enormous pressure. "You have no idea how crazy life was with everyone in the plutocracy viewing me as a heretic. You're living in this weird world, and you find your cop-out. You fall prey to very base temp-tations. That's the human mind."

"In all fairness," he added, "you gotta say this is an act of stupid hubris. I pretend it was nothing other than that. . . . Was I set up? *No*. I was set up by the human psyche." Spitzer says he began on his path to political perdition by perusing the escort ads in the back of *New York* magazine. Emperors Club VIP never advertised there, but Spitzer says that this initial research led him onto the Internet and, ultimately, his first, nervous phone call to the young woman who turned out to be Cecil Suwal. He says he never patronized any other escort service.

Looking back on his public career, Spitzer insists he had arrived in Albany eager to abandon the role of scold. "I was tired of pointing the finger. I was sick of it. You *know* you're not that pure. Nobody can live up to the standards we articulate. That's a reason I was glad I wasn't AG." But Albany had proven far more difficult than he'd ever imagined. After six months as governor, "I was frustrated as hell and angry," Spitzer says. "I was beginning to realize that Albany was going to be harder to reform than Wall Street. Joe Bruno is eating out of the trough in every way possible, and everybody knew it, and had known about it for years."

Spitzer couldn't help but wallow in the opportunity he'd squandered, in Albany and beyond. *What he could have accomplished as governor!* Bruno was gone and the senate was in Democratic hands, just midway through what should have been his first four-year term. "We'd probably be able to get something done," he says, "if I hadn't been such a schmuck." The crisis in the financial system, tragic as it was, posed even more opportunity to make a difference. It would—it *should*—have been Eliot Spitzer's moment.

Now he is left to try to put the pieces back together, determined—even desperate—to find a way to play a satisfying role. Spitzer dismisses the notion that he's somehow violated rehabilitation protocol, that he should have waited longer. "I don't know if there is a conventional model that works. I'm not sure what I went through is conventional." In his case, Spitzer says, "the incoming missiles are going to be there, no matter when or where I'm going. I'll take the incoming missiles. I'm not going to hide under a rock for four years and say, 'Now I've served my time.' If I disappeared for four years, there'd still be people who'd say whatever they wanted to say."

Almost two years after blowing himself up, Eliot Spitzer was palpably itching to get back in the game. "Putting aside the harm to family, it's hard just watching the world go by," he told me. In his heart, Spitzer believes there is still a constituency out there for the man once known as the Sheriff of Wall Street—people who remember what he did for them, what he has to offer. But he also knows running again for public office would be brutal, if not impossible. He understands, all too well, what he's squandered. "Given the horror of the economic collapse, I can at least go home and have three drinks and say, 'You may be insane, but you were *right*.'"

"That's my life," says Eliot Spitzer. "Is it pure agony? Yes, absolutely."

Acknowledgments

Any nonfiction book inevitably depends on the kindness of both friends and strangers. I have been a great beneficiary on both fronts. I conducted more than a hundred interviews for *Rough Justice*, on topics ranging from mutual-fund trading deadlines to the finer points of running an escort service. Most of these conversations were on the record. But for various reasons, a number of people agreed to speak only "on background," allowing me to use the information freely, but not to identify them by name. I am grateful for each and every form of cooperation.

A project like this starts with the people who worked most closely with the protagonist. Virtually all of Eliot Spitzer's longtime aides and advisors, in government and in politics, were remarkably candid and generous with their time, painful as the conversation sometimes was. I spoke to some a dozen times or more. This group includes Rich Baum, David Brown, Lloyd Constantine, Cindy Darrison, Eric Dinallo, Darren Dopp, Michele Hirshman, Marty Mack, David Nocenti, Peter Pope, Mike Schell, Avi Schick, Kristie Stiles, Ryan Toohey, Marlene Turner, Jef Pollock, and Jon Silvan. Among those who signed on during Spitzer's run for governor (or later), special thanks to Christine Anderson, Mike Balboni, Erin Duggan, Paul Francis, Allyson Giard, Jen Givner, Bruce Gyory, Miriam Hess, Danny Kanner, Catesby Perrin, Jimmy Siegel, Chrissy Stevens, Drew Warshaw, Dennis Whalen, and Charles O'Byrne, David Paterson's former top deputy. Thanks to George Arzt, Bill Green, Barbara Kloberdanz, John Marino, Aaron Retica, and Hank Sheinkopf for providing insight into Spitzer's early political career.

Many in Albany were generous with their time. Joe Bruno, Shelly Silver, Malcolm Smith, Jim Tedisco, Mark Weprin, Tom Libous, Richard Brodsky, Richard Gottfried, and John McArdle shared their thoughts on state government and the Spitzer era. Jeff Pearlman and Ryan Dalton, from Governor David Paterson's staff, dealt patiently with my voluminous document requests, as did Jim Folts and his team at the New York State archives. Bob Freeman, executive director of the state committee on open government, helped me navigate state records laws. David Grandeau spoke to me about government ethics. William Kennedy and David Langdon generously served as guides on the history and traditions of Albany.

The business world includes a few remaining Spitzer fans and many notable Spitzer foes. Special thanks to superlawyers Dick Beattie and David Boies, who faced off over AIG and Hank Greenberg. Former Citigroup chairman John Reed granted a rare interview about the Grasso case, offering new details; Jack Morris made that possible. John Whitehead discussed his unpleasant experience as the target of a Spitzer outburst. My account of Ken Langone's characteristically blunt response to being sued comes from my 2004 interviews with him for *Fortune*. Langone declined to speak to me for this book. He did, however, sit for a filmed interview with Alex Gibney. Hank Greenberg also declined repeated interview requests. But my colleague James Bandler generously shared his interview notes from conversations with both men for his terrific 2009 portrait of Greenberg in exile published in *Fortune*. Roger Stone, an agent of Spitzer's enemies, let me treat him to breakfast.

In law enforcement, thanks to former U.S. attorney Michael Garcia; former New York FBI director Mark Mershon; former Manhattan DA Robert Morgenthau and his longtime deputy Dan Castleman; Albany County DA David Soares; and New York City police detective Myles Mahady. Among veterans of the escort business, special thanks to Mark Brener, Cecil Suwal, "Tammy Thomas," Shelley Everett, Natalie McLennan, and Hulbert Waldroup.

I owe a considerable debt to the many talented journalists who have written about Spitzer during his career, many of whom also spoke with me. This list starts with Brooke Masters, now with the *Financial Times*, whose meticulously reported Spitzer biography, *Spoiling for a Fight*, was published in 2006. I am also grateful to *The Village Voice*'s inestimable

Wayne Barrett, who generously shared his keen insights—and research—on Albany and New York politics. I'd also like to acknowledge Ralph Blumenthal, Alan Feuer, Alan Finder, Danny Hakim, Willy Rashbaum, and Ian Urbina of *The New York Times;* James Odato, Bob Port, and Rex Smith of the Albany *Times Union;* CNBC's Charles Gasparino; and Jacob Gershman and Joseph Goldstein of the now-defunct *New York Sun.*

Thanks also, for an assortment of reasons, to lawyers Marc Agnifilo, Barry Agulnick, Sean Berkowitz, Janet Ward Black, Jason Brown, Don Buchwald, Steve Cohen, Jan Constantine, Al Ebanks, Mike Farkas, Ron Gunzburger, Mike Koenig, Andy Lachow, Chip Loewenson, Carl Mayer, Jeff Moerdler, Brian Pakett, Murray Richman, Cliff Sloan, Evan Stewart, and Steve Weissman; professor Robert Faggen; and PR consultants Brandy Bergman, Anna Cordasco, Eric Dezenhall, and Jim McCarthy.

This book was made possible through the extraordinary support of *Fortune* magazine. Andy Serwer, *Fortune*'s managing editor, allowed me to devote almost two years to this project, during which he remained consistently encouraging. Hank Gilman, the magazine's deputy managing editor, offered his sage advice and friendship. Steve Koepp coordinated the book's early stages. Two gifted colleagues, James Bandler and Tim Smith, offered invaluable comments on the manuscript; three others—Carol Loomis, Pattie Sellers, and Marcia Vickers—offered reporting suggestions. Time Inc. editorial director John Huey gave his all-important blessing to my writing a book—*again*.

I have had two remarkable partners throughout this project. The first is Academy Award-winning filmmaker Alex Gibney, who is also a remarkably talented journalist. The second is *Fortune* senior reporter Doris Burke, a fabulous researcher and invaluable sounding board. Alix Colow did a great job rounding up the photographs. Thanks to Maiken Baird and Sam Black, who worked with Alex Gibney. My agent, Liz Darhansoff, perfectly managed multiple roles: advocate, critic, friend; I am grateful. At Portfolio, publisher Adrian Zackheim understood the resonance of this story and believed in my ability to tell it. David Moldawer skillfully refined my prose and shepherded the book through to completion. I'd also like to thank Alex Gigante, Will Weisser, and Amanda Pritzker.

Marius Muresanu did double duty, providing both photographs and an interview. Former *Sports Illustrated* photographer Phil Huber, friend of the Elkind family, generously contributed my picture for the book jacket.

I also owe an enormous debt to my twenty-year friendship with Joe Nocera, now with the *Times*; he has played an instrumental role in my career.

More than anyone, I owe my family. That begins with my wife, Laura Elkind, who endured (usually cheerfully) far too many weeks of single-parent duty. She is my greatest supporter, partner, and friend. My older sons, Stephen, Landon, and George, offered encouragement during visits home from college. Adele and Sam, the little ones, are doing a terrific job growing up. I just *look* like their grandfather.

Index